September 22, 2021

Dear Marissa & Joey,
What a joy to
hear about you for your
sister in law. I hope
you find a blessing
in this book!
Love in christ,
Cristy

Included in Christ

Scripturally unraveling the apparent incongruity between gay Christians and the Church's belief in "one man, one woman"

Cristy Perdue, MD

PUBLISHING

LifeRich Publishing is a registered trademark of
The Reader's Digest Association, Inc.

LifeRich Publishing books may be ordered through booksellers or by contacting:

LifeRich Publishing
1663 Liberty Drive
Bloomington, IN 47403
www.liferichpublishing.com
1 (888) 238-8637

ISBN: 978-1-4897-2843-2 (sc)
ISBN: 978-1-4897-2844-9 (e)

Print information available on the last page.

LifeRich Publishing rev. date: 04/02/2020

CONTENTS

Section 1   **Introduction and Thesis** xiv

Chapter 1   The Traditional Christian Approach to
                  Homosexuality... 1
Chapter 2   Gay Christians?... 7
Chapter 3   Does the Possibility Exist?...................................... 12
   a.   Were Gay People Fearfully and Wonderfully Made? 13
   b.   Traditionalists Consider a Loophole.............................. 13
   c.   Setting the Standard of Proof.. 14
   d.   The Word of God is the Ultimate Standard................... 16
Chapter 4   The Word "Homosexuals" in the Bible................... 18
   a.   Baldock and Oxford's Work.. 20
   b.   Is the Orientation Condemned or the Act?..................... 23

Section 2   **Bible Passages**... 26

Chapter 5   I Corinthians 6:9-11: Those Who Will Not
                  Inherit the Kingdom of God.................................. 27
   a.   The New American Bible Footnote for Clarification 28
   b.   *Arsen + Koite = Arsenokoitai* 29
   c.   The Passion Translation Footnote.................................. 31
   d.   The Word "Homosexuals" Was a Mistranslation............ 34

Chapter 6   I Timothy 1:9-11: The Ungodly and Sinful. 36

Chapter 7   Romans 1:18-32: The Antithesis of Grace by
                   Faith in Christ 42

    a. Were These People Gay, and Is That Important?............46

    b. Reversing Paul's Premise 48

    c. Reversing a Premise, an Example of a Faulty Argument.....50

    d. Shameful, Unnatural, Reprobate.................................51

    e. Temple Prostitution..52

    f. Shameful and Unnatural.......................................53

    g. Reprobate Mind...55

    h. You Who Pass Judgment Do the Same Things.............55

    i. *Porneia*, a Very Important Word...............................57

    j. Due Penalty 58

    k. The Author of Scripture Knew About Gay People..........59

    l. Paul's Description of the People in the Passage.............59

    m. In Summary, the Rebuttal and Response 64

    n. My Final Thought on Romans 1 65

Chapter 8   Genesis 19: The Story of Sodom and Gomorrah 66

    a. Every Man in Town Was Gay?.................................67

    b. The Terms Are Not Interchangeable............................68

    c. In Summary...70

Chapter 9   Two Passages from Leviticus 71

    a. Relations Forbidden During a Woman's Menses 72

    b. Procreation and the Promise of Innumerable
       Descendants...72

    c. Patriarchy..73

    d. Anatomical Complementarity 75

    e. Does the Law Serve as Our Guide? 75

    f. In Summary...79

Chapter 10 One Man, One Woman...............................80

    a. One Flesh...80

    b. Exceptions to "One Man, One Woman" in
       Scripture: God/King David, Jesus/Eunuchs, Paul/
       No Longer Male and Female.................................81

   c. A Commonly Accepted Exception to "One Man, One Woman"..85

   d. Does the "Image of God" Require Heterosexual Marriage?...86

   e. Procreation...86

   f. The Creation Story: His Perfect Plan for Everyone?........87

   g. In Summary...89

Chapter 11   Other Scriptures to Consider With Regard to Gay Christians..90

   a. Go and Sin No More 90

   b. Jesus Defined Marriage: One Man, One Woman...........91

   c. If Anyone Causes One of These to Stumble....................92

   d. Wives, Submit to Your Husbands................................93

   e. Because You Are Lukewarm.......................................95

   f. Wretched, Pitiful, Poor, Blind, and Naked....................96

   g. Converting the Words Sodom and Gomorrah to Homosexuality..97

   h. Strange Flesh...98

   i. A Way that Seems Right 99

   j. Iniquity, Dishonest Scales, Fraud 99

   k. Accept One Another Just as Christ Accepted You 100

   l. Condemning the Innocent......................................100

   m. To Judge God's Servant...101

   n. This Was Not a Result of the Fall of Man 101

   o. What You Know is Good..102

   p. No One Who Continues to Sin Knows Him 102

   q. Do Not Call Anyone Impure or Unclean 103

Chapter 12   Exceptions, Reversals, and Other Labels for Certain Scriptural Topics...................................104

   a. Women in the Assembly 105

   b. Slavery 111

   c. Deacons 111

   d. Elders..112

   e. Eunuchs Forbidden to Enter the Temple 113

f. Food Sacrificed to Idols................................... 114

g. The Earth is the Center of the Universe 114

h. Love Your Enemies 115

i. Pearls, Gold Jewelry, Braids............................. 117

j. Greet One Another with a Holy Kiss 118

k. Head Coverings 118

l. Interracial Marriage is Forbidden 119

m. Remarriage 121

n. Tithe... 123

o. One Man, One Woman 124

p. In Summary... 125

Chapter 13 Eating Defiled Food and Forbidding People
            to Marry 126

a. Consider the Parallel: Eating Defiled Food and
    Forbidding People to Marry............................ 130

b. Sin Requires Harm 131

c. Promoting Homosexuality Among Children............... 133

d. The Early Church Agreed to Disagree...................... 136

e. Seared as with a Hot Iron............................ 137

Section 3   History 142

Chapter 14 God Heals: Ex-Gay Ministries........................ 143

a. Ex-Gay Ministries..................................... 144

b. Do Studies Prove that Change is Possible?................... 152

c. Current Ex-Gay Ministries........................... 156

Chapter 15 Therefore, Celibacy 160

a. Celibate Gay Christians 160

b. Is Celibacy the Answer to Same-Sex Attraction? 164

Chapter 16 Where Did This Extreme Aversion to Gay
            People Come From? 166

Chapter 17 Same-Gender Attraction Does Not Imply
            Pedophilia.. 176

Section 4   Opinions, Positions, Propositions...................... 180

Chapter 18   Should Gay Christians Be Allowed to Serve
             Within Our Churches, or Should They
             Remain Visitors?... 181
Chapter 19   If This Is True, How Could We Have Gotten
             It So Wrong for So Long? 185
    a. Slavery in the Southern Baptist Theological Seminary...... 185
    b. Interracial Marriage 196
    c. Discrimination of Marginalized People in Society........ 196
    d. Bible Translations: "Helpful" Clarifications,
        Opinions, Objections, Errors 197
    e. Job was Actually Impatient 199
    f. Translators Find Jesus's Words Objectionable and
        "Correct" Them 201
    g. It is Time to Reconsider the Premise................... 203
    h. Three Traditionalist Pastors Extend Welcome to
        the LGBTQ Community....................................204
    i. Let's Not Make This Mistake Again....................206
Chapter 20 Consider The Two Main Non-Affirming Positions.. 208
    a. Non-affirming View 1: Gay Christians Must
        Renounce Homosexuality 209
    b. Taking Up the Gay Christian's Cross........................... 212
    c. An Essential Part of Oneself.................................. 214
    d. Advocating (Likely Unfulfilling) Mixed-
        Orientation Marriage 214
    e. Homosexuals Should Just Become Straight.................. 215
    f. Homosexuality is Not Comparable to Adultery,
        Pedophilia, or Bestiality 216
    g. Freedom from Bondage to Sin.............................. 216
    h. Renouncing Presbyopia, Left-Handedness,
        Cancer, and Homosexuality................................. 218
    i. Non-affirming view 2: Christians Can Be Gay but
        Must Be Celibate or Heterosexually Married 221

j.   In the New Covenant, the Holy Spirit Guides Us
     From Within..223
k.   Comparing Homosexuality to a Non-Practicing
     Pedophile, Anorexia, and Singleness............................224
l.   We Will All Stand Before Him 225
m.   Perhaps Only Homosexual Behavior is Sinful 226

Chapter 21   Addressing Other Non-Affirming Arguments......229
a.   Eunuchs Who Were Born That Way.............................231
b.   Let's Talk About a Slippery Slope................................233
c.   Answers to Dr. Michael Brown's Questions 235
d.   Hundreds of Thousands of Person-Years of Experience.....237
e.   Brown: Have We Tried Hard Enough to Convert
     People to Heterosexuality?..238
f.   Holy Sexuality 239
g.   Could We Agree to Disagree?.......................................240

Chapter 22   Heart to Heart..244
a.   My Statement of Faith 245
b.   Am I Saved?...247
c.   No Division in The Body..248
d.   Inconsistencies in the Non-Affirming Argument..........249
e.   Is Christianity's Rejection of Gay People to Blame
     for the Decline in Numbers? 251
f.   Suicide Among Gay Youth and Groups Who
     Combat It 254
g.   Our Identity is in Christ...256
h.   Discrimination versus Religious Freedom: Are
     Gay People Really Gay, or Are They Confused
     Straight People?..257
i.   Accept One Another, Then..260
j.   Churches Led by Gay Christians...................................266
k.   Non-Affirming Same-Sex Attracted Christians 267
l.   Various Analogies...268
m.   The Affirming Church's Answer to Gay Christians 271

Chapter 23 Summarizing the Premise: Is Scripture
           Crystal Clear That Homosexuality Is a Sin?......... 272
    a. The Bible Passages that Address Same-Sex Activity 273
    b. One Man, One Woman and the Whole of
        Scripture, Beginning in Genesis.................................... 274
    c. Historical and Cultural Misconceptions....................... 275
    d. But Isn't Homosexual Activity Unnatural?.................. 276
    e. The Holy Spirit Guides the Believer From Within........ 277

Appendix A: Where Do You Stand?... 279
Appendix B: The Baptism in the Holy Spirit 285
Reference List.. 311
Acknowledgments 327
About the Author.. 333

SECTION 1

....

INTRODUCTION AND THESIS

Chapter 1: The Traditional Christian Approach to Homosexuality
Chapter 2: Gay Christians?
Chapter 3: Does the Possibility Exist?
Chapter 4: The Word "Homosexuals" in the Bible

1

THE TRADITIONAL CHRISTIAN APPROACH TO HOMOSEXUALITY

Thus far in history, many traditional, evangelical, and other mainstream churches have chosen what appears to be the most conservative and safest approach regarding homosexuals, or gay people. Churches have been friendly to gay people but have not allowed them to participate in membership or ministries. Some churches with traditional views may allow those who maintain celibacy to participate, but would not consider a gay couple for membership or ministry. The approach is thought to be safe because the traditional argument holds to the premise, "homosexuality is a sin," and Christians cannot condone sin.

Nevertheless, gay Christians and gay Christian couples are in our churches all over the world. Some Christians were raised in church and attended for many years before they realized that they were gay, or same-sex attracted. Other gay people have come to church later in life, seeking a closer relationship with Christ. Gay people are in virtually every church, whether congregants are aware of it or not. The steadfast witness and undeniable testimony of faithful gay Christians is opening the door for conversation between the traditional church and Christians who support the inclusion of gay people in local churches.

If all gay people are living in sin because of their same-gender attractions, then the church is doing the right thing to condemn them, and probably is not going far enough. However, if God is honored within monogamous, permanent, committed, Christ-centered relationships, and in the lives of single gay Christians, then the church has misinterpreted key Scriptures that have been mistranslated, misunderstood, and misused to condemn gay Christians unjustly.

Proverbs 17:15: "Acquitting the guilty and condemning the innocent - the Lord detests them both." It is my conviction that we must, therefore, consider this matter more thoroughly, as I believe the traditional Christian community has condemned the innocent.

I hold that the traditionalists' premise, "Scripture is clear that homosexuality is a sin," is wrong. I present my case directly from the Bible. For decades, the vast majority of Christendom, including countless trusted leaders, have heralded this phrase. For those in agreement, there is comfort and assurance that this unambiguously reflects the truth. Our modern Bible translations outright condemn homosexuality.[1] Thus, it is not unreasonable that many Christians currently believe that homosexuality is a sin.

What is abundantly clear in Scripture is that male sexual acts involving abuse and exploitation, and all same-gender sexual activity related to idol worship and rejection of our Creator, are sinful. Unfortunately, since 1946, Bible translators have erroneously referred to those acts as a group of people, namely, "homosexuals."

---

[1] I Corinthians 6:9-10, NASB: "Do not be deceived... neither fornicators, nor idolaters, nor adulterers, nor effeminate, nor homosexuals... will inherit the kingdom of God."

Traditional Christians refer to marriage as a sacred institution designed by God exclusively for one man and one woman. There are biblical exceptions to the one man, one woman tenet, which we will explore. Scripture records one of these exceptions in God's voice; Jesus also gave us one exception to "one man, one woman." We will also consider biblical exceptions to other previously held traditional positions within Scripture, to which traditionalists no longer hold.[2]

The Word of God absolutely does not change. It is the same yesterday, today, and forever. God's inspired Scripture, in its original form, is the inerrant, infallible Word of God. Translations and interpretations, however, do change over time. Our understanding of Scripture changes as the Holy Spirit within us guides us to understand His will for our lives and for His Church.[3]

A dear friend of mine is a gay woman who has never known Christ. Over the years, I have prayed for her salvation. She was invited to a megachurch in Atlanta around 2007. When she began attending, I was thankful and optimistic about God's work in her life. She enjoyed the church and community so much that she wanted to volunteer. She signed up to help with the nursery. After her first Sunday volunteering, she was told that she was not allowed to be in the nursery. She requested to meet with the pastor. When she asked why she was not allowed in the nursery, he said, "because you are gay." Genuinely confused, she asked, "what difference does that make?" He said, "I'm sorry. That is our policy."

I am dumbfounded by this event. My friend had never in her life heard the gospel, beyond what the pastor had said from the pulpit. He could have presented the good news of the gospel of Jesus Christ to my friend instead of simply rejecting her. At this point, over a

---

[2] I address this in chapter 12.

[3] In general, I use Church (capital C) to indicate the body of Christ, and church (lowercase C) to represent local church groups.

decade later, I am in a position to present the gospel to her. She graciously declines, but I continue to pray that she will one day see that God loves and adores her and does not reject her. The church desperately needs to look more carefully into this matter and engage gay people, rather than reject them.

Consider another example, this one involving a gay Christian who believes that Scripture condemns homosexuals.

> As a gay Christian [man], I am looking at two possibilities for my life: I could marry another man, and live the rest of my life with nagging doubts that I have sacrificed my relationship with God for this marriage. Or, I could choose not to marry a man, and blame God for the loneliness that I feel. There's a third option, and that's to kill myself now, while I still am in good relationship with God.
> -Anonymous

The following are statistics from a study published by Andrew Marin in 2016[4]:

- 86% of LGBT (lesbian, gay, bisexual, and transgender) people were raised in church.
- 54% leave by the age of 18, and many of them did not want to leave.
- 76% of them are open to returning to church.
- 92% of those who want to return to a local church are not asking the church to change its theology, but to accept, welcome, and love them.

---

[4] Marin, Andrew. (2016). *Us versus Us: The Untold Story of Religion and the LGBT Community*. Carol Stream, IL: NavPress.

In general, Christian churches want to welcome people into a saving relationship with Christ. However, the church leadership cannot condone sin. Churches recognize that people are imperfect, and everyone sins. There are statistics, for example, that reveal that addiction to pornography is prevalent in churches today.[5] The unique situation with gay Christians, however, is present when gay Christians do not agree with the church and believe that same-gender attractions and monogamous, covenantal relationships are not sinful. In other words, the church will accept someone who sins, provided that the person agrees he is sinning. But the church cannot accept someone who believes his relationship is not sinful when the church believes he is living in sin.

Can a monogamous, permanent, Christ-centered, same-gender relationship be blessed by God, or is it sinful? Our failure to agree on the answer to this question is the crux of this issue.

There exists within the Scripture an excellent example of this unusual phenomenon. There was a fundamental issue that divided Christians in the New Testament, some of whom believed the act was sinful, and some of whom believed that God blessed it. I will examine this carefully.[6]

As churches continue to exclude gay Christians from membership and ministry, please recognize the bigger picture. Exclusion from church suggests exclusion from the family of God. Gay people in the community are not welcomed into these churches, and many believe that God's saving grace does not extend to them. Throughout

---

[5] Statistics from the Barna Group and Covenant Eyes include the following: 68% of church-going men and over 50% of pastors view porn regularly. Of young Christian adults 18-24 years old, 76% actively search for porn. TruNews Team. (2018 September 19). "15 Stunning Statistics about Porn in the Church". Retrieved October 5, 2019 from www.TruNews.com.

[6] This is covered in chapter 13.

this book, I will refer to the issue of excluding gay Christians from membership and ministry in traditional churches, but this argument extends to sharing the gospel with those who do not know Christ.

As gay Christians and their Christian allies have become more outspoken, this issue is gaining attention. My goal is to present the scriptural basis held by those Christians who believe that gay Christians and Christ-centered, covenantal, permanent, same-gender relationships are blessed by God.

I plan to demonstrate that the Bible does not condemn gay people or monogamous, loving, gay couples. Many people believe, based on I Corinthians 6:9-10, that homosexuals will not inherit the kingdom of God. I will explain that translation and clearly define its error. One can believe the Bible to be the sacred Word of God and faithfully, confidently determine that there is no biblical reason to disapprove of gay people or gay couples.

For those readers who believe that marriage is only appropriate between one man and one woman, I am not asking you to give up your view of marriage or to change your theology. I only ask that the reader be willing to hear on what basis some Christians, holding the Scripture as the absolute highest authority in our lives, honestly believe that God blesses gay Christians, even those within committed, same-gender relationships.

Until churches realize the possibility that gay people can and should be included in the local church, even while gay, we will not be able to effectively minister the love of God and the gospel of Jesus Christ to this beautiful segment of God's creation.

For those who cannot consider homosexuality to be anything other than a sin against God's design for humanity, I humbly request and thank you for hearing me out through the pages of this book.

2

GAY CHRISTIANS?

Imagine if you will, a room full of 400 people who have all come together to worship the Lord. There's a band up front. There's praise music. People are worshiping the Lord, some with hands in the air, some prostrate on the floor. Someone in the crowd has a beautiful giant orange and red flag, and he's waving it rhythmically with the music. It's a beautiful scene of worship. The leader says into the microphone, "if you have your prayer language, just begin to pray in tongues as the Spirit leads." And then gently, softly, people are praying in the Spirit, worshiping and thanking the Lord. The music continues, and another song is sung. Thereafter the voices of people praising God can be heard. Eventually, among the sounds of worship to the Lord, one voice stands out. This one voice is singing, and all the other voices and sounds die down.

Amazingly, the man holding the flag is now in the center of the auditorium in front of the stage, singing, beautifully, slowly, in tongues. And the whole crowd is silent. Then it ends. You could hear a pin drop. Seven seconds later, the bassist on the platform sang the interpretation: "I dwell among you. I call you My friends. I dwell among you, and I hold your hand. I am the Lord your God, and I go before you now. Lift up your head in this place, and wear My heavenly crown." The tongues and interpretation were both sung in the same tune. It was incredible.

More people lay down, prone, on the floor, on their faces before God. Many were crying; some were laughing and jumping and praising God out loud. There was an atmosphere of worship in that room unlike anything I have ever experienced. I have seen the Lord give a word through tongues and interpretation countless times in my life. Until that day, I had never once seen it happen in song.[7]

This event involved 400+ Christians, approximately 95% of them from the LGBTQ[8] community. The Immersed Conference 2018 was titled Healing and Miracles by Faith. It took place in July 2018 in Atlanta, Georgia. I have since attended several LGBTQ Christian conferences, and I find that a scene like this is not unusual. Most of the attendees are in covenantal relationship or marriage with a same-gender partner. These Christians love and honor the Lord with their lives. They are walking with the Lord.

There are large groups of LGBTQ Christians all over the world who meet periodically. The Reformation Project and Q Christian Fellowship are other examples of LGBTQ-affirming Christian groups who hold annual meetings. The Covenant Network, which hosts the Immersed Conference every year, held ten conferences in 2019 in cities throughout the United States. The European Forum of LGBT Christian Groups hosts conferences throughout Europe.

---

[7] For those unfamiliar with the idea of "tongues," I have included a simple yet thorough explanation in appendix B.

[8] LGBTQ is an acronym for lesbian, gay, bisexual, transgender, queer. "Queer" is typically a blanket term referring to anyone who is non-heterosexual or gender non-conforming in some way. For a brief discussion of gender non-conforming, see the last subheading at the end of chapter 19. Some choose to add Questioning, Intersex, Asexual, Allies. I do not purposely exclude these, but will use the standard LGBTQ. I think the entire list could one day be represented by "Q."

I describe this worship scene because I know that many people do not realize that gay Christians even exist. Some cannot imagine that gay people would take any interest in Christianity since the church typically rejects them. Conversely, others assume that homosexuals could not even be Christians because they believe homosexuality to be sinful.

Throughout this book, I hold that gay Christians are, in fact, Christians, having trusted in Christ, His life, death, and resurrection. I break this down carefully in chapter 20. If the reader believes that a gay person could not be a Christian, I encourage you to consider a simple example, a 17-year-old Christian boy who has just realized that he has same-gender attractions, or a 25-year-old Christian man who has prayed since he was a teenager to be straight. This man follows Christ, is celibate, and recognizes that he is a sinner in need of a savior. But he simply cannot and does not deny that he is attracted to men, despite never having acted on his feelings. Importantly, despite the placement of the two words, his identity in Christ is more important than any other identity he has. Gay Christians are Christians, first.

The word gay does not imply any action. It refers to something that one senses from within himself. It is as if one is left-handed or right-handed. Some may reject even that notion and believe that gay people have chosen to be gay. Here, the word gay simply refers to someone who realizes that they feel most comfortable in a romantic relationship with someone of the same gender. For a gay person, a relationship with someone of the opposite gender may be wonderful as a friendship but does not feel natural as a romantic relationship.

The terms same-sex attracted and gay are used interchangeably throughout this book. The terms apply both to people who wish they were not same-sex attracted, who are asking God to change their orientation, and to those who accept that they are gay. Some gay Christians believe that romantic intimacy within a covenantal relationship can be blessed by God. Some gay Christians do not think that same-gender, romantic expression is permitted, and thus choose celibacy. Whether celibate or in a committed, monogamous relationship, both of these examples refer to gay or same-sex attracted Christians.

For those traditionalists who cannot believe that one could be both gay and Christian, as you read this book, please consider the word gay to simply mean same-sex attracted.

Christians who believe that God blesses permanent, monogamous, committed, Christ-centered, same-gender relationships are referred to as gay-affirming, or simply, affirming. Those who hold that God does not bless any same-gender intimacy are referred to as non-affirming, or non-gay-affirming. In this book, the terms non-affirming and traditionalist are equivalent. Some gay Christians are non-gay-affirming and thus do not believe that God blesses same-gender relationships. They typically advocate celibacy for gay Christians but do not deny that they are same-sex attracted. Some Christians prefer the term "same-sex attracted" because they feel that the word "gay" reflects a sinful identity. A small minority of gay couples feel that God calls them to celibacy within a gay relationship. It is not uncommon for gay Christians to enter into heterosexual marriages in order to uphold the traditional view of marriage.[9]

I am a Bible-believing, evangelical, Holy Spirit filled Christian. I am also a gay woman in a permanent, Christ-centered, committed relationship with my partner, Sue. For purposes of communicating, I must be able to say, "I am a woman," or "I am gay." However,

---

[9] Kathy Baldock has presented significant research on mixed-orientation marriages in her book, *Walking the Bridgeless Canyon*. Baldock, K. (2014). *Walking the Bridgeless Canyon: Repairing the breach between the Church and the LGBT community*. Reno, NV: Canyonwalker Press, chapter 12.

these terms only describe me to the extent that "rollerblader" and "beachgoer" describe me. My identity is in Christ, first and foremost. The other words are used to communicate a point, not to define who I am.

Importantly, I have recently completed a re-reading and a study[10] of the Bible before beginning the writing of this book. I want to show Christians that one can maintain one's faithfulness to God and His Word and affirm gay Christians, despite all that we were taught and grew up believing. I understand the non-affirming position well, and years ago I could have written that book. I recognize that many non-affirming people are well-meaning Christians, including some of my friends and close family members. My goal is to expose God's heart and His truth on this matter, as He chooses to use me, to the best of my understanding of His purpose. I want only to honor Him in my life.

To my beloved non-affirming reader, I owe a great debt for your time. I recognize the vulnerability it takes for some of you to read something so far out of the bounds of your experience and walk with God. Some of you have been mature Holy Spirit filled, Bible-believing Christians for decades, and cannot imagine that you could have possibly been wrong on this topic. I thank God for you, and I pray that the Holy Spirit brings you and me into agreement with His heart on this issue very soon.

---

[10] I study the Bible under Dr. Bill Creasy at LogosBibleStudy.com. He is an excellent teacher of the Bible, and I highly recommend him to anyone interested in a thorough study of Scripture. (I do not know whether Dr. Creasy is affirming or non-affirming of gay Christians.)

3

DOES THE POSSIBILITY EXIST?

My goal is to demonstrate that God lovingly, legitimately, purposefully creates some people without the capacity for heterosexuality and that He does not exclude them from His kingdom. Some Christians immediately assume that one must disregard the Bible to believe this, as they think that homosexuality is a sin.

Conversely, based on their understanding of the teachings of Christ, others cannot imagine that the exclusion and disapproval of gay people is justified. Nevertheless, modern Bibles read that homosexuals will not inherit the kingdom of God.[11] Thus, many people do not consider the Bible to be sacred Scripture.

The Bible is the Word of God and can be trusted as such. I will carefully unravel the apparent incongruity between the traditionalists' claim that homosexuality is a sin and the faithful Christian witness of countless gay Christians and straight Christian allies.

---

[11] I Corinthians 6:9-10, NASB: "Do not be deceived... neither fornicators, nor idolaters, nor adulterers, nor effeminate, nor homosexuals... will inherit the kingdom of God."

Were Gay People Fearfully and Wonderfully Made?

"For You created my inmost being; You knit me together in my mother's womb. I praise You because I am fearfully and wonderfully made." (Psalm 139:13-14a)

Affirming Christians believe that Scripture suggests we are fearfully and wonderfully made, even while gay. Non-affirming arguments would not disagree that even gay people were fearfully and wonderfully made. However, traditionalist Christians believe that God created everyone with the capacity for heterosexuality, but that the results of sin in the world have led to same-gender attractions. The idea that same-gender attraction is a result of the fall is prevalent in the traditional arguments.[12]

Traditionalists Consider a Loophole

One view that some traditionalists consider is that "God's best" for everyone would be heterosexual marriage. However, perhaps God allows same-gender expression, although it was not His original plan, just as He allowed for divorce and for Israel to have a king. Jesus explained to the Pharisees in Matthew 19 that God had not planned for divorce "from the beginning," but that due to their "hardness of heart," Moses permitted divorce. Similarly, God allowed Israel to have a king, despite His profound disappointment that His people had rejected Him as King over them. (I Samuel 8:7-8) God called King David a man after His own heart,[13] despite having intended from the beginning that He, God alone, would be Israel's only King. The people demanded a king, and although the idea displeased God, He agreed to allow it.

---

[12] I discuss this in chapter 11.

[13] Acts 13:22b: "I have found David son of Jesse, a man after my own heart; he will do everything I want him to do."

While the idea that God *perhaps reluctantly* allows same-gender relationships may be illogical to many gay-affirming people, it may be a way to begin this conversation with the traditional faith community.

Setting the Standard of Proof

If there were a gay couple blessed by God in Scripture, the church would be inclusive of gay Christians. If we knew that there existed, now or in the past, a gay couple whose relationship was blessed by God, then the church would be inclusive. Likewise, if the church believed that the possibility exists that a gay couple could be blessed by God, that is, that a particular gay couple's relationship brought honor to Him, then the church would probably want to be inclusive of this small Christian minority in their midst. In other words, I am setting the standard of proof here very low purposely.

The standard I propose is whether or not even the possibility exists that God is honored in the lives of some gay Christians, even while gay, and that God is honored within some same-gender relationships. Is it possible that the church is wrong on this topic? If that possibility exists, and if we can find the error in our long-held premise, then the church would not want to continue to reject gay Christians and gay people.

Consider a different scenario. If a man took his father's wife as his own and the two began attending church as a couple, the church would rightly question this situation. Adultery is a grave sin. The local church would have to take the man aside and explain that living in an adulterous relationship is forbidden in the church, and taking one's own father's wife (likely his stepmother) makes the act especially heinous. There is no possibility that this situation or one like it would honor God. Since that possibility does not exist, the local church must deal with the couple, and if they do not repent, then exclude them. This situation is described in I Corinthians 5:1-13.

But why, one may wonder, would the author not propose a higher, more confident-sounding standard? The answer is simple. Christians are diametrically opposed to one another on this topic. I visualize this rejection of LGBTQ Christians crumbling, but traditionalists believe that God, in His divine providence, would never allow such "sin" into His Church. If I could offer even a hint of doubt into the premise that gay people should be rejected from church, then traditionalist Christians would be faced with the reality that they are rejecting people whom God welcomes, on possibly incorrect assumptions. One does not want to "stretch" Scripture to reject people.

Let's find common ground. If that common ground is that the possibility exists that Scripture does not condemn gay Christians, and that some same-sex couples and gay Christians bring honor to God, then LGBTQ rejection must end.

The current common ground is that certain same-sex activity, such as promiscuity and abuse, are sinful. However, this does not address gay Christians. The church needs to address this issue specifically with regard to gay Christians who love, honor, and serve Christ wholeheartedly.

The idea that homosexuality is a grave sin against God is seared, as with a hot iron, into the consciences of many Christians.[14] However, the premise is not maintained under careful scrutiny of Scripture. If Christians re-examine their assumptions and remain confident that homosexuality is sin, as we know that adultery is sin, then traditionalist Christians will proceed with that view and continue

---

[14] I Timothy 4:2

to reject gay Christians in our churches. If re-examination provides evidence that calls these assumptions into question, then the church has the opportunity to make this right.

The Word of God is the Ultimate Standard

Neither side, the traditionalists nor gay-affirming Christians, condones or promotes sin. As Paul noted in I Corinthians 4:4, "My conscience is clear, but that does not make me innocent. It is the Lord Who judges me." I recognize soberly that God judges me in all of my thoughts, attitudes, words, and actions, including everything written here. I do not take this matter lightly. Holding Scripture as the highest authority in my life, I will present my case, that God is not dishonored, but rather, He is pleased and honored by gay Christians and permanent, loving, monogamous, Christ-centered, same-gender relationships.

Until recently, in Christian circles, most gay Christians remained closeted, and the Christian community did not realize that there were sober-minded, disciplined gay Christians in their midst. The gay Christian community has seen a move of God in recent years. Spiritually mature gay Christians and gay Christian couples are increasingly free to worship God openly. Furthermore, anointed and passionate Christian straight allies are working tirelessly to see the inclusion of all LGBTQ Christians in our churches.

If the traditional, non-affirming argument reflects God's heart and His will, then the information presented here will not be of any consequence, and what I refer to as "a move of God" among gay Christians will fade. However, if God's heart is reflected in the pages of this book, and if the world begins to recognize a move of God among gay and all LGBTQ Christians, then the church should consider this evidence. The traditional teaching on this subject is flawed. Scripture does not call for the rejection of gay Christians in the church. On the contrary, God's saving grace through Christ is extended to all people, including gay people and gay couples.

4

The Word "Homosexuals" in the Bible

The word "homosexuals" did not appear in any Bible until 1946. The Revised Standard Version (RSV) New Testament intended to translate the Bible using modern language. In the 1940s, when the translators were working on these passages, homosexuality was defined by the authoritative medical experts and psychoanalysts as a mental illness. There was no understanding in society of consensual attraction among adults of the same gender. At that time, the idea of a stable, happy, committed, same-gender relationship simply did not exist. Almost all gay people were closeted. As the reader will see in chapter 16, over twenty years later, in 1967, Americans still had no concept of a stable, happy, committed, same-gender relationship. The scientific and medical communities regarded all homosexual people as broken, sick, and perverted, and in general, mainstream society, including Bible translators, did not see any reason to question the assertions of the professionals.

In 1946, the Revised Standard Version New Testament combined two Greek words, *arsenokoitai* and *malakos,* as "homosexuals." This was thought to refer to the active and passive partners in male-male sex acts. (We will explore these two words in detail in the next chapter.)

When the translators of the Bible first translated the original Greek text of I Corinthians 6:9 using the word "homosexuals," the word in society meant something different than it means today. A homosexual, or gay person, refers to an otherwise normal member of society who has a same-gender orientation, which may include emotional, romantic, and physical attractions. In decades past, society typically referred to male abusers of male children as homosexuals because there was no understanding of a homosexual person in a faithful, monogamous relationship. If a man abused a boy, it was thought, then that man must be a homosexual. However, someone who commits such crimes could be either a gay person or a straight person. These crimes have nothing in common with loving, committed, monogamous, same-sex relationships. Today, many older people have difficulty uncoupling the two.[15] For several decades leading up to the 1970s, experts in the medical and research communities mistakenly stated that all homosexuals were at best mentally ill, and at worse, capable of these types of horrific crimes.

There is a technical term for the molestation or exploitation of a male (child, teenager, prostitute, or slave, for example) by a man. The term is "homosexual molestation." The word homosexual refers to the genders of the two people, not to the sexual orientation of the abuser. Pederasty, which was common in the Greco-Roman world of the New Testament through the middle ages, is a good example of homosexual molestation. Pederasty refers to a sexual relationship between a man, most typically a heterosexual man, married or unmarried, and a boy or prostitute. To be clear, exploitation of a young, male teenager by a heterosexual, married man would still be called "homosexual molestation," even though the offender is heterosexual. Unfortunately, the term, "homosexual molestation," led people in society to believe that homosexuals molested children.

---

[15] Some people continue to believe that all homosexuals are pedophiles.

Once the Revised Standard Version New Testament (RSV) translated these Greek words as homosexuals, many translations followed their lead. While the original Greek Scripture in these passages referred strictly to male sex acts, as the two passages containing the word *arsenokoitai* (I Corinthians 6:9, I Timothy 1:10) were more loosely translated over time, they lost any sense of gender specificity or behavior. The original Scripture condemned a specific sin, committed specifically by males. However, the passages erroneously became a blanket condemnation of anyone with same-gender attraction, regardless of whether they were male or female, and regardless of whether they committed the sin described in the original text or not.

In my opinion, this was an egregious mistake which has cost the gay community irreparable harm and countless lives to suicide. Furthermore, it has cost the Church the talents, gifts, and contributions of an entire segment of beautiful, loving, talented people whom God never intended to be excluded from His family.

Baldock and Oxford's Work

Kathy Baldock, author of *Walking the Bridgeless Canyon: Repairing the Breach Between the Church and the LGBT Community* (2014), and Ed Oxford, co-author of Baldock's upcoming book (tentatively titled, *Forging a Sacred Weapon: How the Bible Became Anti-Gay*) have uncovered new evidence, through exhaustive research involving tens of thousands of documents from the archives at Yale University. They have determined that the initial inclusion of the word "homosexuals" was done within a cultural context.[16]

---

[16] Baldock, K. (2019 June 13). "The word 'homosexual' in the 1946 RSV Bible – a moral wrong based on a factual error". Retrieved June 2019 from www.CanyonWalkerConnections.com.

The head of the translation team for the Revised Standard Version New Testament, Dr. Luther Weigle, communicated with a young seminarian in 1959. In a series of letters that Baldock and Oxford found in the archives, a man named David questioned the use of the word "homosexuals" in the RSV translation. He wrote that he feared that the "incorrect usage of this word" could be used

> as a sacred weapon, not in fact for the purification of the Church, but in fact for injustice against a defenceless minority group which includes the sincere, convicted, spiritually re-born Christian who has discovered himself to be of homosexual inclination from the time of his memory.[17]

Baldock explains that Dr. Weigle agreed after some communication with (now) Reverend David that the RSV team would need to revise that particular Scripture in the following edition.

Through "the most amazing series of events,"[18] David's identity was discovered, and Baldock's team has befriended him. Now in his eighties, he has participated in LGBTQ Christian conferences recently. The details of this unprecedented, monumental discovery will be available to us in Baldock's highly anticipated second book, co-authored with Ed Oxford, which is expected to be released in 2020.[19] Sharon "Rocky" Roggio and her team are creating a documentary chronicling Baldock and Oxford's research. The

---

[17] (Last name withheld), David. 1959, The letter is presented in the following article: Baldock, K. (2019 March 26). "How the Bible Became Anti-Gay: Forging a Sacred Weapon". Retrieved October 2019 from www.CanyonWalkerConnections.com. This has been included with Reverend David's permission.

[18] Ibid.

[19] Baldock, K. (2019 March 26). "How the Bible Became Anti-Gay: Forging a Sacred Weapon". Retrieved May 2019 from www.CanyonWalkerConnections.com.

documentary is titled *Lost in Translations* and is expected to be completed in 2020.[20]

In a blog post, Ed Oxford revealed further findings that will be presented in their upcoming book. Their team has been collecting old Bibles, dictionaries, and lexicons from various countries (including some countries that no longer exist). They found that in a German Bible from the 1800s, the passages in Leviticus which currently read "man shall not lie with man," read, "man shall not lie with young boys." For the New Testament translation of *arsenokoitai*, the 1800s translation reads "boy molesters." In the Luther Bible from 1534, the German translation for *arsenokoitai*, which today is often translated "homosexuals," was translated *knabenshander* in German. This term in German means "violator of boys," or "boy molesters." Oxford's 1674 Swedish translation and 1830 Norwegian translation[21] reveal the same sentiment, "boy abusers" or "boy molesters."[22]

Modern translators of the Bible had a misunderstanding about homosexuality, stemming from misinformation from within the medico-scientific community in the early to middle decades of the twentieth century. The inclusion of the word "homosexuals" appears to have been cultural and ideological in origin. This is just now beginning to be clarified and understood. The modern translations are not consistent with the ancient translations. In fact, the modern translations have introduced a completely new idea into these verses.

Importantly, newer translations have noted these inconsistencies in translating these two Greek words. The Passion Translation and the

---

[20] See their trailer here: https://vimeo.com/371082273. New title: 1946

[21] Oxford brought these valuable Bibles and other books to The Reformation Project in Seattle, Washington in November 2019, so that we were able to see these incredible findings firsthand.

[22] Hershey, J. (2019 March 21). "Has 'homosexual' always been in the Bible?". Retrieved June 22, 2019 from www.ForgeOnline.org.

New American Bible both include footnotes which reveal that the word translated as "homosexuals" has a more specific meaning of exploitation and abuse. I will address this carefully in the following chapter.

If, as the ancient translations suggest, the words refer to exploitative and abusive forms of male sexual acts, then we should ask ourselves whether this is appropriately extrapolated to apply to all gay people, as the translators have done.

Is the Orientation Condemned or the Act?

Consider this list of potential behaviors that could apply to someone who is heterosexual or to someone who is homosexual. The entries within each category are actually the same.

Heterosexuality:	Homosexuality:
-Marriage, monogamy, commitment	-Marriage, monogamy, commitment
-Divorce	-Divorce
-Dating	-Dating
-Singleness, celibacy, devotion to Christ	-Singleness, celibacy, devotion to Christ
-Chastity before marriage in honor to God	-Chastity before marriage in honor to God
-Sex/promiscuity before marriage	-Sex/promiscuity before marriage
-Adultery	-Adultery
-Rape/abuse	-Rape/abuse
-Promiscuity	-Promiscuity
-Child/adult pornography	-Child/adult pornography
-Prostitution/exploitation	-Prostitution/exploitation
-Idol worship	-Idol worship
-Rejection of Christ	-Rejection of Christ

Many forms of *hetero*sexuality are condemned in Scripture. It would be inappropriate to ascribe any condemned heterosexual act to "heterosexuality" in general. This is the error in the traditionalists' premise on *homo*sexuality. Non-affirming arguments have ascribed every passage referencing same-sex acts to "homosexuality." For example, pederasty, or exploitation and abuse of younger males represents only a subset of homosexual acts, not "homosexuality" in general, and not gay people.

I must parenthetically clarify the following: engaging in a same-sex act does not by definition make someone homosexual. Consider straight men married to women, involved in a "swingers" club in America. A biblical example would be male-male cult prostitution as part of idol worship in ancient Rome. These men engage in all manner of sexual immorality, including promiscuity and same-sex acts with other men. These are examples of straight men (heterosexual) who participate in same-sex (homosexual) acts. Another example would be a pedophile. A heterosexual man, married or unmarried, who abuses young men or boys, would be an example of a straight man involved in same-sex sexual acts. He would not appropriately be labeled "homosexual," but rather "abuser of male children."

On the other hand, there are gay people who engage in heterosexual acts. Dr. Nate Collins is the founder and president of Revoice,[23] a group of same-sex attracted Christians committed to a traditional, biblical view of marriage. He is a gay man married to a woman. In an interview, Collins specifically stated that he was neither straight nor bisexual.[24] That is, he is a homosexual man who engages in heterosexual acts.

In other words, performing the act does not define someone one way or the other. In ancient times, people did not use the words gay and straight or think of people in terms of who they were attracted to. This concept is relatively new, but it does not change Scripture,

---

[23] Revoice is discussed further in chapter 15.

[24] Sprinkle, P. (2015 February 3). "A Simple Reason to Get Married: 'We Were in Love'". Retrieved August 7, 2019 from www.SpiritualFriendship.org.

and should not cause confusion. One who engages in a same-sex act could be either gay or straight.

Every explicit same-sex act in the Bible is condemned. But it would be a mistake to refer to one who engages in those acts "homosexual," without knowing if that person were gay or straight. Today, homosexual simply means someone who is attracted to people of the same sex, whether it be emotionally, romantically, or physically.

The orientation, or inclination, itself does not suggest involvement in any particular activity. If the translators of the Bible were to translate condemnation of the sinful acts appropriately, then a faithful rendering of the text does not convert that condemnation to an entire segment of people, namely all gay people, but rather to the individuals who perform those acts.

Dr. Luther Weigle and the RSV translation team did in fact change the translation in the revised version. The new term was rendered "perverts," referring to anyone, gay or straight, who participates in the sinful acts.

SECTION 2

....

BIBLE PASSAGES

Chapter 5: I Corinthians 6:9-11
Chapter 6: I Timothy 1:9-11
Chapter 7: Romans 1:18-32
Chapter 8: Genesis 19:1-29
Chapter 9: The Levitical Prohibitions
Chapter 10: One Man, One Woman
Chapter 11: Other Scriptures to Consider With Regard to Gay Christians
Chapter 12: Exceptions, Reversals, and Other Labels for Certain Scriptural Topics
Chapter 13: Eating Defiled Food and Forbidding People to Marry

There are six passages in Scripture which refer to same-sex activity. Many people believe these "clobber passages," as they are sometimes called, condemn gay people. In chapters 5 through 9, we will consider the evidence that these Scriptures have been mistranslated, misinterpreted, and misunderstood.

5

I Corinthians 6:9-11: Those Who Will Not Inherit the Kingdom of God

> Or do you not know that the unrighteous will not
> inherit the kingdom of God? Do not be deceived;
> neither fornicators, nor idolaters, nor adulterers,
> nor effeminate [*malakos*], nor homosexuals
> [*arsenokoitai*], nor thieves, nor the covetous, nor
> drunkards, nor revilers, nor swindlers, will inherit
> the kingdom of God. Such were some of you; but
> you were washed, but you were sanctified, but you
> were justified in the name of the Lord Jesus Christ
> and in the Spirit of our God. (NASB)[25]

The Greek word *arsenokoitai* has, throughout centuries of history, been thought to refer to exploitative male sexual acts involving abuse of power. The King James Version, published in 1611, translated *arsenokoitai* as "abusers of themselves with mankind." *Arsenokoitai* is used two times in the Scripture, in I Corinthians 6:9 and I Timothy 1:10. When used in other ancient texts, it is in lists, not unlike the

---

[25] I have included the Greek words in brackets for clarification.

lists that Paul uses in these two passages. It appears from the order of the lists in other ancient texts that the word *arsenokoitai* refers to injustice and exploitation.[26]

Malakos, the other Greek word used in I Corinthians, is translated soft or lazy, including having weakness of moral character, degeneracy, decadence, and lack of courage.[27] In 1611, in a society where women were of lesser value than men and thought to be morally weak, the term was translated "effeminate." The only other biblical use of *malakos* is in the context of fine or soft clothing. (Luke 7:25, Matthew 11:8)

These two words were combined in the 1946 Revised Standard Version and were translated "homosexuals."

The New American Bible Footnote for Clarification

The New American Bible uses the words "boy prostitutes" and "sodomites" in place of "effeminate" and "homosexuals" in the NASB. The New American Bible has a clarifying footnote for this passage:

> The Greek word translated as *boy prostitutes* [*malakos*] may refer to catamites, i.e., boys or young men who were kept for purposes of prostitution, a practice not uncommon in the Greco-Roman world. In Greek mythology this was the function of Ganymede, the "cupbearer of the gods," whose Latin name was Catamitus. The term translated

---

[26] Martin, Dale. (2006). *Sex and the Single Savior: Gender and Sexuality in Biblical Interpretation.* Louisville, KY: Westminster John Knox Press, pages 39-41.
[27] Ibid, pages 43-4.

sodomites [*arsenokoitai*] would then refer to adult males who indulged in homosexual practices with such boys.²⁸

The New American Bible goes on to say, "See similar condemnations of *such practices* in Romans 1:26-27, 1 Timothy 1:10." (The emphasis is mine.) In other words, The New American Bible suggests that each reference to "homosexuality" in our modern translations may refer to exploitative (perhaps mutually so, as in the case of prostitution) male sexual acts.

Arsen + Koite = Arsenokoitai

Paul apparently coined the word *arsenokoitai*. The Greek translation of the Old Testament (the Septuagint) is the Scripture that was available to Jews and Christians before the New Testament was written. In the Hebrew text, the Greek terms *arsen* (meaning, man) and *koite* (meaning, to lie with) appear together six times. It is assumed that Paul combined *arsen* and *koite* to create *arsenokoitai*.

There is no reason to believe that *arsenokoitai* refers to homosexuals when one considers the usage of *arsen* and *koite* in both Numbers 31:17-18 and Judges 21:11-12. All four of these verses refer to men (*arsen*) having sexual relations (*koite*) with women. (These are the transliterated Greek words from the Septuagint in parentheses.)

There are two instances in the Hebrew text when *arsen* and *koite* refer to men having sexual relations with males. The words from Leviticus 20:13 are as follows: "if a man (*arren*, or *arsen*) has sexual relations with (*koite*) a man...." There is a similar statement in Leviticus 18:22.

---

²⁸ Again, the bracketed words, for clarification, are mine.

In the Levitical passages, the two Hebrew words for man are different, indicating a distinction between the two males.[29] Ancient translations recognized the Levitical passages to prohibit pederasty (relations between a man and a child or teenager). If it was from the Levitical passages that Paul coined the word *arsenokoitai*, then it may refer to male sexual acts involving exploitation and abuse of power, such as pederasty.

However, there are four instances in the Old Testament when *arsen* and *koite* together refer to men having sex with women. In other words, these two terms only definitively refer to males and a sexual act, but there is no reason to assume that the term *arsenokoitai* necessarily involved sex between two males.

As an example, a man who sexually abuses a person who is under his authority certainly could refer to a man who abused a boy, teenager, or man. This could also describe a man who abused a girl, teenager, or woman.

Yale New Testament scholar Dale Martin wrote the following:

> I suggest that a careful analysis of the actual context of the use of *arsenokoites*, free from linguistically specious arguments from etymology or the word's separate parts, indicates that *arsenokoites* had a more specific meaning in Greco-Roman culture than homosexual penetration in general.... It seems to have referred to some kind of economic exploitation by means of sex, perhaps but not necessarily homosexual sex.[30]

---

[29] This is addressed in chapter 9.
[30] *Sex and the Single Savior*, page 40.

In other words, it is apparent that *arsenokoitai* referred to a sinful act, such as prostitution or pederasty. There is no evidence that it refers to a person's same-gender orientation.

The Passion Translation Footnote

Regarding *arsenokoitai*, The Passion Translation states, in a footnote in I Timothy 1:10, under the word "homosexuals," "The Aramaic can be translated 'molesters of male children.'"

The word homosexuals, as it is known and used today, is not a proper translation of a term that means "molesters of male children." Many homosexuals, or gay people, are involved in consensual, loving, committed partnerships. However, the term meaning "molesters of male children" does not refer to consensual relationships. The condemned act is not gay people in committed relationships, but rather, abuse of power involving men who commit exploitative and abusive sexual acts.

We can confidently say that *arsenokoitai* in the I Corinthians passage refers to male sexual acts. The Levitical prohibitions using the words *arsen* and *koite* refer to male same-sex acts. The terms in Numbers and Judges refer to male sexual acts. We understand from the Scriptures that sinful male sexual acts were prohibited. The question is, what was the reason for the prohibition of *arsenokoitai*, and how does it apply to us today? Consider the following points:

- *Arsenokoitai* refers to male sexual acts that were abusive to children.
  In I Timothy 1:10, The Passion Translation footnote reads, "abusers of male children."
- The acts involved male prostitution.

In I Corinthians 6:9, the New American Bible footnote reads, "the Greek word [is] translated as boy prostitutes" and "adult males who indulged in homosexual practices with such boys."

- *Arsenokoitai* is not best rendered by "homosexuals," but rather sexual exploitation involving a power differential, which is often described between a man and a boy, teenager, or man, but does not preclude abuse and exploitation between a man and a girl, teenager, or woman.

- Note that non-*arsenokoitai* male same-sex acts were part of idol worship and did not necessarily involve a power differential.

  Romans 1:25: "They worshiped and served created things rather than the Creator." The same-sex acts in Romans 1 (addressed in chapter 7) were not necessarily exploitative and appear to be mutually consensual. This passage does not use the word *arsenokoitai*.

The act of *arsenokoitai* did not refer to equal status, consenting relationships. In the condemned act, one participant of the sex act had power, and the other participant was being used, degraded, and exploited.[31] These acts were exploitative and abusive, as was originally, appropriately translated.

In early 2019, New York Governor Andrew Cuomo signed The Child Victims Act,[32] reopening the window for civil and criminal lawsuits for heinous crimes of sexual abuse committed by those in power. Fourteen other states have done this as well.[33] On August 14,

---

[31] *Walking the Bridgeless Canyon*, page 237.

[32] "Governor Cuomo Signs The Child Victims Act". (February 14, 2019). Retrieved November 15, 2019 from www.Governor.NY.gov.

[33] Condon, B., Mustian, J. (2019 December 7). "Surge of New Sexual Abuse Claims Threatens Church Like Never Before". Retrieved December 10, 2019 from www.CharismaMag.com.

the first day that victims were allowed to sue in New York under the new ruling, hundreds of lawsuits were filed, including alleged abuse by little league coaches, doctors, priests, Boy Scout leaders, and high school employees, among many others.[34] The crimes described by some of these lawsuits may represent the Greek word *arsenokoitai*.[35]

I maintain that the Holy Spirit was not condemning same-gender couples, people with same-gender attractions, or even sexual acts within same-gender, covenantal relationships. The sin was exploitative male sexual acts, such as pederasty, pedophilia, and homosexual cult prostitution, which were very common in the Greco-Roman world of the New Testament. In other words, I hold that the Scripture has been mistranslated. In my opinion, the initial inclusion of the word "homosexuals," after which all modern translations followed, was not malicious, but simply, tragically, ill-informed.[36]

The footnotes (in the New American Bible and The Passion Translation) and the recent translations cannot both be correct. If the terms in I Corinthians 6:9-10 mean "boy prostitutes" and "men who indulged in homosexual practices with such boys," then the terms do not mean "homosexuals." They would only refer to a subset of male homosexual acts and would require an exploitative action, not merely a person or a consenting couple.

---

[34] Siemaszko, C. (2019 August 14) "Hundreds filed lawsuits under Child Victims Act in New York". Retrieved November 16, 2019 from www.NBCnews.com.

[35] My inclusion of this paragraph is a result of a talk given by Dr. Cheryl Anderson on November 9, 2019 at the Reformation Project annual conference. Her talk can be seen here: https://www.facebook.com/ReformationProject/videos/464487600847246/, beginning at 1:02:47 into the video.

[36] For a fantastic review of the scholarship in this area, I highly recommend Kathy Baldock's first book, *Walking the Bridgeless Canyon*, 2014, and her soon-to-be published second book.

Similarly, the current translations and the older translations cannot both be correct. Ed Oxford's Bibles, from as far back as the 1500s, translate this passage, "boy molesters will not inherit the kingdom of God."[37] If the terms refer to young male prostitutes and the men who commit exploitative sexual acts with young males, then the translation using the word "homosexuals" is inaccurate.

Unfortunately, the modern misinterpretation of these verses has potentially two devastating consequences. First, it has led to a misplaced focus on homosexuality or same-sex attraction, which does not involve abuse or predatory behavior. Secondly, it has distracted us from the true sin, which is abuse of the vulnerable. Leaders within the Christian Church have made the painful mistake over the decades of protecting the powerful rather than the vulnerable. That is, they have covered up *arsenokoitai* within the churches to protect the churches. And they have allowed predators to remain in positions of power and thus have not protected the vulnerable from abuse and exploitation.[38] In the meantime, they reject gay people from involvement in the same churches.

The Word "Homosexuals" Was a Mistranslation

When the aforementioned 21-year-old seminarian student first read the word "homosexuals" in his new Bible in 1959, he recognized the potential for erroneously condemning certain people. Reverend David feared that the Bible could be used as "a sacred weapon" against people who were gay. He had recently completed a seminary course in the Greek language. He presented Dr. Luther Weigle, the head of the RSV translation team, with resources to support the

---

[37] Hershey, J. (2019 March 21). "Has 'Homosexual' always been in the Bible?" Retrieved July 5, 2019 from www.ForgeOnline.org.

[38] The ideas within this paragraph are attributable to Sue Peters. Personal conversation, February 2019.

position that the word homosexuals had been translated in error. Dr. Weigle agreed with Reverend David, but had just three weeks prior, signed with the publisher that there would be no changes to the RSV Bible for ten years. As noted previously, the word homosexuals was removed in the revised edition, but the damage had been done.

The Message Bible paraphrases these verses as follows:

> Don't you realize that this is not the way to live? Unjust people who don't care about God will not be joining in his kingdom. Those who use and abuse each other, use and abuse sex, use and abuse the earth and everything in it, don't qualify as citizens in God's kingdom. (I Corinthians 6:9-10)

6

I Timothy 1:9-11:
The Ungodly and Sinful.

We know that the law is good if one uses it properly.
We also know that the law is made not for the
righteous but for lawbreakers and rebels, the ungodly
and sinful, the unholy and irreligious, for those
who kill their fathers or mothers, for murderers,
for the sexually immoral, for those practicing
homosexuality [*arsenokoitai*], for slave traders and
liars and perjurers, and for whatever else is contrary
to the sound doctrine that conforms to the gospel
concerning the glory of the blessed God, which He
entrusted to me.[39] (2011 NIV)

Note that the latter portion of the list includes the following:

Those who kill their fathers or mothers,
murderers,
sexually immoral,
those practicing homosexuality,

---

[39] The bracketed Greek word for clarification is mine.

slave traders,

liars,

perjurers.

As noted in chapter 5 above, The Passion Translation and the New American Bible (original and Revised Edition) footnote verse 10 to clarify that the original Scripture refers to exploitative male sex acts typically involving men with boys or teenagers. Some newer translations simply maintain the erroneous blanket term "homosexuals." However, other translations are finally considering the injustice that blanket term has done to gay people, when the sin referred to was not *being gay*, but rather, some form of abusive, exploitative male sexual act. Some scholars also believe that "slave traders" referred to those who traffic male sex slaves,[40] which thus appropriately follows *arsenokoitai* in the list.

Recall that *arsenokoitai* combines two terms meaning "male" and "to lie with." This word requires, for a proper translation, a sinful sexual act performed by a man. Consider other translations in place of "those practicing homosexuality" in the 2011 NIV.

- Older editions of the New International Version, published before 2011, use the term "perverts." The 2011 edition reads, "those practicing homosexuality." Perverts is a more appropriate translation, as it could refer to either gay or straight people; however, "perverts" lacks gender specificity. *Arsenokoitai* refers explicitly to males.
- The Living Bible (1971): "homosexuals." This translation also dropped the gender specificity and the sinful action of the word *arsenokoitai*, and refers not to any action, but instead to any person, man or woman, boy or girl, who realizes that he or she has same-gender attraction. The

[40] Keen, K. (2018 December). "Dialogue with Preston Sprinkle on Same-Sex Relationships". Retrieved January 5, 2019 from www.KarenKeen.com.

Living Bible has condemned as "ungodly and sinful" anyone with same-gender attraction, regardless of how they handle it. That would include, for example, a 12-year-old boy who has just realized that he is interested in boys at school and goes to bed every night, begging God that it's not true. Similarly, that would include a 40-year-old celibate man who was never given the gift of celibacy, but with the intent to observe the historic, Christian doctrine of marriage and sexuality,[41] has maintained lifelong celibacy and debilitating loneliness. This mistranslation encompasses every person with same-gender attraction. Same-gender attraction cannot be manufactured or chosen. Whether this mistranslation was sincerely and honestly misstated, or careless, it is a truly egregious miscarriage of justice that is responsible for countless suicides and the loss of innumerable souls who would never consider darkening the door of a church.

- Amplified Bible (1987): "those who abuse themselves with men." This version appropriately maintained the gender of the word as well as the sinful act. Clearly, this sin requires abuse. However, gay Christians are in consensual relationships. Abusive relationships bear no resemblance to Christ-centered, committed relationships. This Amplified version was copyrighted with six different dates between 1954 and 1987.
- Amplified Bible (2015): "homosexuals." Unfortunately, this modern translation does what previous translators did, and simply removes any action or any gender, implying that anyone with same-gender attraction is "ungodly and sinful."
- American Standard Version (1901): "abusers of themselves with men." Again, this is a reasonable translation. It requires abuse and maintains gender specificity.

---

[41] Keen, K. (2019 April 30). "In Defense of Revoice: A Response to Robert Gagnon". Retrieved May 4, 2019 from www.KarenKeen.com.

- King James Version (1995): "them that defile themselves with mankind." This is a reasonable translation as well, maintaining both the gender and sinful act.
- Revised Standard Version (1971), New Revised Standard Version (1989), New King James Version (1982), Young's Literal Translation (1898), New American Bible (1992): "sodomites." As noted above, the New American Bible refers to sodomites as "adult males who indulged in homosexual practices with such boys [young prostitutes]." This is consistent with exploitative sex, or rape, which is abuse, a miscarriage of justice, in keeping with the remaining items in the list, including slave traders.
- The Message (2002): "riding roughshod over God, life, sex, truth, whatever!" Eugene Peterson did not list homosexuality in his paraphrase.
- New Life Version (2003): "for people who do sex sins with their own sex." This translation has also dropped the gender specificity of the word *arsenokoitai*. However, it does require that there be a sinful act. It refers to same-sex sin, for example, child pornography, male cult prostitution, and pedophilia, as we have seen within the Catholic Church of men abusing children. We can all agree that those acts are included within the phrase "sex sins with their own sex." I point this out because this translation does not condemn all homosexual people, as other translations wrongly do.
- New Century Version (2005): "who have sexual relations with people of the same sex." This appropriately excludes the 12-year-old virgin boy and the 40-year-old celibate man. However, to be faithful to the original text, it should include gender specificity and a sinful act, such as abuse or exploitation, as many older translations do, and as the footnotes (in The Passion Translation and the New American Bible) explain.

- As noted above, The Passion Translation (2017): "homosexuals," footnote: "The Aramaic can be translated, 'molesters of male children.'" I am eternally grateful for this clarification. There is a glaring question here. How could the translators equate "molesters of male children" with "homosexuals"? The media in our country have always referred to child molestation by men (for example, priests) as "homosexual molestation." This may be one reason. However, the term homosexuals also refers to gay individuals and gay couples who are not involved in abusive or exploitative activity. I appreciate what I assume was a compromise for this committee, adding the footnote that gave the world a glimpse into the real meaning behind this verse, which has caused so much pain and suffering to innocent men, women, boys, and girls.

- As noted in chapter 4, the Luther Bible from 1534 translates this text using the word *knabenschänder*, in place of "homosexuals." *Knaben* is translated "boy;" *schänder* is translated "molester" or "violator."[42] This German word is translated, "boy molesters." The German translation of the Bible did not use the word "homosexuals" until 1983, more than a century after the word homosexual was coined, by the Germans. Interestingly, in 1983, the German translation that first included the word homosexuals was funded by the American company, Biblica, which owns the New International Version (NIV).[43]

As previously noted and worth repeating, the translations and the footnotes cannot both be correct. Similarly, the modern translations and the ancient translations cannot both be correct. This passage does not refer to homosexuals.

---

[42] www.Dictionary.Cambridge.org/dictionary/German-English.
[43] Hershey, J. (2019 March 21). "Has 'Homosexual' always been in the Bible?" Retrieved June 2019 from www.ForgeOnline.org.

Based on this research, including the footnotes in our modern Bibles, ancient translations of the text, and Dr. Luther's correspondence with Reverend David admitting error in using "homosexuals" in the I Corinthians passage, I would humbly suggest the following list:

> Those who kill their fathers or mothers,
> murderers,
> sexually immoral,
> men who practice exploitative, abusive sexual acts,
> slave traders,
> liars,
> perjurers.

7

ROMANS 1:18-32: THE ANTITHESIS OF GRACE BY FAITH IN CHRIST

In the book of Romans, the apostle Paul presents a beautifully structured argument centered around salvation by grace through faith in Christ. He states his thesis in Romans 1:16-17, that is, the gospel is the power of God that brings salvation to everyone who believes, and in it is revealed the righteousness of God by faith. Following this thesis, he begins his formal argument by presenting the antithesis of his topic.[44]

As an example, consider a teacher who wants to convince students that they should do their homework. To make an argument by antithesis, he may point out that those who do not do their homework do not do as well in their final grades.[45]

In the first chapter of Romans, in order to show that faith in Christ leads to righteousness and salvation, Paul describes the antithesis of

---

[44] I learned these concepts from a study of the book of Romans under Dr. Bill Creasy at LogosBibleStudy.com.
[45] Ibid.

a life lived by faith. Those who suppress the truth and reject God live lives of evil and depravity.

Romans 1:18-32 in the New International Version:

> The wrath of God is being revealed from heaven against all the godlessness and wickedness of people, who suppress the truth by their wickedness, since what may be known about God is plain to them, because God has made it plain to them. For since the creation of the world, God's invisible qualities— His eternal power and divine nature—have been clearly seen, being understood from what has been made, so that people are without excuse.

> For although they knew God, they neither glorified Him as God nor gave thanks to Him, but their thinking became futile and their foolish hearts were darkened. Although they claimed to be wise, they became fools and exchanged the glory of the immortal God for images made to look like a mortal human being and birds and animals and reptiles.

> Therefore God gave them over in the sinful desires of their hearts to sexual impurity for the degrading of their bodies with one another. They exchanged the truth about God for a lie, and worshiped and served created things rather than the Creator—who is forever praised. Amen.

> (Verse 26) Because of this, God gave them over to shameful lusts. Even their women exchanged natural sexual relations for unnatural ones. In the same way the men also abandoned natural relations

with women and were inflamed with lust for one another. Men committed shameful acts with other men, and received in themselves the due penalty for their error.

Furthermore, just as they did not think it worthwhile to retain the knowledge of God, so God gave them over to a depraved mind, so that they do what ought not to be done. They have become filled with every kind of wickedness, evil, greed and depravity. They are full of envy, murder, strife, deceit and malice. They are gossips, slanderers, God-haters, insolent, arrogant and boastful; they invent ways of doing evil; they disobey their parents; they have no understanding, no fidelity, no love, no mercy. Although they know God's righteous decree that those who do such things deserve death, they not only continue to do these very things but also approve of those who practice them.

From a traditionalist's perspective, this passage clearly states that all same-gender sexual activity is condemned as shameful and unnatural. Let's consider the following questions, first briefly and thereafter in more depth.

- Were these people gay, and would that make a difference?
  - o Traditionalists: It does not matter. It is the act of same-gender sexual activity that is clearly forbidden.
  - o Affirming Christians: It is important because same-gender activity to a gay person is completely natural, but to a straight person, it is unnatural.
- Can a passage about idol worshipers who hated God apply to people who love and worship God?
  - o Traditionalists: Yes. The passage is condemning a specific behavior. It does not matter if the same-sex

couples are monogamous or claim to be Christians. It is the activity that is condemned.

o Affirming Christians: No. One must reverse Paul's premise to claim that this passage can refer to people who love God.

- Isn't homosexuality what God gives some sinners over to when they reject Him?
  o Traditionalists: Yes. God gave them over to shameful lusts because they rejected Him.
  o Affirming Christians: People who reject God are given over to all manner of sexual immorality including promiscuity and expressions of sexual excess outside of their own natural desires.

- Doesn't "natural relations" refer to God's perfect design, His divine order, as seen in the creation story?
  o Traditionalists: Clearly, it represents the whole of Scripture, God's perfect design.
  o Affirming Christians: No, "natural relations" refers to the heterosexual individuals Paul is describing. For a gay person, same-gender intimacy is not unnatural.

- Does the text say that everyone who has engaged in a same-sex act has been given over to a reprobate mind, meaning they are irredeemable?
  o Traditionalists: No, even homosexuals can be redeemed if they renounce homosexuality. (Some traditionalists say yes, that all homosexuals are irredeemable.)
  o Affirming Christians: No. The text says that everyone who rejects the Creator has been given over to a reprobate mind.

- Is there anything in the original text that my Bible leaves out?
  o Traditionalists: Scripture is clear. There's no need to try to read into it to make it fit your perspective.

- o   Affirming Christians: Several translations, including the NIV, left out the Greek word *porneia*, which is important to this argument.
- Does the due penalty represent death from AIDS in the gay community?
  - o   Traditionalists: Yes. (However, some may disagree.)
  - o   Affirming Christians: Death is the due penalty for everyone who rejects Christ.
- Was Paul unaware of loving, monogamous, same-sex couples?
  - o   Traditionalists: The Author of Scripture is omniscient. Whether Paul was aware of this is irrelevant.
  - o   Affirming Christians: The Author of Scripture certainly knows about same-gender couples. This passage addresses wicked people who hated God and participated in all manner of sexual immorality, not faithful Christian couples.
- Who do the descriptors at the end describe, only gay people or anyone who rejects God?
  - o   Traditionalists: Those words describe, at least in general, homosexuals. It is not necessary for every single word to describe every single gay person. In general, this is God's description of homosexuality.
  - o   Affirming Christians: These words describe anyone who has rejected God, whether gay or straight, but Christ has redeemed us, and we respond to each descriptor with what God's Word says about us.

Were These People Gay, and Is That Important?

First of all, to a traditionalist, it does not matter if the people were gay. All same-gender sexual activity is condemned. If that is the case, then it should extend to monogamous, loving, gay couples. Let's briefly examine the other perspective.

What Paul describes is not same-gender attraction, but rather unbridled lust and sexual excess. Traditionalists typically equate this passage to all homosexual relationships, even monogamous, committed relationships. However, Paul was not referring to gay couples. This passage describes heterosexual men and women participating in outrageous sexual activity, including involvement in same-sex acts. While homosexual orientation was not known, defined, or understood during this time, it may be reasonable to note that even today, in America, it is estimated that only 4.5% of the population is gay.[46] Paul was not addressing homosexuals.

Further evidence that this passage is discussing heterosexual people is the use of the phrase "their women" in verse 26. Let us attempt to examine this with a fresh mindset, despite the baggage of decades of anti-gay messages that have been seared into our hearts and minds. Briefly, consider that these two simple words alone make it clear that this entire passage is referring to *hetero*sexual idol worshipers. "Their women" actually means that neither the men nor the women were gay. These women, likely the wives of the men, were participating in something unnatural.

One cannot faithfully extrapolate this passage and apply it to a gay couple in a loving, monogamous, Christ-centered relationship. The people that Paul described were, very simply, straight. The passage does not refer to all same-gender sexual activity for all people, for all time. It refers to people who rejected God and engaged in all manner of sexual immorality, including promiscuity.

Today, some people attend clubs and parties devoted to "swinging" and sexual excess. Heterosexual people who engage in unbridled promiscuity, adultery, and orgies involving both men and women are prime examples of the scene Paul described. Of course, this passage

---

[46] "In U.S., Estimate of LGBT Population Rises to 4.5%". Retrieved November 14, 2019 from Gallup.com.

could apply to homosexual people as well. Anyone who rejects his Creator is subject to a life of depravity. Just as a term meaning "abusers of male children" does not describe gay Christians, neither does this scene of unbridled, shameful, sexual excess describe gay Christians.

Reversing Paul's Premise

Some non-affirming arguments use this passage to suggest that anyone who participates in same-gender sexual practice of any kind, monogamous or otherwise, hates God and rejects the truth. However, that is not a valid argument. In this passage, there were people who rejected God and committed indecent acts with members of the same sex. However, there are gay people who do not reject God, who express intimacy in Christ-centered, covenantal relationships exclusively. This type of loving relationship bears no resemblance to the situation that Paul described.

In this passage, Paul explains what becomes of people who reject their Creator. The people Paul describes "neither glorified Him as God, nor gave thanks to Him." The eleven verses that follow refer to those people who "worshiped and served created things rather than the Creator." What is described from that point on, is people who reject their Creator. This point never changes within the illustration. It is the very foundation of Paul's position in this passage.

Thus, one can argue that this passage could describe some non-Christian homosexuals. One could just as easily argue that it could describe some non-Christian heterosexuals. But one cannot faithfully apply this argument to a person who does glorify God and gives thanks to Him. A Christian simply cannot be described by this passage.

The Holy Spirit leads and guides us to understand Scripture today. Consider the following simplification, in order to understand the importance of the word "therefore."

> If one were to break down the passage, it looks like this:
>
> 1. Certain people rejected God and worshiped idols.
> 2. Therefore, God gave those people over to shameful lusts.
> 3. Therefore, they engaged in shameful, unnatural, same-gender sexual acts.
> 4. They have a depraved mind, filled with wickedness, murder, and hatred toward God.

The word "therefore" in line 2 follows the premise laid out in line 1. Without that premise, one cannot move on to line 2. This is why one may apply this illustration to people who reject God, who "neither glorify Him as God nor give thanks to Him," but one cannot faithfully apply this passage to any person who glorifies God and gives thanks to him. To use this passage as an illustration of "homosexuality," one would have to reverse Paul's premise as follows.

> Non-affirming arguments mistakenly imply that the passage reads like this:
>
> 1. Certain people engaged in shameful, unnatural, same-gender sexual acts.
> 2. Therefore, they must have rejected God and worshiped idols.
> 3. God gave them over to shameful lusts.
> 4. They have a depraved mind, filled with wickedness, murder, and hatred toward God.

This passage includes same-gender sexual acts, but it does not address "homosexuality" in general, or gay people. In other words, all of the people in Paul's passage rejected God. That is his premise. He is talking about non-Christians who participate in same-sex acts. If one uses this passage to suggest that people who commit same-sex acts are non-Christians, they have reversed Paul's premise, and that would be an invalid argument. I will give another example of reversing a premise to demonstrate the fallacy in that approach.

Reversing a Premise, an Example of a Faulty Argument

Consider a group of people born to exceedingly rich parents. These people were "trust fund babies" who never had to work, but were always given everything they needed or wanted. Therefore, they developed an entitlement mentality, and typically expected, and usually got, other people to cover the costs of activities for them. They never developed a sense of the joy of hard work and had no interest in pursuing careers. They became selfish and petty. Because of this, once the money ran out, they maxed out their credit. When all the credit was exhausted, they declared bankruptcy, and using a very gracious law in society, received a clean slate. However, despite having had the debt wiped off their record, thereafter, they did it all over again, maxing out all of their credit a second time. They are selfish, ignorant people who disobey their parents and take money from people with no intention of repaying it.

One might point out that this story is about people who max out their credit, declare bankruptcy, and max out their credit again. These "trust fund babies" took advantage of other people and did not work hard to earn money to cover their expenses and carry their weight in society. Most people in life simply do not have the option to live off of other people, but these people did, and took advantage of it. Even after receiving a completely clean slate, they didn't learn a lesson, but returned to the same activity, spending other people's money, they again maxed out their credit. These are truly selfish people, as described.

Now consider a couple whose young daughter was diagnosed with a rare form of cancer. They were not trust fund babies, and both worked full-time jobs taking care of their responsibilities. The cancer treatment was expensive, and they soon spent all of their savings early on in the course of treatment. Therefore, they ran their credit up, paying for treatments until they had no more credit, and they filed for bankruptcy. At some point, graciously, the cancer went into remission. However, some years hence, the cancer returned, and the parents again exhausted their savings and maxed out their credit on cancer treatments for their young daughter. This couple does not fit the premise outlined in the original story, nor do they fit the descriptors at the end. They are not selfish or ignorant, nor do they dishonor their parents or borrow money with no intention of repaying it.

Although in both situations, people maxed out their credit, declared bankruptcy and again maxed out their credit, the two groups are different based on the premise, which is the information prior to the word "therefore." If one were to use this story to suggest that all people who max out their credit twice have an entitlement mentality, then they would have reversed the premise of the story. That would be an invalid argument. In other words, one could not faithfully use this illustration to describe all people who max out their credit twice. Similarly, one cannot accurately use Paul's example to describe a gay Christian couple.

Shameful, Unnatural, Reprobate

Let's carefully address each of the following negative descriptors:

1. Shameful (NIV) / vile (KJV)
2. Unnatural: "against nature"
3. Depraved (NIV) / reprobate (KJV)

Recall that there are many different aspects to both heterosexuality and homosexuality. Some are shameful. For example, promiscuity, adultery, abuse, and prostitution represent shameful acts in both gay and straight communities. Likewise, monogamy and commitment, as well as singleness and celibacy, represent honorable acts.

In other words, not all homosexual acts are shameful and unnatural. This is the point at which traditionalists and gay-affirming Christians disagree. Traditionalists believe that all forms of homosexual activity are shameful and unnatural. However, if Paul's illustration focuses on temple prostitution, it is very possible that he is not condemning all same-sex sexual acts.

Temple Prostitution

Paul had not been to Rome when he wrote his letter to the Romans. (Romans 1:10) He was most likely writing from the city of Corinth. Corinth was a large commercial city, a double seaport town. Per the NIV Study Bible, Corinth was "a center for open and unbridled immorality." In Corinth, "the worship of Aphrodite fostered prostitution in the name of religion. At one time, 1,000 sacred prostitutes served her temple."[47] This is likely the context from which Paul took his Romans 1 illustration. The temple served as a place for blatant sexual immorality as a form of idol worship.

The people who were involved in this activity rejected their Creator, worshiped and served idols, and likely participated in all manner

---

[47] Barker, K. (1985). "Introduction to I Corinthians: Its immorality". *The NIV Study Bible*, Grand Rapids, MI: Zondervan, page 1732.

of shameful sexual activity, including adultery, promiscuity, and unnatural same-sex acts, committed mostly by heterosexuals. Paul is not talking about a small group of homosexuals; he is describing the most licentious activity he knew existed within the pagan temple worship. Pagan worship and shrine prostitution was no different in the city of Rome. Paul's audience understood this passage to refer to idol worship, which was commonplace.

Shameful and Unnatural

The same-gender acts described in the Romans 1 passage are unequivocally and indisputably both "shameful" and "unnatural." There is another situation described using these same words in Scripture. Paul wrote to the church at Corinth, "Does not the very nature of things teach you that if a man has long hair, it is a disgrace to him?" (I Corinthians 11:14) That is, long hair on a man is both shameful and unnatural, according to the Scripture. The Greek words for shameful/disgrace (*atimia*) and unnatural/nature (*physis*) are the same two words in both Romans 1:26 and I Corinthians 11:14.[48]

The shameful and unnatural act of wearing long hair for the men in Corinth came as a fundamental understanding of the culture of their day. Just as it would be disgraceful and against the nature of normal day to day life for me to show up at work wearing a nightgown, it was not sensible, not natural, not appropriate for men to wear hair that resembled a woman's hair in a patriarchal society.[49] In that context, long hair on a man was both shameful and unnatural.

---

[48] www.BlueLetterBible.org.
[49] I took this idea from the following article: Piper, J. (2018 August 20). "Is It Wrong for Men to Have Long Hair?" Retrieved July 4, 2019 from www.DesiringGod.org.

If one were to take each of these situations out of this particular context and describe it within another context, the possibility exists that they are no longer shameful and unnatural. For example, in society today, it is somewhat trendy for men to wear long hair. It is not seen as either unnatural or shameful today. In almost every depiction I can recall, Jesus is shown as wearing long hair. Consider the Nazarite vow described in Numbers 6. Samson, a lifelong Nazarite, had long hair. Outside of the context in which Paul wrote, and in our context today in America, it simply is neither unnatural nor shameful for a man to have long hair. Similarly, there is another context, far different from the scene that Paul described in the first chapter of Romans, in which same-gender intimacy is expressed, and is neither shameful nor unnatural. That context, of course, is within a monogamous, covenantal, permanent, gay Christian couple's relationship.

Traditional arguments state that all same-sex behavior is "unnatural," for all people, for all time. The suggestion is that "nature" is depicted in Genesis as God's perfect design, and is definitively described by "one man, one woman." When addressing the portrayal of men's long hair as "unnatural," traditionalists typically appeal to cultural arguments. They believe that "unnatural" with regard to long hair was not a matter of God's perfect, natural design, while the same word referencing same-sex acts *was* a matter of God's perfect, natural design.

Consider a different example of the same term, "unnatural," which is a very positive use of the word.[50] In Romans 11:24, Paul describes Gentiles as having been, against nature, grafted into the vine, and into reconciliation to God. The term "against nature" in Greek is "*para physis*," the same Greek term used in Romans 1:26 (referring to the same-sex acts) and in I Corinthians 11:14 (referring to men

---

[50] I was first introduced to this idea by Daniel Helminiak. Helminiak, D. A. (1995). *What the Bible Really Says about Homosexuality*. San Francisco, CA: Alamo Square Press, pages 67-8.

with long hair). In the context in Romans 1, the term "unnatural" is appropriately viewed as negative, but that term is not always seen in Scripture as negative. Importantly, "unnatural" cannot faithfully be extrapolated from the Romans context to describe all same-gender relationships as unnatural, for all people, for all time.

Reprobate Mind

Regarding the word "reprobate," there are groups who call for the execution of LGBTQ people in America based on the idea that they are irredeemable, having been given over to a "reprobate mind."[51] (Romans 1:28, KJV) To refute the suggestion that there is no redemption for LGBTQ people, I offer two arguments.

1. The premise, "homosexuality is a sin," simply is not demonstrated in Scripture, as this book argues. Specifically, the people who were given over to a "reprobate mind" in Romans 1 were those who had rejected God and therefore lived lives of evil and depravity. There was same-gender sexual activity in Romans 1, but it did not apply to gay people who love and trust in their Creator. It applied only to people who rejected God.
2. Paul's readers did "the same things" that he described in Romans 1. That includes those of us reading Romans 1 today.

You Who Pass Judgment Do the Same Things

Let's consider two sentences, back to back (with my emphases in italics), from the end of Paul's description of these idol worshipers who hated our Creator. Romans 1:32-2:1:

---

[51] www.nifbcult.com.

> Although they know God's righteous decree that
> those who *do such things* deserve death, they not
> only continue to *do these very things* but also approve
> of those who practice them. You, therefore, have
> no excuse, you who pass judgment on someone
> else, for at whatever point you judge another, you
> are condemning yourself, because you who pass
> judgment *do the same things.*

Recall the moment when Peter heard the rooster crow; he had done exactly what he had promised Jesus he would not do: he had denied his Lord in the most painful moments of Jesus's life. Reader, please humbly consider the possibility that Scripture suggests that those who judge based on Romans 1 do the "same things" in God's eyes. If the passage is about homosexuality, then they do not actually do the same things, since many have never participated in a same-sex act. Thus, the passage must be about rejecting God, not about homosexuality. If that is the case, then yes, it is true, we have all done the same things.

Paul's audience and those, in the name of Scripture, calling for the executions of LGBTQ people, at some point in time, also rejected God and did the same ungodly, idolatrous things. This passage does not describe homosexuality. It describes people who rejected God. Some of them turned from their evil ways, repented, and believed in Christ for the remission of sins and eternal life. Some may have been among Paul's original readers in Rome. Even those who reject Him have the option to repent and receive Christ's forgiveness. Remember that Paul once rejected Christ, before his conversion on the road to Damascus. Every Christian at one point believed in Christ for eternal life, and no longer rejected Him.

In the context in Romans, the unnatural, shameful homosexual activities were committed by people because they rejected God.

Christian gay couples who participate in same-gender activity only within the confines of a covenantal, monogamous relationship are not appropriately described by a passage referring to people who reject God. As a trustworthy confirmation, notice that the descriptors at the end of the passage do not describe gay Christians.

Porneia, a Very Important Word

Paul describes these people beginning in verse 29. The first half of that sentence is as follows: "They have become filled with every kind of..."; in the Greek, the five words that follow are translated in the King James Version as follows: 1.) unrighteousness, 2.) fornication, 3.) wickedness, 4.) covetousness, 5.) maliciousness. Notice the second word. They were filled with every kind of fornication.

Fornication in the KJV is translated from the Greek word *porneia*.[52] Interestingly, some of the modern translations, including the New International Version (NIV) and the Amplified Bible, simply do not translate that word in this passage. *Porneia* is the Greek word from which we get the word pornography. Jesus used it in Matthew 19 as the one exception He gave for divorce. It refers to all manner of sexual immorality.

These people in Paul's illustration who rejected God and served idols have been filled with every kind of sexual immorality. Does that strike the reader as describing a loving, monogamous relationship? That these people Paul describes were filled with every type of *porneia* suggests even more strongly that this passage cannot faithfully be applied to committed, monogamous, Christ-centered relationships.

Inexplicably, the NIV uses four words, "wickedness, evil, greed, depravity," none of which refers specifically to sexual sin, to cover five

---

[52] www.BlueLetterBible.com.

Greek words, one of which specifically refers to sexual sin. When the NIV translates *porneia* in Matthew 19, "sexual immorality" is used, but it simply is not translated in Romans 1:29. There is no reference to sexual immorality in verses 29-32 in the translations that omit this essential word.

Nevertheless, the original text in Romans specifies that these idol worshipers were filled with every kind of sexual immorality. This discovery provides further confirmation that this passage cannot be used to condemn Christians in monogamous, Christ-centered, same-gender partnerships. It would be very difficult to argue that "filled with every kind of *porneia*" could be represented by love and monogamy.

Due Penalty

Some readers will recall television evangelists beginning in the 1980s who used Romans 1:27 to say that the death of homosexuals due to AIDS was "due penalty" for their error. The Scripture states that death is the due penalty to everyone since we were all born into sin (Romans 6:23) but that Christ came so that whosoever believes in Him would not perish but have everlasting life. (John 3:16) John 3:36 states that whoever rejects the Son will not see life, because the wrath of God remains on him.

The due penalty for sin is applied in this passage in Romans because every single person in the story rejected God: "for although they knew God, they neither glorified Him as God nor gave thanks to Him." (Romans 1:21a)

Rejection of the Creator is the very premise of Paul's argument. Thus, they will all receive the due penalty for their error, as will anyone who does not acknowledge and call on the name of Jesus. Jesus is the only One to become our substitute and thus take our punishment on Himself. Those people who turn to Christ and believe in His atoning sacrifice on the cross do not receive the penalty of death, but rather, eternal life.

The Author of Scripture Knew About Gay People

Traditionalists often erroneously suggest that affirming Christians simply hold that Paul did not know about sexual orientation. That point is irrelevant, since the Holy Spirit authored Paul's works. The Holy Spirit is omniscient. Paul's original audience likely did not consider the idea of sexual orientation. But his current audience does. The Holy Spirit Who inspired the writing of the passage leads and guides us as we study this topic.

Paul's Description of the People in the Passage

Non-affirming arguments hold that the passage in Romans 1 refers to all people who participate in same-sex practices. However, I believe that it refers to people who reject God. In the last paragraph of the passage, Paul described the people that he was referring to. The Amplified Bible (1987) lists 30 specific terms that describe these people. I have listed them one by one. Notice that the descriptor is a word or phrase which is opposed to Christ and all that Christians stand for. In italics, I have listed a Christian's response[53] to each descriptor (specifically, my response to the suggestion that the descriptor describes me). The idea as you read through these specific descriptors is to determine whether they seem to describe gay Christians or people who reject Christ.

---

[53] Each Scripture citation is a reference, and is appropriate as such in any translation. I do not necessarily quote verbatim in this section.

- They were filled, permeated and saturated, with every kind of the following:
  - o Unrighteousness
    I am the righteousness of God in Christ. II Corinthians 5:21; He atoned for my sins on Calvary. I John 2:2; I have received the gift of righteousness. Romans 5:17; I am made righteous by believing in the Lord Jesus in my heart. Romans 10:10
  - o Iniquity
    My sins and unrighteousness He remembers no more. Hebrews 8:12
  - o Grasping
    Perfect love casts out all fear. I John 4:18; The Holy Spirit works in me to will and to do for His good pleasure. Philippians 2:13; He makes my paths straight. Proverbs 3:6
  - o Covetous envy
    I love my neighbor as myself. Matthew 22:39; I take captive every thought to the obedience of Christ. II Corinthians 10:5; I rejoice with those who rejoice and weep with those who weep. Romans 12:15
  - o Malice
    I am crowned with loving kindness and tender mercies. Psalm 103:4
- They were full of the following:
  - o Envy
    I walk in the fruit of the Spirit, which is love, joy, peace, patience, gentleness, goodness, faith, meekness, temperance. Galatians 5:22-23
  - o Jealousy
    I rejoice with those who rejoice. Romans 12:15
  - o Murder
    I love my neighbor as myself. Mark 12:31; I do not repay anyone evil for evil. Romans 12:17
  - o Strife

I make every effort to keep the unity of the Spirit through the bond of peace. Ephesians 4:3

o Deceit

The Holy Spirit guides me into all truth. John 16:13

o Treachery

In love, I do no wrong to my neighbor. Romans 13:10

o Ill will

The Holy Spirit puts in me to will and to do for His good purpose. Philippians 2:13

o Cruel ways

I hate what is evil and cling to what is good. Romans 12:9; I live in harmony with everyone as much as possible. Romans 12:18

- They were the following:
  o Secret backbiters

  I honor others above myself. Romans 12:10

  o Gossipers

  I take every thought captive to the obedience of Christ. II Corinthians 10:5

  o Slanderers

  I love my neighbor as myself. Matthew 22:39

  o Hateful to and hating God

  I love the Lord my God with all my heart, and with all my soul, and with all my mind, and with all my strength. Mark 12:30

- They were full of the following:
  o Insolence (rude and disrespectful behavior)

  I live and conduct myself honorably and becomingly as in the day. Romans 13:13; I am a new creation in Christ. II Corinthians 5:17; God writes His laws in my heart and on my mind. Hebrews 10:16; I am a child of God, and I am led by the Holy Spirit. Romans 8:14

- o Arrogance
  I do not overestimate or think of myself more highly than I ought, but I rate my ability with sober judgment, according to the degree of faith apportioned by God to me. Romans 12:3
- o Boasting
  I boast only in Christ's finished work on my behalf, as did Paul. Galatians 6:14
- They invented new forms of evil.
  Anyone who continues to sin has neither seen Him or known Him. I John 3:6
- They were disobedient and undutiful to parents.
  I honor my father and mother with the fruit of my work. Matthew 15:4-6
- They were without understanding.
  He gives wisdom to all who ask without finding fault. James 1:5
- They were conscienceless.
  The Holy Spirit is in me and guides me in all truths. John 16:13; He puts in me to will and to do for His good pleasure. Philippians 2:13
- They were faithless.
  I am saved by grace through faith. Ephesians 2:8; I have been given a measure of faith. Romans 12:3
- They were heartless.
  The love of God has been poured into my heart by the Holy Spirit. Romans 5:5
- They were loveless.
  I operate in the fruit of the Spirit, including love. Galatians 5:22-23; I love my neighbor as myself. Mark 12:31
- They were merciless.
  I have been given a crown of mercy, and am merciful to others. Psalm 103:4
- They do such things even though they know that those who do deserve to die.

> *The wages of sin is death, but the gift of God is eternal life*
> *through Jesus Christ. Romans 6:23; In Christ I have abundant*
> *life. John 10:10*

- They approve of and applaud others who practice them.
  I do not conform to this world, but I am transformed by the
  renewing of my mind, that I may prove what is that good,
  acceptable, and perfect will of God. Romans 12:2

If this passage from Romans 1 is describing all people who engage in any form of same-gender intimacy, then these thirty specific items will accurately describe me and any gay Christian that you know. It is my position that Paul was not describing gay Christians and that gay Christians would be better described by those phrases from Scripture listed in italics. Those words could describe any of us before we came into a relationship with Christ and experienced His forgiveness and atonement for sin. However, Paul is not describing Christians.

Many kind-hearted, non-affirming Christians who agree that the thirty descriptors above do not describe gay Christians, still maintain that Romans 1 is discussing "homosexuals." This inconsistency reveals a fallacy in the non-affirming argument. To be clear, if one holds that Romans 1 is condemning homosexuality, then a faithful, consistent argument must hold that those words, at least in general, describe homosexual people, including gay Christians. If one cannot agree that the words "wickedness, evil, greed, depravity" describe gay Christians, then a valid argument must conclude that Paul is not referring to all gay people.

On the other hand, if one holds that these words describe all gay people, I would ask if that person believes they describe him also. In other words, as per Romans 2:1, these words describe all of us at any moment in time that we were not living according to Scripture and God's will for our lives.

In Summary, the Rebuttal and Response

Traditionalists' rebuttal: The passage is about same-sex sexual activity. It does not matter that these people were not gay nor that they were not Christians. People who engage in same-sex sexual activity have rejected God's design for His creation. They worship and serve their own idols, which is their same-sex activity. All same-sex sexual activity is unnatural, and one must have been given over to a reprobate mind in order to engage in it. The descriptors at the end of Romans 1 may not specifically describe every gay person, but in general, this is how God describes homosexuality. Same-sex sexual activity is a rejection of God's design and is explicitly condemned in Scripture.

My response: The passage is about idol worshipers who participated in temple prostitution in ancient Rome. Paul described people who hated God and engaged in all manner of depravity including same-sex sexual orgies among straight people. These acts were shameful and unnatural. However, gay Christians do not reject God. They engage in natural acts, not unnatural acts. The idol worshipers were engaged in same-sex activity that involved sexual excess and unbridled passions. This does not apply to a faithful, monogamous, Christ-centered, gay Christian couple or a faithful gay Christian.

Only one of these perspectives can accurately reflect God's heart.

If the church *might* be wrong on this issue, then we must stop the rejection of gay Christians in our churches, and by extension, LGBTQ people in our communities.

My Final Thought on Romans 1

Does the church's rejection of gay Christians, which has left countless suicides and broken families in its wake, really hinge on a passage about the same-sex orgies of idol worshipers who hated God? How long will Christians continue to gamble the souls of gay people on their misunderstanding of this passage?

8

GENESIS 19: THE STORY OF SODOM AND GOMORRAH

This is a story about gang rape. The men of the town sought out Lot's guests, who were angels, in the hopes of raping them. The men were struck blind by the angels and thus did not succeed in their quest. The suggestion that this story has anything whatsoever to do with loving, same-gender couples or gay Christians is simply invalid. Gang rape is wicked, and God brought down His judgment on the men of these towns, destroying them.

The Bible mentions Sodom and Gomorrah several times. It never refers to any same-gender attractions or actions that led to the destruction of the cities. Scripture records,

> Now this was the sin of your sister Sodom: She and her daughters were arrogant, overfed and unconcerned; they did not help the poor and needy. They were haughty and did detestable things before Me. Therefore, I did away with them as you have seen. (Ezekiel 16:49-50)

Jesus compared Sodom and Gomorrah to towns that did not welcome His disciples. (Matthew 10:14-15)

There is a terrible parallel story in Judges 19 where the men of the town sought to gang rape a man but were offered a woman instead. They accepted the offer. The Scripture states that the men raped, abused, and ultimately killed her that night. This story has never been held up as a biblical text against heterosexuality, and neither should any gang rape be compared to homosexuality, Christian or otherwise.

New Testament scholar Jeffrey Siker writes,

> As for the Sodom and Gomorrah story, one can certainly conclude that homosexual rape (just like heterosexual rape, though this seems of little concern to Lot in the story) is an abomination before God, but it does not follow from this that all expressions of homosexuality are prohibited. (David's sin of adultery with Bathsheba does not make all heterosexual expressions sinful!)[54]

Every Man in Town Was Gay?

Sadly, it has become commonplace for Christians to simply equate Sodom and Gomorrah with homosexuality. I think that one can sense at the very least, that this interpretation is a stretch beyond what is clearly seen in Scripture. We are told that every single man, both young and old, came to rape Lot's guests. (verse 4) If one

---

[54] Siker, J. S. (1994). How to Decide?: Homosexual Christians, the Bible, and Gentile Inclusion. *Theology Today, 51*(2), 226.

equates this story with homosexuality, then I suggest that person must be willing to consider carefully the following two ideas:

1. Do traditionalist Christians honestly believe that every single man in the cities was gay? That's a statistical impossibility. How could anyone in the towns reproduce if all the men were gay? This idea is completely illogical. However, if one believes that this story is about homosexuality, then it follows that one must believe that the people intending to rape the guests were all homosexuals.

2. Do traditionalist Christians honestly believe that the motivation to rape Lot's guests was sexual desire? Matthew Vines wrote,

> The men of Sodom demanded that Lot bring out his guests so that the men could have sex with them. But this was not an expression of sexual desire. It was a threatened gang rape. In the ancient world, for a man to be raped was considered the ultimate degradation.... Men seeking to shame a conquered foe often would rape him in order to complete his humiliation. Aggression and dominance were the motives in these situations, not sexual attraction.[55]

The Terms Are Not Interchangeable

I was stunned to hear a senior pastor at Bethel Church in Redding, California, "quote" a portion of Jeremiah 23:14. Below are both his quote and the actual Scripture in the NIV. I cannot find any Bible translation or paraphrase that reads this verse as he did.

---

[55] *God and the Gay Christian,* page 65.

- Pastor Kris Vallotton: "He [God] rebukes the prophets for, get this, I will read it to you: 'for strengthening the hands of those who commit adultery and fornication and homosexuality.'"[56]
- Jeremiah 23:14:

> And among the prophets of Jerusalem I have seen something horrible: They commit adultery and live a lie. They strengthen the hands of evildoers, so that not one of them turns from their wickedness. They are all like Sodom to me; the people of Jerusalem are like Gomorrah.

As the reader can see, the traditional view simply converts any mention of "Sodom and Gomorrah" into "homosexuality." In my opinion, this is an egregious misrepresentation of Scripture. I would offer, for those who disagree with me, that at the very least, converting "Sodom and Gomorrah" to "homosexuality" is not a faithful application of Scripture. Clearly, people who sit under teaching like that trust their leaders and accept that Jeremiah 23 condemns "those who commit homosexuality." However, Jeremiah 23:14 does not refer to homosexuality. To suggest otherwise, in my opinion, is an embarrassment to modern scriptural scholarship.[57]

Furthermore, please note that God declared the prophets and the people of Jerusalem to be like Sodom and Gomorrah to Him. This

---

[56] Vallotton, K. (2019 December 8). "Sovereign Providence". Sermon delivered at Bethel Church, Redding, CA. Retrieved December 27, 2019 from https://www.bethel.tv/en/podcasts/sermons/episodes/478. This quote begins at 26:19 in the audio.

[57] This is Daniel Helminiak's phrase. Helminiak, D. A. (1995). *What the Bible Really Says about Homosexuality*. San Francisco, CA: Alamo Square Press, page 99.

alone provides very strong evidence that Sodom and Gomorrah is not about homosexuality.[58]

In Summary

The story of Sodom and Gomorrah is about treating guests, the poor, and the needy, detestably. In short, it is about gang rape. Arguments suggesting that the Sodom and Gomorrah story has anything to do with gay Christians lack merit. Nevertheless, for decades, mainstream Christians have wrongly used this passage to suggest that gang rape is equivalent to same-gender attraction and same-gender relationships, even Christ-centered, loving, monogamous, gay Christian relationships.

---

[58] This idea is attributable to my friend Mary, personal text conversation, January 13, 2020.

9

TWO PASSAGES
FROM LEVITICUS

Leviticus 18:22, RSV: "You shall not lie with a male as with a woman; it is an abomination."
Leviticus 20:13, RSV: "If a man lies with a male as with a woman, both of them have committed an abomination; they shall be put to death, their blood is upon them."

The word "abomination" in these passages has been very effectively used like a sledgehammer to condemn gay people. It is important to note that in Leviticus 11:11, God also referred to eating shellfish as an abomination. Yet, we do not deem it inappropriate to eat shellfish, despite knowing that God described it with such strong language. Furthermore, in the law, we see the death penalty applied to a number of sins, including anyone who disobeyed his parents. "A stubborn and rebellious son who does not obey his father and mother" was to be stoned to death. (Deuteronomy 21:18-21)

Relations Forbidden During a Woman's Menses

Let's examine a different law within the same chapter. In Leviticus 18:19, Scripture records that sexual relations between a male and a female were forbidden during a woman's menses. The punishment was that the couple be cut off from the nation of Israel. (Leviticus 20:18) Today, this practice is not considered sinful. We must ask ourselves, what was the reason for the prohibition, and does that reason apply to us today? That specific law concerned ceremonial uncleanliness related to separation from the practices of surrounding nations. Anyone who was ceremonially unclean was not able to come before the assembly of the Lord. Prior to the atoning work of Christ on the cross, certain cleansing rituals were performed to cover ceremonial uncleanliness. However, because of Christ's sacrifice, in the new covenant, we no longer regard these ceremonial laws. "We have been made holy through the sacrifice of the body of Jesus Christ once for all." (Hebrews 10:10) Therefore, the prohibition against sexual activity during a woman's menses is no longer applicable.[59]

Procreation and the Promise of Innumerable Descendants

It was crucial for the Israelite nation to increase in number. Procreation was so important to what would become the people of Israel, that when Onan "spilled his seed on the ground" in Genesis 38:9-10, the Lord, in His anger, had him put to death. The blessings that God promised to Abraham involved descendants "as numerous as the stars in the sky and as the sand on the seashore." (Genesis 22:17)

---

[59] A beautiful and thorough discussion of the literature and research which clarifies this position was done by Matthew Vines in his book, *God and the Gay Christian*, 2014.

Procreation was the blessing for the people of Israel. However, in Christ, the blessing comes via spiritual rebirth, having been buried with Him and raised again to newness of life. (Romans 6:4, Colossians 2:12) In Christ, the family of God grows and is blessed through people coming into relationship with Him, not through procreation.

Patriarchy

Patriarchy is a social system in which men hold primary power and predominate in roles of leadership.[60] Patriarchy is present throughout Scripture. Recall that Lot was deemed righteous (II Peter 2:7) despite having offered his virgin daughters up for rape. (Genesis 19:8) Trying to understand the Bible today without considering its patriarchal context would be unreasonable and disheartening. The status that males held over females was so great that it would be preferable, even righteous, for a man to allow his daughters to be raped than for his male guests to experience such torture. Lot stated to the men of Sodom and Gomorrah, "Let me, I beg of you, bring [my virgin daughters] out to you; only do nothing to these men, for they have come under the protection of my roof." (Genesis 19:8, Amplified Bible) The similar situation in Judges 19:24 (ESV) is as follows: "Behold, here are my virgin daughter and his concubine... Violate them and do with them what seems good to you, but against this man do not do this outrageous thing."

In the Old Testament, males and females were not peers of equal status. Within that framework, it may be easier to understand that sex was seen as an act "done to" someone of lower status. (Think, active partner, passive partner.) The prohibition against male same-sex activity had to do with the status of the partners. Male-male sex

---

[60] Wikipedia contributors. (2019 November 14). Patriarchy. In Wikipedia, The Free Encyclopedia. Retrieved November 24, 2019, from www.Wikipedia.org.

acts would denigrate the passive partner to the role of a woman. Note the wording in both Levitical passages, "as with a woman." This is abhorrent in a patriarchal culture. The practice of pederasty (male same-sex acts with younger boys, typically prostitutes or slaves), was historically accepted in most cultures, but such exploitative and abusive behavior was forbidden by God and thus by the Jewish people. As noted in chapter 4, the German Bibles from the 1800s recognized the passages in Leviticus to be a prohibition of pederasty.

Importantly, in the original Hebrew text, there are two different words for man.[61] This suggests that the passage is not simply about an ordinary man lying with another ordinary man; there is some distinction. The Blue Letter Bible tool reveals the following Hebrew text: "If a man (*iysh*) also lie with mankind (*zakar*)...."[62] The word *zakar* is translated as "man child" or male child four times in the King James Version.[63]

Although much debate has centered around temple prostitution as the reason for the same-sex prohibitions in Leviticus, recent scholarship suggests there may not be sufficient evidence of this.[64] Interestingly, even within that debate, the main argument against the act is the denigration of the passive partner to the role of a woman.[65] The same is said of the common practice of pederasty.[66] The practice, which was condemned, was exploitative and forbidden in a culture that found women to be of much lower status than men.

---

[61] Gerig, B. L. (2004). "The Clobber Passages: Re-examined". Retrieved July 23, 2019 from www.Epistle.us.

[62] www.BlueLetterBible.org.

[63] Ibid.

[64] Keen, Karen R. (2018). *Scripture, Ethics & the Possibility of Same-Sex Relationships*. Grand Rapids, MI: Wm. B. Eerdmans Publishing Company, page 119, number 3.

[65] Ibid, page 17.

[66] *God and the Gay Christian*, page 87.

Anatomical Complementarity

It must be noted that anatomical complementarity (the "fittedness of the parts") was not the issue here. If anatomical complementarity were the reason behind prohibition of male same-sex acts, then that would necessarily extend to women. There is no prohibition of female same-sex acts in the Mosaic law. Some may consider that the Bible simply failed to address women since it was a patriarchal society. However, that is not the case, as prohibitions are declared for sex acts between a man and an animal, as well as, specifically, between a woman and an animal. (Leviticus 18:23) Importantly, there is no passage in Scripture which alludes to anatomical fittedness. I will discuss this further in chapter 10.

Does the Law Serve as Our Guide?

Most importantly, Christians are not under the law. Likewise, the law was never given to Gentiles (non-Jews). When Gentiles came into the Christian faith in the first years after Christ's life, death, and resurrection, the Christian leadership met at the famous Council of Jerusalem, circa 50 AD, to declare that Gentiles are not under the Law of Moses, and do not require circumcision and adherence to the Mosaic law. (Acts 15:1-31)

Many traditionalists categorize the laws of the Old Testament. Some categories include moral laws, food laws, purity laws, ceremonial laws, and social laws. This categorization is not biblical. But it provides a way for scholars to sort out and study the various rules. Some people make distinctions between those laws that they believe Christians should keep versus those that are no longer kept. Some believe that the "moral laws" must continue to be upheld today. For example, we maintain the law against murder but do not keep dietary restrictions.

Galatians 3:24b-25 (NLT): "The law was our guardian until Christ came; it protected us until we could be made right with God through faith. And now that the way of faith has come, we no longer need the law as our guardian."

In various translations, that Scripture reads, the law was our guardian (NIV), trainer (BLB), tutor (NKJV), schoolmaster (KJV), teacher (CEV), guide (Aramaic Bible in Plain English), before Christ. However, after Christ fulfilled the law, we are no longer under the guardianship of the law.

If the law is no longer our guide, how are we to live? Jesus addressed that.

Matthew 22:37-40:

> Jesus replied: "Love the Lord your God with all your heart and with all your soul and with all your mind." This is the first and greatest commandment. And the second is like it: "Love your neighbor as yourself." All the law and the prophets hang on these two commandments.

Paul also addressed it. Galatians 5:13-14:

> You, my brothers and sisters, were called to be free. But do not use your freedom to indulge the flesh; rather, serve one another humbly in love. For the entire law is fulfilled in keeping this one command: "Love your neighbor as yourself."

The author of Hebrews wrote that the new covenant, which required Christ's atoning sacrifice for sin, "has made the first one [the old covenant] obsolete." (Hebrews 8:13) Paul referred to the law as "the ministry of death." (II Corinthians 3:7, ESV) In Colossians 2:13-14 (1984 NIV), it is written, "God made you alive with Christ. He forgave us all our sins, having canceled the written code, with its regulations, that was against us and that stood opposed to us; He took it away, nailing it to the cross." Christ fulfilled the law; thus, Christians are not under obligation to the law, but rather to faith in Christ and the guidance of the Holy Spirit.

Scripture records that He "canceled the written code;" thus, we consider the written code canceled. Nevertheless, every single word in Scripture is important. We categorize the laws because that helps us to study them. However, should Christians create a category of laws and declare that we should uphold them? There are at least three good reasons that this would be a bad idea.

1. First and foremost, God declared the written code canceled. Why should man decide that some part of the written code is not canceled, but meant to continue to be a guide for us?

2. If we created a category which is not found in Scripture, we may make a fundamental mistake in creating that list. In fact, typically, the "moral laws" include "homosexuality." However, previous translations saw the Levitical passages as a prohibition of pederasty, not of people with a homosexual inclination. Furthermore, there is nothing in the Old Testament law about women having relations with women; yet the word "homosexuality" is gender-neutral. In other words, man has added a "sin" to the "moral laws" that is not even present in the Old Testament law.

3. Galatians 3:10 states, "For all who rely on the works of the law are under a curse, as it is written: 'Cursed is everyone who does not continue to do everything written in the Book of the Law.'" Why would a Christian, who has been redeemed from the law because of Christ's sacrifice on Calvary, (Colossians 2:14) put himself under the law? The

law is described as "the ministry of death," (II Corinthians 3:7, ESV) something that "stood against us and condemned us," (Colossians 2:14) something that is "not based on faith." (Galatians 3:12) We are free from the law! Let us not, like the "foolish Galatians," put ourselves back under the law. (Galatians 3:1-3) But by all means, if one chooses to be under the law, it is important to keep all of it, as the above Scripture (Galatians 3:10) states.

In the new covenant, we live by faith, not by the law. In order for us to accomplish living without an external code of law, God has deposited the Holy Spirit into our hearts and minds to guide us. Scripture specifically says that we no longer need the law as our guardian. Thus, the idea that man must create a category of the law that should serve as our guide does not reflect the heart of God. If the Holy Spirit in us guides us to study and memorize Scripture, to honor our parents, and to avoid covetous thoughts, then we are living according to the commandments of Jesus, via the Holy Spirit of God within us. He bears witness from within, that we are to love God and love each other. We live by faith in the guidance of the Holy Spirit, not by the written code.

"All Scripture is God-breathed and is useful for teaching, rebuking, correcting and training in righteousness." (II Timothy 3:16) This includes the written code, which has been deemed "canceled." It is very important for Christians to study and understand the law, for whom and why it was given, from our perspective on this side of the cross and Christ's resurrection. In Christ, the law of the spirit of life has set us free from the law of sin and death. Jesus came to live among us, in the likeness of sinful flesh, and condemned sin through His righteousness. Thus, through Christ, we Christians, all of us who are included in Christ, have fulfilled the righteous requirements of the law. (Romans 8:2-4) We cannot fulfill the righteous requirements of the law by attempting to keep them. The only option for fulfilling the law is through faith in Christ.

In Summary

Although we are no longer under the written code, we study it carefully, as the Holy Spirit guides us. The prohibition against male same-sex acts in Leviticus was grounded in a patriarchal culture that is not relevant in our lives today, even as the prohibition against sexual activity during a woman's menses is not relevant in our lives today. In Scripture, we see the increasing status of women, beginning from the time when Lot's daughters were offered to rapists. Recall that Phoebe was a deaconess, (Romans 16:1) that Paul and Luke both referred to Aquila and Priscilla using the woman's name first in some instances, that Paul considered husbands and wives to be mutually responsible to each other sexually, (I Corinthians 7:4) and importantly, the declaration in Galatians 3:28, "there is neither Jew nor Gentile, neither slave nor free, nor is there male and female, for you are all one in Christ Jesus." Again, above all, Christians are not under the law.

10

ONE MAN, ONE WOMAN

In Genesis 1:27 and 5:2, the Word of God states, "Male and female He created them." In Genesis 2, Scripture states that "a man shall leave his father and mother and cling to his wife, and the two shall become one flesh." In Matthew 19 and Mark 10, Jesus repeats this. In Ephesians 5, Paul repeats it.[67] This is the Church's foundation for "one man, one woman." Importantly, for those without a thorough knowledge of Scripture, the particular phrase "one man, one woman," is not actually in the Bible. It is simply a phrase used to illustrate the Church's view of "God's design," that is, their vision of Christian marriage.

One Flesh

Many assume that "the two shall become one flesh" has some sense of anatomical complementarity associated with it; that is, the "fittedness" of anatomical parts. However, this is not the case. In Scripture, "one flesh" is seen in terms of the ties of kinship. When Adam met Eve in Genesis 2:23, he stated, "this is now bone of my bones and flesh of my flesh." Uncle Laban declared when he saw his

---

[67] This is how my pastor began a sermon one Sunday in 2018.

nephew Jacob, "you are my own flesh and blood." (Genesis 29:14) In II Samuel 5:1 (NKJV), the tribes of Israel said to King David, "we are your bone and your flesh." In Leviticus 18, it is written that a man's grandchildren are his "own flesh."

When Paul wrote (in I Corinthians 6:16) that to unite oneself to a prostitute would be to become "one flesh" with her, he was denouncing the act that would unite a couple physically but not otherwise.[68] However, kinship ties, although not always sexual (as in the case of Laban and Jacob, for example), refer to unity in many and various aspects of a kinship relationship. A marriage necessarily requires this one flesh unity, but one flesh unity does not require anatomical complementarity.

There is nothing anywhere in Scripture regarding anatomical complementarity. The idea of anatomical complementarity is a social construct, one that appeals to common sense, as follows: God made male and female, and their parts fit together appropriately and allow for procreation, and this is His perfect plan for everyone. Within the traditional evangelical world, this idea seems wise, and the disagreement of it seems foolish. But the latter half of this statement is simply not found anywhere in Scripture.

Exceptions to "One Man, One Woman" in Scripture: God/
King David, Jesus/Eunuchs, Paul/No Longer Male and Female

There is an important problem with this seemingly obvious, unambiguous tenet that marriage is exclusively between one man and one woman. That is, God Himself gave King David many wives.

---

[68] The study of "one flesh" is beautifully articulated in Dr. Brownson's book. Brownson, James. (2013). *Bible Gender Sexuality: Reframing the Church's Debate on Same-Sex Relationships*. Grand Rapids, MI: William B. Eerdmans Publishing Company, page 102.

God's best for David, although I do not fully understand it, was not one man, one woman. God said, through the prophet Nathan, "I gave your master's house to you, and your master's wives into your arms." (II Samuel 12:8) If it were simply recorded that David had his master's wives, we could assume that God was displeased, as we know He was displeased with Solomon's 700 wives and 300 concubines.[69] However, God made it clear that He, God Himself, gave David several wives. God even said that if that had been too little, "I would have given you more." Scripture has given us many examples of marriages that do not fit the idea of one man and one woman. This particular example with King David is one exception to that rule that does not dishonor God.

Jesus also gave us an exception to the idea of one man, one woman. In Matthew 19, the Pharisees asked Jesus about divorce. He responded with the creation story from Genesis, affirming marriage between a man and a woman. Subsequently, the Pharisees pressed Jesus based on their discussion about divorce, saying perhaps it would be better for a man not to marry. Consider if this question were presented to a pastor of a typical church today. He would take the opportunity to reaffirm marriage as a biblical institution, defined by one man and one woman. However, when Jesus was asked about marriage the second time, He did something truly remarkable. Rather than affirming the traditional view of marriage again, Jesus affirmed an exception to one man, one woman.

He spoke of eunuchs, the sexual minority of His day.[70] He stated, in answering their question,

---

[69] I Kings 11:1-13

[70] If you ever wondered what Jesus was referring to in this verse, I highly recommend Sandra Turnbull's book. Turnbull, Sandra. (2012). *God's Gay Agenda*. Bellflower, CA: Glory Publishing.

> Not everyone can accept this word, but only those
> to whom it has been given. For there are eunuchs
> who were born that way, and there are eunuchs who
> have been made eunuchs by others—and there are
> those who choose to live like eunuchs for the sake
> of the kingdom of heaven. The one who can accept
> this should accept it. (Matthew 19:11-12)

Is there one thing that everyone could agree on regarding eunuchs? Recall Hegai, the eunuch who groomed Ester to be chosen by King Xerxes as his new queen. (Esther 2:8-17) As was typical, a king's harem was overseen by a eunuch. A eunuch could be trusted because he had no sexual interest in women.

Jesus Himself pointed out that not everyone will be able to accept this statement. I believe that includes some of those reading this book today. Jesus took the opportunity during a discussion on marriage and divorce to point out that some people, which we know to be a small minority, will not fit within the one man, one woman category, and actually were "born that way." He never suggested healing, restoring, reprogramming, or fixing these natural-born eunuchs.[71]

Another exception to the traditional view of marriage between a man and a woman is a Scripture most Christians are very familiar with. Paul, reading the Greek Septuagint, knew well that God created mankind, "male and female." Paul uses this specific phrase in Galatians 3:28. The NIV reads, "There is neither Jew nor Gentile, neither slave nor free, nor is there male and female, for you are all one in Christ Jesus."

Please note the use of the conjunction "nor" for Jew/Gentile and slave/free, but Paul used "and" for male/female. In fact, Paul used in Greek the exact words that were written in the Greek Septuagint

---

[71] Ibid, page 137.

in both Genesis 1:27 and 5:2. I have underlined the Greek words, "male and female," which are identical in the following passages.

- Genesis 1:27: "ἄρσεν καὶ θῆλυ" - "Male and female" He created them.
- Genesis 5:2: "ἄρσεν καὶ θῆλυ ἐποίησεν αὐτούς" - "Male and female" He created them.
- Mark 10:6: "Ἄρσεν καὶ θῆλυ" - "Male and female" He created them.
- Galatians 3:28: "οὐκ ἔνι Ἰουδαῖος οὐδὲ Ἕλλην οὐκ ἔνι δοῦλος οὐδὲ ἐλεύθερος οὐκ ἔνι ἄρσεν καὶ θῆλυ πάντες γὰρ ὑμεῖς εἷς ἐστε ἐν Χριστῷ Ἰησοῦ." This reads, "There is neither Jew nor Gentile, neither slave nor free, nor is there male and female, for you are all one in Christ Jesus."[72]

Please take a moment and consider this. The very words in the creation story, "male and female He created them," are used in Galatians 3:28, "nor is there male and female." Paul actually interrupted the structure of his sentence. He did not follow "Jew nor Gentile, slave nor free," with "male nor female." Rather, using the exact phrase as it was written in the Septuagint, he wrote, "nor is there male and female." This must account, at the very least, as an exception to the one man, one woman principle.

We saw in Scripture the fulfillment of "there is neither Jew nor Gentile" when Cornelius and his family were brought into the Christian faith. Approximately twelve years later, the church leaders met at the famous Council of Jerusalem, described in Acts 15, allowing for Gentiles to become Christians and declaring that they were not required to adhere to the Mosaic law or circumcision. In the first years of the early Church, the believers were mostly Jewish. We therefore see "there is neither Jew nor Gentile" of Galatians

---

[72] The Greek translation of the Old Testament Scriptures is taken from the Septuagint as found on www.BibleHub.com.

3:28 fulfilled in Scripture. Today, the Church is almost exclusively Gentiles.

Regarding the dissolution of the distinction between slave and free, we see a trajectory within Scripture of the fulfillment of this. Specifically, slavery was accepted in biblical times, yet we see in Scripture Paul's request that his friend Philemon free a particular slave who had become a brother in Christ. Today, we recognize that the Bible's overarching principles of love, and Paul's declaration that there was neither slave nor free, signaled an end to the practice of slavery.[73] This issue is now settled within the Church.

The final principle in the Galatians 3:28 verse is that there is no longer male and female; for we are all one in Christ Jesus. This use of the exact phrase from the creation story to declare that in Christ Jesus, "nor is there male and female," must constitute at the very least an exception to the traditional view of marriage between one man and one woman.

A Commonly Accepted Exception to "One Man, One Woman"

Another obvious example of an exception which is allowed today, even within mainstream churches, is remarried couples.[74] A man who is remarried once would no longer be described by one man, one woman, but rather, one man, two women. Scripture states that remarriage constitutes adultery, with three exceptions: sexual immorality, (Matthew 19:9) the death of a spouse, (Romans 7:2) and if the unbeliever leaves the marriage. (I Corinthians 7:15) Nevertheless, there are many remarried couples in mainstream,

---

[73] This sentence is attributable to someone else; however, I am unable to locate the source.

[74] I discuss this in greater depth in chapter 12.

traditional churches today, including those whose divorces did not fall within the three exceptions.

Does the "Image of God" Require Heterosexual Marriage?

Another aspect of complementarity is considered in the suggestion that male and female together make up the image of God. However, this is not biblical, as all of mankind has been created in the image of God. One cannot correctly assert that single men or women are not created in God's image. Jesus was fully human and unmarried, yet He was still the complete image of God. (Colossians 1:15)

Procreation

Some suggest that a couple must be capable of procreation to fulfill "God's best," or "God's design." New Testament scholar Dr. James Brownson writes,

> The moral logic of the Bible is thus fairly clear on this subject; procreation is an important purpose of marriage, and marriage is the sole context where procreation should happen, but marriage has something more than procreation as its essential reason for being. When we consider some of the most extensive discussions on marriage in Scripture, including Genesis 2, Song of Songs, Ephesians 5:21-33, and I Corinthians 7, procreation is entirely absent from the discussion, and the focus falls on kinship, sharing, mutual support, self-control, and intimacy. And nowhere in Scripture is the absence

of children a justification for dissolving the marriage bond itself.[75]

Procreation is emphasized for the nation of Israel. God's blessing to Abraham involved descendants as numerous as the sand on the seashore. (Genesis 22:17) However, in many key parts of the biblical text, procreation is scarcely mentioned. Churches today do not consider the ability to procreate when marrying couples.

The Creation Story: His Perfect Plan for Everyone?

Let's examine each part of the idea of complementarity separately.

1. *God made male and female, and their anatomical parts fit together appropriately and allow for procreation.* No one on either side of the debate questions this. Without a doubt, God made males and females who together, as a family unit, may have and raise children. Couples consisting of a man and a woman, with or without children, make up the vast majority of Christian families.
2. *"One man, one woman" is His perfect plan for everyone.* This is the crux of the issue. We all agree that God created Adam and Eve, not Adam and Steve. Certainly the very first male would not have been homosexual, nor would he have been a eunuch, nor would he have been given the gift of celibacy. However, there is no biblical reason to extrapolate from the creation story that the union of a man and woman is the *only* allowable union.

Dr. Jeffrey Siker wrote,

---

[75] *Bible, Gender, Sexuality*, page 118.

> To use the creation stories to argue for heterosexuality as the exclusive norm is largely an argument from silence, since nothing there is said about homosexuality. Heterosexuality may be the dominant form of sexuality, but it does not follow that it is the only form of appropriate sexuality.[76]

Reverend Bruce Lowe agreed. He wrote,

> [The creation story] does not mention friendship, for example, and yet we do not assume that friendship is condemned or abnormal. It does not mention the single state, and yet we know that singleness is not condemned, and that in certain religious circumstances it is held in very high esteem.[77]

For decades Americans did not recognize that gay people could be healthy, sober-minded, upstanding citizens. Thus, the traditional view that heterosexuality was the exclusive norm was not questioned. However, we realize now that gay Christians worship in our churches with us, and many declare the lordship of Christ in their lives. The presence of healthy gay Christians among us should cause traditionalists to reconsider the long-held notion that heterosexuality is His perfect design for everyone. This idea is never described in the Bible. It is simply extrapolated from Scripture and declared by those who hold this view. We see heterosexuality throughout Scripture, but nowhere in Scripture is it suggested that *everyone* must be heterosexual. In fact, there are scriptural exceptions to one man, one woman in general and even to heterosexuality specifically. Not

---

[76] Siker, J.S. (1994). How to Decide?: Homosexual Christians, the Bible, and Gentile Inclusion. *Theology Today, 51*(2), 226.

[77] Lowe, B. (2001). "A Letter to Louise: A Biblical Affirmation of Homosexuality". Retrieved September 2019 from www.GodMadeMeGay. blogspot.com.

all people were created with the capacity for heterosexuality; thus, it is not His plan for *everyone*.

In Summary

Without a doubt, the traditional marriage between a man and a woman is appropriate for the vast majority of Christians, but there are exceptions. King David, to whom God gave many wives, was one exception. Jesus's acknowledgment of people who were born as eunuchs, that is, without the capacity for heterosexuality, is another valid exception. Paul's letter to the churches in Galatia represents another exception. Remarried couples and gay Christians are still other exceptions to this "one man, one woman" rule.

11

OTHER SCRIPTURES TO CONSIDER WITH REGARD TO GAY CHRISTIANS

The first ten include Scriptures which are quoted within non-affirming arguments to support the idea that homosexuality is a sin. I address these carefully. The seven verses that follow list Scriptures that affirm gay Christians.

Go and Sin No More

John 8:11b (KJV): "Go and sin no more." Christ has atoned for our sins by His sacrifice on the cross. We have been forgiven and set free from bondage to sin. (Romans 6:6) As Christians, our highest goal is to bring glory and honor to God in every aspect of our lives. We agree wholeheartedly with this saying. We want no sin in our lives.

Non-affirming arguments use this verse because they believe the premise, "homosexuality is a sin." When this Scripture is used referring to gay people, it typically means, go and renounce homosexuality, and do not act on homosexual desires.

However, I believe that their premise is wrong. In the context of a monogamous, permanent, same-gender partnership, there is no sin. Similarly, a single gay Christian is not living in sin in either his quest for celibacy or his desire for loving, monogamous partnership.

Faithful gay Christians repent of all sin in our lives, as do straight Christians. We trust in the atoning work on the cross, with humility and enormous gratitude that our sins are forgiven.

In summary, this would only be an argument against sin. If homosexuality in general is not sinful, as I assert, then this verse does not apply to gay people any differently than it applies to all people.

Jesus Defined Marriage: One Man, One Woman

Matthew 19:3-12: As noted in the previous chapter, Jesus affirmed the appropriate marriage for the vast majority of people in this passage as between a man and a woman. We cannot ignore that He also affirmed an exception to that marriage. When asked by the Pharisees about divorce, Jesus replied,

> Haven't you read that at the beginning the Creator "made them male and female," and said, "For this reason a man will leave his father and mother and be united to his wife, and the two will become one flesh"? So they are no longer two, but one flesh. Therefore what God has joined together, let no one separate.

The Pharisees had brought up divorce, referring to the Law of Moses. Jesus had appealed to an earlier precedent,[78] that is, the creation story, to demonstrate that divorce was not God's original intention

---

[78] *Scripture, Ethics, & the Possibility of Same-Sex Relationships,* page 31.

and plan, but rather, committed marriage. However, Jesus explained that God allowed for divorce because of their "hardness of heart," but that divorce and remarriage would be equivalent to adultery.

When the Pharisees asked if perhaps it was better not to marry at all, Jesus actually affirmed the sexual minorities of His day, referring to "eunuchs who were born that way," (Matthew 19:12) recognizing that many eunuchs are called into service to God.

Does that have implications for the typical, non-affirming view that all people were fearfully and wonderfully made with the capacity for heterosexuality, as I noted in chapter 3? I think to be faithful to this Scripture, one must conclude that some people are fearfully and wonderfully made, even without the capacity for heterosexuality.

If Anyone Causes One of These to Stumble

In Mark 9:42, Jesus states, "If anyone causes one of these little ones—those who believe in Me—to stumble, it would be better for them if a large millstone were hung around their neck and they were thrown into the sea." Some non-affirming arguments suggest that this refers to gay people, because some children may be enticed *to be gay* if they know older gay people. This is not an appropriate interpretation of Christ's words. Gay Christians and their straight allies have no interest in the idea of "promoting homosexuality," as the media presented in previous decades. We do not believe it is possible to cause someone to be gay. That idea is entirely illogical.

Imagine the following scenario: a gay couple is invited to and attends a church that appears to be friendly and welcoming. During the fourth service they had attended, they both answer an altar call early in the service to trust in Jesus and receive salvation. They cry, they pray with the leaders of the church, and they go back to their seats, and sit, one with their arm around the other, for the sermon. They learn that week that they are in a non-affirming church and their consideration of joining it would not be an option for them. They were never called, never invited back, and in fact, ran into one of the church leaders at their child's school from time to time, who never invited them back to church or acknowledged that they used to come. They had felt the call of Jesus in their lives, and they wanted to answer that call and become a couple of faith. But they started to realize that they were not wanted in that church. That really became a difficult hurdle. This story does not yet have an ending. Sadly, based on Christ's words above, I think this is a valid example of causing people to stumble in their walk with Jesus.

In summary, non-affirming arguments believe Jesus is condemning gay people for "causing children to become gay" (which we don't believe to be possible or desirable). Affirming arguments believe that Jesus is referring to Christians rejecting people from the church. If you stand in agreement with the premise, "homosexuality is a sin," then any gay person who believes that they cannot be a Christian has been caused to stumble by this ongoing, widespread belief. If the possibility exists that the premise is wrong, then we need to do the work to correct this. If by chance a gay couple responds to the altar call in our local church, let's be available to welcome and disciple them, rather than reject them.

Wives, Submit to Your Husbands

Ephesians 5:22-25: "Wives, submit to your husbands." "Husbands, love your wives, just as Christ loved the Church." In the churches, women were not allowed to speak. No woman was allowed to usurp the authority of any man. (I Timothy 2:11-14) Deacons, elders, teachers were all men, with one possible exception for deacons. If any woman had a question, she was not allowed to ask the question within the assembly; she was instructed to ask her husband at home. (I Corinthians 14:34-35)[79]

This was a patriarchal culture that did not allow for equality between males and females. We continue to apply this rule today, that wives must submit to their husbands. We confess it, we agree with the principle, but in reality, marriage is typically between men and women of equal status, and decisions are agreed upon. Nevertheless, when a decision must be made, and a compromise is not possible, then, just as the husband loves the wife as Christ loves the Church, it is appropriate that the wife submit to the husband. In gay relationships, there is typically a spiritual leader who assumes this role, in love, as Christ loved the Church.

The use of the words husbands and wives in Paul's teachings does not preclude partnerships between couples of the same gender. Consider the Constitution of the United States, which refers to the president as "he,"[80] and does not preclude a female president.

Paul's original audience likely did not have openly gay couples. Today it does. As the Holy Spirit led Paul to write and leads us to understand Scripture, He reveals His purpose and pleasure to us. Just as the Holy Spirit bears witness with our spirits that women are allowed to ask a question during a question and answer session at church, and, in some churches, to teach men at times, although both of these were strictly forbidden in Scripture, and just as the Holy Spirit bears witness that we should not reject remarried couples, although the Scripture refers to it as adultery in some cases, so the Holy Spirit used the language of husbands and wives for Paul's audience. Yet, it applies even to same-gender couples today, who read Scripture under the guidance of the Holy Spirit.

---

[79] I address this in depth in chapter 12.
[80] United States Constitution, Article II, Section 1.

Because You Are Lukewarm

Revelation 3:16-17: "So, because you are lukewarm, neither hot nor cold, I am about to spit you out of my mouth. You say, 'I am rich; I have acquired wealth and do not need a thing.' But you do not realize that you are wretched, pitiful, poor, blind and naked." I attended a small church for several years that, to me, did not resemble anything that I read about in the Scripture. There were some wealthy tithers at the church at some points in time. I did not know Christ personally or experience the power of the Scriptures and the indwelling of the Holy Spirit at that church. I think this is the type of situation Christ is describing at the church in Laodicea in this passage.

Many gay Christians cannot be described as lukewarm, simply because coming to God through Christ is an uphill battle for many, as family and churches have denounced their "behavior" as such that would never allow entry into the kingdom of God. (There is often the implication of sexual impurity even when gay Christians do not engage in sexual relations.) For some Christians who realized they were gay, there was a struggle and deliberate searching for the possibility of a relationship with God. For some gay people who came to Christ, there was the same struggle, the searching, as if upstream against all of the negative beliefs that they could be accepted by God. The stigma surrounding gay Christians and the rejection they face cause many intense pressure to run full speed into the arms of a loving God in Whom there is no condemnation and no rejection. Christ Jesus said, "and whoever comes to Me, I will never cast out." (John 6:37, ESV) To a gay Christian, those precious words from our Savior are the opposite of those we have heard in the churches.

Wretched, Pitiful, Poor, Blind, and Naked

Again, from Revelation 3:17, "you are wretched, pitiful, poor, blind, and naked." This was written to a church. Let's consider the Scripture, specifically on blindness, as it applies to believers. In II Peter chapter one, Peter lists the following characteristics: faith, virtue, knowledge, self-control, steadfastness, godliness, brotherly affection, and love. Peter then wrote about Christians who lacked these qualities. He didn't condemn people for lacking these qualities. He didn't tell them to try harder, go to church more often, read the Scripture more frequently, or pray more earnestly.

Peter said, "For whoever lacks these qualities is so nearsighted that he is blind, having forgotten that he was cleansed from his former sins." (II Peter 1:9, ESV) Blindness in a believer is due to failure to realize his sins are forgiven. In many mainstream churches, gay people may hear and believe that God cannot forgive them for their ongoing same-gender attraction or their behaviors. Non-affirming arguments suggest that gay Christians are blind to their sin. But the Scripture says that blindness in a believer is failure to recognize that Christ has cleansed us from all unrighteousness.

All Christians have been forgiven for all sins, based on Christ's atoning work on the cross. The blood of Christ, the indwelling of the Holy Spirit, and the desire to serve Him are necessary and sufficient to live the abundant life in Christ that the gospel offers. Many believers remain in bondage to sin because they believe that their sins are not forgiven. This is especially true for many gay people who want to follow Christ, because, as they understand it, the only way to be forgiven is to become *not gay*. However, as Paul teaches us in Romans 3, the punishment for all sin fell on Him, and we are "justified freely by His grace through the redemption that came by Christ Jesus." (Romans 3:24)

The non-affirming response will be that the gay Christian has not repented of the "sin" of homosexuality, and thus cannot receive forgiveness. Again, this is the crux of the issue, as affirming Christians hold the premise, which calls homosexuality sinful, to be wrong. We, gay Christians, repent of all sin in our lives, just as do straight Christians. However, we do not "repent" for the relationships that we believe are instituted and blessed by God. Instead, we thank God for His blessing.

In Christ, we have favor, (Psalm 5:12) we are blessed, (Ephesians 1:3) we are rich, (II Corinthians 8:9) our eyes have been opened by the gospel, (Acts 26:17-18) and we are clothed in the garments of salvation. (Isaiah 61:10) Failure to continually recognize Christ's atonement for our sin, however, leaves believers wretched, pitiful, poor, blind, and naked. Let us not continue to tell gay Christians that their sins are not forgiven. Christ stated that He had come so that we could live abundant lives. (John 10:10) That includes the opposite of the characteristics of the church at Laodicea. In Christ we have favor, blessedness, peace, sight, and provision!

Converting the Words Sodom and Gomorrah to Homosexuality

Jeremiah 23:14:

> And among the prophets of Jerusalem I have seen
> something horrible: They commit adultery and live
> a lie. They strengthen the hands of evildoers, so that
> not one of them turns from their wickedness. They
> are all like Sodom to me; the people of Jerusalem
> are like Gomorrah.

As noted previously, this passage does not read, as one pastor claimed, "those who commit adultery and fornication and homosexuality."

It is inappropriate to convert any mention of Sodom and Gomorrah to "homosexuality." This passage is not about people with same-gender attractions in any way.

Strange Flesh

Jude 1:7 refers to the men of Sodom and Gomorrah going after "strange flesh." Traditionalists and translators prefer the term "unnatural" lusts or desires, and suggest that this Scripture condemns homosexuality. "Strange flesh" refers to the fact that Lot's guests were angels. In Genesis 6:1-6, we read of God's great displeasure that the "sons of God," that is, angels, had relations with "the daughters of humans," or women. The relations between women and angels produced Nephalim, men of great size, according to Numbers 13:32-33.

Dr. James Brownson provides a concise explanation of "strange flesh":

> The Greek text here... cannot refer to same-sex desire. The phrase [in Greek] *sarkos heteras* literally means "other flesh," and the word "other" means "another of a different kind." It is the same word from which we get the English word *heterosexual*! The sin envisioned in the text is not lusting after someone of the same sex, but the sin of lusting after the angelic visitors - who are not human - hence [the translator's] rendering of the phrase "unnatural lust."[81]

---

[81] *Bible, Gender, Sexualtity,* page 42, number 2.

A Way that Seems Right

"There is a way that appears to be right, but in the end it leads to death." (Proverbs 14:12) This does not refer to gay Christians. In fact, death is not the fate of any believer. Solomon had many wives who worshiped other gods. To Solomon, it seemed right to build "high places" for his wives' "detestable gods." (I Kings 11:7-8) Whether the end of that led to the death of him or not, I cannot say, but to those who worshiped and served idols in the "high places" he created, the end was death unless the Lord intervened. There are many appealing ideas in the world about how to live one's life. Some really seem right. Those that do not include the Lordship of Christ absolutely end in death. However, a Christian's end is never death. Christ conquered death for everyone who believes in Him.

Iniquity, Dishonest Scales, Fraud

One evangelical Christian pointed me to Hosea 12:8, suggesting that the same could be said of gay Christians. Regarding Israel, the Scripture reads, "Ephraim boasts, 'I am very rich; I have become wealthy. With all my wealth they will not find in me any iniquity or sin.'" The suggestion is that affirming Christians erroneously state that gay people are not living in sin. The context of this verse is important. The previous verse reads, "The merchant uses dishonest scales and loves to defraud." Verse 14 reads, "But Ephraim has aroused his bitter anger; his Lord will leave on him the guilt of his bloodshed and will repay him for his contempt." In the new covenant, the blood of Christ washes away all of the iniquities, all of the deception, oppression, and fraudulence that has ever been brought about by a believer.

The sin of a believer will never be on him; for Christ has borne those sins on the cross. The believer does not continue to walk in sin. Having been redeemed, he is filled with the Holy Spirit and lives out a life to God's purpose. Gay Christians are humbled by the overwhelming love of God, in the face of so much rejection in their lives. God is not provoked to bitter anger by gay Christians; He sees us through His sinless Son, Christ Jesus, and He adores us like no other has ever loved us.

The following Scriptures appear to affirm gay Christians.

Accept One Another Just as Christ Accepted You

Paul was writing to the Christian church in Rome when he said,

> May the God Who gives endurance and encouragement give you the same attitude of mind toward each other that Christ Jesus had, so that with one mind and one voice you may glorify the God and Father of our Lord Jesus Christ. Accept one another, then, just as Christ accepted you, in order to bring praise to God. (Romans 15:5-7)

If the reader would imagine himself to have the privilege and responsibility to vote on important matters within his local church, I humbly suggest that he strongly consider this admonition by Paul before voting to reject the gay Christians or gay Christian couples from the local church. To reiterate, Paul wrote, "Accept one another, then, just as Christ accepted you, in order to bring praise to God."

Condemning the Innocent

Christ said, "If you had known what these words mean, 'I desire mercy, not sacrifice,' you would not have condemned the innocent." (Matthew 12:7) To my non-affirming reader, let it never be said of you that you condemned the innocent. If you could possibly be wrong one way or the other, would you rather reject someone (and later find out you were wrong), or accept them (and later find out you were wrong)?

To Judge God's Servant

"Who are you to judge someone else's servant? To their own master, servants stand or fall. And they will stand, for the Lord is able to make them stand." (Romans 14:4) I am a child of God, a believer in the gospel, a member of His Church. I have received the abundance of grace and the gift of righteousness, according to Romans 5:17. I am His servant. I believe the Church should recognize this and discontinue their rejection of God's gay children.

This Was Not a Result of the Fall of Man

"'Neither this man nor his parents sinned,' said Jesus, 'but this happened so that the works of God might be displayed in him.'" (John 9:3) The Pharisees had asked Jesus if a man was born blind because of his own sin or the sin of his parents. Our traditional, non-affirming response to someone who declares he is gay, is that he was born into sin because of Adam's original sin. Thus, we live in a fallen world, and same-sex desires must be a result of the fall of man. In other words, as noted in chapter 3, traditionalists believe that everyone was fearfully and wonderfully made with the capacity for heterosexuality, but that sin in the world brought about same-gender attractions. However, when this question was presented to Jesus with regard to a man born blind, Jesus did not respond that way. Importantly, Jesus healed the blind man, but never suggested the need to "heal" a eunuch, even one who was "born that way."

What You Know is Good

"Therefore do not let what you know is good be spoken of as evil." (Romans 14:16) I have spent the last three years on the back row of my church, and the four years prior to that completely silent in church, trying not to ruffle any feathers. Thus far, I have only wanted to be allowed to attend, even if I'm not allowed membership or participation in ministries. But I feel God calling me to write this book, and express, as I understand it, His heart on this topic.

There is something "good" in earthly terms, in my life, and that is my covenantal partnership with Sue. I know that people recognize my relationship as "evil," and many Christians who know me believe that "homosexuality is a sin." Furthermore their Bibles (erroneously) read that homosexuals will never enter the kingdom of God, so I understand why they believe my relationship is evil. However, I'm quietly speaking out. I recognize that my relationship is good, in earthly terms, as are the covenantal partnerships of countless gay Christian couples, and that the Church should not call this evil.

No One Who Continues to Sin Knows Him

"No one who continues to sin has either seen Him or known Him." (I John 3:6b) I love the Lord, and I don't want any sin in my life. Unfortunately, I still have very real flaws that the Holy Spirit is working on. But I see Him, His work in my life. I know Him, His mercy and compassion, His redemption, His still, small voice, His peace. I know Him through His Word, through music, nature, and His children in my local church. I know that people believe that I "continue to sin" in my same-gender relationship. However, one who is sinning cannot continue in a relationship with Him. Light cannot have fellowship with darkness. (II Corinthians 6:14b)

Do Not Call Anyone Impure or Unclean

"But God has shown me that I should not call anyone impure or unclean." (Acts 10:28b) I believe that this powerful statement should inform our decision making when voting whether or not to include LGBTQ Christians in our churches.

12

EXCEPTIONS, REVERSALS, AND OTHER LABELS FOR CERTAIN SCRIPTURAL TOPICS

In Scripture, we see many examples of clear-cut, established rules or practices. Some are eternal and unchangeable. For example, Jesus said,

> Love the Lord your God with all your heart and with all your soul and with all your mind. This is the first and greatest commandment. And the second is like it: Love your neighbor as yourself. All the law and the prophets hang on these two commandments. (Matthew 22:37-40)

This is a foundational teaching. No Christian would disagree under any circumstances with this tenet, nor is there any exception to it in Scripture or in culture today. Finally, there is no use of figurative language in this passage.

Other rules in Scripture, which on the surface appear to be unambiguous and clearly stated, have exceptions within Scripture, and some no longer apply to us. Some biblical practices show a trajectory away from the original intention within Scripture. For others, there has been a complete reversal of the rule or practice. In at least one situation, we have to conclude that Scripture uses figurative language, which alters what it appears to say. I will not consider commonly discussed points from the Mosaic law, but rather, topics mainly from the New Testament Scripture, most of which are relevant today.

I will give fifteen examples of these topics, and will attempt to apply any or some of the following labels or tags[82] to each topic:

- Exceptions within Scripture
- Exceptions today
- Rules that no longer apply
- Trajectory in Scripture away from original intent
- Reversals within Scripture
- Reversals in society today
- Figurative language

Consider the biblical stance on the following topics. Notice how unambiguous the Scripture is.

Women in the Assembly

I Timothy 2:11-14:

> A woman should learn in quietness and full submission. I do not permit a woman to teach or to assume authority over a man; she must be quiet. For Adam was formed first, then Eve. And Adam was not the one deceived; it was the woman who was deceived and became a sinner.

---

[82] I use the terms labels and tags interchangeably, as in social media hashtags.

I Corinthians 14:33b-35 (Amplified Bible):

> As [is the practice] in all the churches of the saints
> (God's people), the women should keep quiet in the
> churches, for they are not authorized to speak, but
> should take a secondary *and* subordinate place, just
> as the law also says. But if there is anything they
> want to learn, they should ask their own husbands
> at home, for it is disgraceful for a woman to talk in
> church [for her to usurp and exercise authority over
> men in the church].

In the NIV, verse 34 states that women must be *silent* in church. Paul did not specify this for a particular church, but rather, for "all the churches." When Paul wrote to Timothy (as noted above), he explained why women must be quiet. He did not suggest that particular women were loud, or that the culture did not allow for women to speak. He referred back to the creation story in Genesis 2 to make his point that women must be silent in the church. He stated that Adam was formed first, then Eve and that Eve had been deceived.

Even the most conservative churches allow women to speak and sing in church, even if they do not allow a woman to preach from the pulpit. John MacArthur, a well-known pastor and author, considered one of the most influential preachers of our time,[83] recently delivered a sermon titled, "Does the Bible Permit a Woman to Preach?" Dr. MacArthur read from I Corinthians 14 (quoted above). He stated, "There is no lack of clarity with regard to what the Bible says about women who preach.... It is improper for a woman to speak in church.

---

[83] Wikipedia contributors. (2019 November 25). John F. MacArthur. In Wikipedia, The Free Encyclopedia. Retrieved November 26, 2019, from www. Wikipedia.org.

That's not ambiguous. That's not at all unclear. It is improper for a woman to speak in church. That is an absolute prohibition."[84]

MacArthur quoted the following from I Corinthians 14:35: "The women are to keep silent in the churches....If they desire to learn anything, let them ask their own husbands at home." However, when Dr. MacArthur opens his church service to questions, he takes questions from women. Yet the Bible specifically addressed how the church was to handle the situation when a woman had a question. She was to remain silent in church and ask her husband at home.

What does "just as the law also says" mean? For those who believe "women are to remain silent in church" to be a declarative statement by Paul for all people, for all time, "the law" refers to Genesis 3:16, in which God punished Eve by declaring that her husband would rule over her. However, I do not find adequate evidence that this is "the law" to which Paul is referring. Paul is typically very specific when he refers to Old Testament passages.[85] There are at least seven other instances in this letter to the Corinthians in which Paul references the Old Testament and then writes out the specific quote from the Old Testament.[86] There is no Old Testament law among the 613 laws of Moses that addresses women being forbidden to speak. I believe this phrase, "just as the law also says," refers to a Roman law or a law

---

[84] MacArthur, J. (2019 November 8). "Does the Bible Permit a Woman to Preach?" *YouTube*. Retrieved November 21, 2019 from www.YouTube.com. This is within the first 3 minutes of the video.

[85] Preato, D. J. (undated) "Did Paul Really Say, 'Let the Women Keep Silent in the Churches'?" Retrieved December 5, 2019 from www.GodsWordtoWomen.org.

[86] For examples, consider I Corinthians 1:19 and 2:9, where Paul quotes from Isaiah, I Corinthians 1:31, where he quotes from Jeremiah, I Corinthians 3:19, where he quotes from Job, I Corinthians 9:8-9, where he quotes from Deuteronomy, I Corinthians 10:7, where he quotes from Exodus, and I Corinthians 15:45, where he quotes from Genesis. This list is from Dennis Preato's article, cited above.

in the city of Corinth. For example, women likely did not participate in municipal meetings in the city of Corinth.

Those who see the prohibition of women speaking as a declarative statement for all time will point out that the reason behind the prohibition, noted in I Timothy 2 (quoted above), went back to the creation story in Genesis, indicating that this prohibition must refer to God's original design and plan. However, those same people do not argue that women must wear head coverings, even though the Scripture also linked the mandate that women cover their heads to the creation story. (I will address head coverings within this chapter.)

Why do so many churches no longer follow these rules about women? Consider two reasons:

1. The New Testament Church could not conceive of a woman in a leadership role, or in any way independent of a man. Paul, under the guidance of the Holy Spirit, wrote to his audience in Corinth. The recipients of the letter would have conducted themselves within their own cultural framework. Just as our United States Constitution refers to the President as "he,"[87] so did the writers of the Bible, addressing their audience, refer to leaders, including elders, deacons, and pastors, for example, using language assuming only males in those roles. The original readers of Scripture could not have imagined the idea that a woman could be called by God to lead.

    Similarly, in the late 1700s in America, there was no concept of the possibility of a female president. The Author of the Bible, however, is alive within us, and He continues to direct and guide us to understand Scripture. The Holy Spirit leads us to determine whether those Scripture verses refer to "an

---

[87] United States Constitution, Article II, Section 1.

absolute prohibition" for all people, for all time, or whether women should be allowed, for example, to ask questions during the question and answer service at church today or preach from the pulpit.

2. Many Christian leaders testify that they have seen the hand of God on women. In many cases, the Holy Spirit has borne witness within the spirits of believers that God is using women in our churches and in various ministries worldwide. God has called women to speak and, in some churches, to teach. Yet, this is unambiguously forbidden in Scripture. Again, some traditionalists, such as Dr. MacArthur, maintain that women are not allowed to preach. However, many traditional churches no longer believe that women are prohibited from preaching or teaching.

There may have been exceptions in Scripture to Paul's mandate that a woman must remain silent in the churches. Philip's four daughters prophesied. (Acts 21:9) Although it is possible, it seems unlikely that these women would have been given the gift of prophecy only for gatherings of women. Pastor MacArthur stated, "It was the daughters of Philip who on one occasion were used by the Lord to speak, not in a church service."[88] The Scripture states that Philip "had four unmarried daughters who prophesied." (Acts 21:9) However, it is not suggested in the text that they prophesied only once, or that it did or did not happen in a church service.

Similarly, I Corinthians 11:5 suggests that women prophesy, referring to "every woman who prays or prophesies." These appear to be exceptions to Paul's unambiguous mandate in Scripture that women remain silent in all the congregations. In the overwhelming sense of

---

[88] MacArthur, J. (2019 November 8). "Does the Bible Permit a Woman to Preach?" *YouTube*. Retrieved November 21, 2019 from www.YouTube.com. This begins at 29:41 in the video.

the day, however, Paul's mandate likely did hold. At the time, women were not allowed to speak in church, but there were exceptions.

As noted previously, we have seen throughout the Bible that the status of women improved. In Genesis it was appropriate to offer a woman up for rape to save a man. In Acts, we met Lydia, apparently a single (perhaps widowed) woman, with her own business dealing in purple fabrics, with room enough in her home to invite Paul and his traveling companions. (Acts 16:14-15) In Galatians, Paul declared that "there is neither Jew nor Gentile, neither slave nor free, nor is there male and female, for you are all one in Christ Jesus." (Galatians 3:28)

Consider also, today women are allowed to speak, ask questions, and sing in church. In some cases women teach men. Furthermore, in many churches it is not uncommon for a woman to deliver the message from the pulpit. This represents a reversal of the original mandate.

With regard to women remaining quiet in the assembly, I think we can give the following labels: exceptions within Scripture, a trajectory within Scripture away from the original rule, in some assemblies of believers, this rule no longer applies to us today, and a reversal of the rule today.

Even the most conservative mainstream churches who hold that women are not allowed to preach still invite women to speak and ask questions into the microphone. This is clearly an exception to the otherwise unambiguous rule that women are to be silent. Silence encompasses asking questions, speaking, and singing in church. This rule appears, therefore, to not hold for all people, for all time, as some otherwise suggest.

Slavery

Leviticus 25:44: "Your male and female slaves are to come from the nations around you; from them you may buy slaves."

Ephesians 6:5: "Slaves, obey your earthly masters with respect and fear, and with sincerity of heart, just as you would obey Christ."

This was appropriate, Christians believed, because of the curse that Noah had declared over Ham's son, Canaan, stating that he would be a servant to his brethren, in Genesis 9. But in Philemon, we see Paul requesting freedom for a particular slave, Onesimus, who had become a brother in Christ. Paul asked that Onesimus be allowed to return to the home but not remain enslaved. However, Paul did not ask that Philemon free all of his slaves.

This depicts a "clear-cut" view of Scripture, that slavery is scripturally sanctioned, that changes within the Scripture itself. Today, slavery is not allowed under any circumstances, and no one would tell a slave, "obey your master."

I give the idea, that slavery is appropriate, the following tags: exceptions within Scripture, a trajectory in Scripture away from the original understanding, this rule no longer applies to us today, and a reversal of the principle today, meaning, slavery, although unfortunately still practiced, is forbidden by Christians and by law.

Deacons

Deacons were to be "the husband of one wife," (I Timothy 3:12, ESV) and "their wives" were to have certain characteristics as well. (I Timothy 3:11, ESV) It seems that deacons must be men. But there appears to be an exception within Scripture. In Romans 16, Paul greeted "our sister Phoebe, a deacon of the church." (Romans 16:1)

Some suggest that Phoebe served within the church, but was not an *official* deacon, because they believe that only men could be deacons. Alternatively, while some believe "their wives" to be the correct translation in verse 11, others think that this phrase should be translated, "the women," meaning, women deacons, suggesting that there were female deacons in the early Church.

Today, women are free to be deacons in many churches. This rule, that deacons must be men, has the following tags: exceptions within Scripture, exceptions today, and in some churches, this rule no longer applies. If you hold that the Scripture suggests women were to be deacons in the New Testament, then there is no exception. This illustrates a problem when Christians maintain that Scripture is "clear" on a controversial topic.

Elders

Titus 1:6: "An elder must be blameless, faithful to his wife, a man whose children believe and are not open to the charge of being wild and disobedient."

I Timothy 3:2 (NLT): "So an elder must be a man whose life is above reproach. He must be faithful to his wife. He must exercise self-control, live wisely, and have a good reputation. He must enjoy having guests in his home, and he must be able to teach."

In the early Church, elders were men. There do not appear to be exceptions to this rule in Scripture (as we see with deacons and Phoebe, a deaconess). Today, women often serve as elders. These appointments are made after careful prayer and submission to the guidance of the Holy Spirit by the pastor, board members, and congregants.

One important distinction between deacons and elders is that, according to I Timothy 3:1-2 (in some translations), elders "must be able to teach." In Scripture, teaching was reserved for men only, because women were not to usurp men or to have authority over them in any way. However, today, women are allowed to be elders and to teach.

Regarding elders being men only, I suggest the following tags: Exceptions today, and in some churches, this rule no longer applies.

Eunuchs Forbidden to Enter the Temple

Eunuchs were not allowed to enter the temple. According to Deuteronomy 23:1 (ESV), "No one whose testicles are crushed or whose male organ is cut off shall enter the assembly of the Lord."

In Isaiah 56, we see a reversal of this rejection.

> To the eunuchs who keep My Sabbaths, who choose what pleases Me and hold fast to My covenant, to them I will give within My temple and its walls a memorial and a name better than sons and daughters; I will give them an everlasting name that will endure forever. (Isaiah 56:4-5)

Jesus referred to eunuchs, the sexual minority of His day, in Matthew 19:11-12. He affirmed those eunuchs "born that way," and of those, "made that way by man." Thereafter, in the first few years of the early Church, in Acts 8:27-39, we see that the Lord sent Philip to minister to a eunuch and baptize him in water.

The idea that eunuchs were forbidden to enter the congregation of the Lord has the following tags: trajectory in Scripture away from the original intent, this no longer applies today, and reversal in Scripture of the original premise.

Food Sacrificed to Idols

At the Council of Jerusalem in Acts 15, the leaders of the Church determined that there were three laws that needed to be kept by the new Gentile converts to Christianity. One of them was to abstain from eating food sacrificed to idols. However, in I Corinthians, thought to have been written about five years later, all food was to be received without raising any questions of conscience, (I Corinthians 10:27) and that included food sacrificed to idols. In I Timothy 4:4, referring to food, Paul states that everything God created is good, and we are to receive it with thanksgiving.

To this rule (Christians must abstain from food sacrificed to idols), I propose the following tags: reversal of the rule within Scripture, and the rule no longer applies to us today.

The Earth is the Center of the Universe

Psalm 93:1b and I Chronicles 16:30b (ESV): "Yes, the world is established; it shall never be moved."

Psalm 104:5 (ESV): "He set the earth on its foundations, so that it should never be moved."

For centuries, Christians believed that the earth was the center of the universe. Joshua 10:13 recorded that the sun stood still in the sky and delayed going down, which suggested that the sun normally moves around the earth. Ecclesiastes 1:5 states, "The sun rises, and the sun sets." Christians believed these passages to unambiguously reveal that the earth stood still and the sun revolved around it. There appeared to be no wiggle room, no possible leg to stand on, should someone suggest that the earth moved around the sun. That was considered heresy.

However, with the invention of the telescope, Galileo discovered what others had proposed, that in fact, the earth was not the center of the universe. That is, the sun is the center of our solar system, and the earth revolves around it. Galileo explained the apparent incongruity between Scripture and the discovery, saying that the Bible used figurative language. In 1616, the Roman Catholic Church condemned Galileo's position. It contradicted society's understanding of Scripture for the previous 1,500 years.[89]

What should a Christian believe when the Bible states, "the sun rises, and the sun sets"? To the idea that the sun rises and the sun sets, I have to label this, figurative language, which actually flips the understood meaning. Scripture is infallible. In this case, it is understood fully to this day to have been written in the language that we use daily, regarding the sunrise and the sunset.

Love Your Enemies

King David wrote in Psalm 139, "Do I not hate those who hate You, O Lord, and abhor those who are in rebellion against You? I have nothing but hatred for them; I count them my enemies." (verses 21-22) Our Lord Jesus, Who was the fulfillment of the law, (Matthew 5:17) stated, "You have heard that it was said, 'Love your neighbor and hate your enemy.' But I tell you, love your enemies and pray for those who persecute you." (Matthew 5:43-44)

---

[89] I was introduced to this idea in Matthew Vines's book, *God and the Gay Christian* (2014), page 23.

In the old covenant, there was no provision for the indwelling of the Holy Spirit; thus, there was no abundance of grace nor gift of righteousness. (Romans 5:17) In the Old Testament, those of God's chosen people who feared God and practiced the law did not have the Holy Spirit leading and guiding them from within. Their sins were covered annually by the blood of bulls and goats.

However, in the new covenant, Christ has atoned for our sin in His sinless body, once for all. (Hebrews 10:10) He took our sin, that we might take His righteousness. (II Corinthians 5:21) He made a way, that the Holy Spirit of God might dwell inside us. As we are led and guided from within by the Holy Spirit, God's righteousness is at work. We are filled with His love, no longer with hate. We are filled with His Holy Spirit and manifest the fruit of His Spirit in our lives: love, joy, peace, patience, gentleness, goodness, faith, meekness, temperance. (Galatians 5:22-23, KJV[90]) We have the capacity to take every thought captive to the obedience of Christ. (II Corinthians 10:5)

In the new covenant, we simply no longer live in a manner consistent with hate. Scripture states that we cannot love God if we hate our brother or sister. (I John 4:20) In Christ, we are called to love our neighbors and our enemies. "Whoever does not love does not know God, because God is love." (I John 4:8)

The psalmist's idea to hate one's enemies has the following tags: exceptions within Scripture, exceptions today, rule that no longer applies, trajectory in Scripture away from original intent, reversal within Scripture, reversal in society today. This does not appear to use figurative language.

---

[90] This is my paraphrase from the KJV, converting "long-suffering" to "patience."

Pearls, Gold Jewelry, Braids

I Timothy 2:9 (ESV): "also that women should adorn themselves in respectable apparel, with modesty and self-control, not with braided hair and gold or pearls or costly attire."

The United Pentecostal Church (UPC) and other holiness groups teach against wearing jewelry. At one point, the UPC allowed women to only wear a watch to tell time and a wedding band to indicate wedlock, according to their website.[91]

Most churches simply dismiss this. However, please consider this sentence from the bylaws of my church: "While the Bible was set during certain times and cultures, we believe it supersedes them and it is our culture that needs to change not The [*sic*] Word of God." Yet on the issue of pearls, if you were to ask the staff why we do not adhere to this Scripture, you would likely be told that was a cultural issue that does not hold for us today.

As we determine how to live life in accordance with the Scripture, it is important that we carefully examine the intent and the context within Scripture. Otherwise, we may find ourselves making illogical rules, as was noted by a former UPC churchgoer. That is, women were allowed to braid their hair but were not allowed to wear gold, silver, or pearls.[92]

The tags here are as follows: exceptions today (assuming some churches still hold to this rule), and for others, this rule no longer applies to us. Today it could be considered a reversal. In general, women often wear jewelry to church.

---

[91] Spiers, J. (2007 Oct 21). "What Does the Bible Say about Wearing Jewelry?" Retrieved November 12, 2018 from www.WhyILeft.org.
[92] Ibid.

Greet One Another with a Holy Kiss

Paul and Peter both exhorted believers (five separate times in the Scripture[93]) to greet each other with a holy kiss. This is another example of a cultural issue. We follow the intended meaning, greeting one another warmly, but we do not feel the need to kiss everyone we greet.[94] Tags: exceptions today, the rule no longer applies to us today.

Head Coverings

In I Corinthians 11, Paul again referred back to the creation story (as he did regarding women speaking in church) when stating that a woman must cover her head. He argued, "for man did not come from woman, but woman from man."

Most conservative churches today do not uphold this as a rule. People who advocate for the silence of women in churches argue that Paul referred to the creation story in I Timothy 2:11-14, suggesting that it thus refers to God's order or God's design for all people, for all time. However, although this passage commanding women to cover their heads also uses the creation story, the same people refer to this as a cultural rule, which no longer holds for us today.

Labels regarding the rule that a woman must cover her head in church: rule that no longer applies, and today there is a reversal in general. Most women in church do not wear head coverings.

---

[93] I Thessalonians 5:26, Romans 16:16, I Peter 5:14, II Corinthians 13:12, I Corinthians 16:20. Thank you, Matthew Vines.

[94] As I write this on March 23, 2020, it is actually unlawful to greet friends within six feet of one another, due to COVID-19.

Interracial Marriage is Forbidden

In a Gallup poll in 1958, 96 percent of Americans disapproved of interracial marriage.[95] In Scripture, Noah pronounced a curse on Ham's son Canaan. This was known as "the curse of Ham," and it was used to justify slavery in the past. Similarly, some Christians believed that God's declaration in Genesis 28:1 (KJV) that "thou shall not take a wife of the daughters of Canaan" held for people in modern times. Thus, interracial marriage was forbidden.

In 1912, Representative Seaborn Roddenbery (a democrat from Georgia) proposed a constitutional amendment banning interracial marriage, as follows: "Intermarriage between negros or persons of color and Caucasians... within the United States... is forever prohibited." In his statement before Congress on December 11, 1912, he stated, "Intermarriage between whites and blacks is repulsive and averse to every sentiment of pure American spirit." In the sentences that followed, he used these words: abhorrent, repugnant, subversive, destructive, debasing, ultra-demoralizing, un-American, inhuman, beast, and leprosy.[96]

As an aside, a century after these words were spoken, we can recognize that this congressman's speech displayed blatant racism, barely veiled inside an argument against interracial marriage. It is reminiscent of similar words used to describe homosexuals over the decades, often in the name of science or Christianity. I will cover this in chapter 16.

In 1967, the Supreme Court took the case of Loving versus Virginia. The Lovings were an interracial couple from Virginia who had

---

[95] Carroll, J. (2007 August 16). "Most Americans Approve of Interracial Marriages". Retrieved December 2018 from www.News.Gallup.com.
[96] Congressional Record, *62d. Congr., 3d. Sess.,* December 11, 1912, pages 502–503.

traveled to Washington DC to marry because the laws in Virginia forbade interracial marriage. Nonetheless, the Lovings were arrested in Virginia for living as an interracial couple. The judge in the case suspended their jail sentence on the condition that they leave Virginia for 25 years. The Lovings appealed the decision.

In 1965, Virginia trial court judge Leon Bazile defended the decision, stating that,

> Almighty God created the races white, black, yellow, Malay, and red, and placed them on separate continents, and but for the interference with His arrangement there would be no cause for such marriages. The fact that He separated the races shows that He did not intend the races to mix.[97]

That, it was believed, was biblical. Acts 17:26 reads, "From one man he made all the nations, that they should inhabit the whole earth; and he marked out their appointed times in history and the boundaries of their lands."

Despite the wishes of the overwhelming majority of Americans, the Court ruled in favor of the Lovings, condemning as unconstitutional all laws forbidding interracial marriages. Chief Justice Earl Warren wrote, "Marriage is one of the basic civil rights of man, fundamental to our very existence and survival."

In 2015, the Supreme Court ruled that the fundamental right to marry is also guaranteed to same-sex couples.

---

[97] Tucker, N. (2006 June 13). "Loving Day Recalls a Time When the Union of a Man And a Woman Was Banned". *Washington Post*. Retrieved December 2018 from www.WashingtonPost.com.

Tags on the prohibition of interracial couples: no longer applies, and reversal, as interracial couples are celebrated today.

Remarriage

In the Scripture, both Jesus and Paul viewed divorce and remarriage during the first spouse's lifetime as adultery, with only limited exceptions. In Mark's[98] and Luke's[99] versions of the story, no exceptions were recorded. Jesus stated that if one were to remarry after divorce, this would be equivalent to adultery. As recorded in Matthew 5:32 and 19:9, Jesus included one exception, that is, *porneia* in Greek, which is often translated "sexual immorality." (Some translations refer to *porneia* in this case as infidelity.) Paul addressed the topic as well, stating that divorced couples must remain unmarried, but he included a different exception, stating that if the unbeliever wants to leave, then the believer should be released from the marriage. (I Corinthians 7:15)

Many churches, under the guidance of the Holy Spirit, add another exception that is not found in Scripture, that is, abuse. Abuse was not grounds for divorce in biblical times, given the law that states a rapist must marry his victim. (Deuteronomy 22:28-29) In modern times, the Bible's overarching principle of love and the good news of the gospel of Christ have allowed for churches to welcome remarried couples, often without raising objections. Today, mainstream churches have many remarried congregants as members.

If a person trusts in the atoning work of Christ on the cross and believes that God raised Christ from the dead, that person is a Christian, a member of the body of Christ. The Holy Spirit dwells in that person and guides him to live a life pleasing to God, to the

---

[98] Mark 10:11-12
[99] Luke 16:18

extent that he trusts in the Lord and allows the Holy Spirit to reign in his life. I would argue that such a person cannot continue to live in sin while walking with God. That is, if he is living a life guided by the Holy Spirit, in peace, then he is not living in sin. The Holy Spirit is well able to guide a person who trusts in Him but who is not living according to God's good pleasure.

For example, if the believer is in an adulterous relationship, or in any relationship not pleasing to God, the Holy Spirit would guide him out of that relationship. A committed Christian simply cannot live in sin in peace in his relationship with God. Light and darkness cannot live together. Thus, when a church encounters a remarried couple in their midst (who do not fit within the three scriptural exceptions), and that couple loves the Lord and wants to serve Him in the local church, does the church encourage them to break up their marriage and each return to their previous spouse? The Scripture does clarify that the marriage, if the divorces did not fall within the exceptions, constitutes ongoing adultery.

So how do we justify it? The Holy Spirit simply does not bear witness in the heart and spirit of the leadership of the church that the couple should divorce and return to their original spouses. We have to trust in the Lord to guide us in these difficult decisions. And the Church has done this in love with couples who are remarried.

Recall that a person's original marriage represents "one man, one woman." However, that no longer holds once someone is remarried. As noted above, the Bible specifies that someone is free to remarry in three situations, the death of a spouse, (Romans 7:2) sexual immorality, (Matthew 19:9) and once an unbeliever has decided to end the marriage. (I Corinthians 7:15) Thus, any remarriage is an exception to "one man, one woman," and those that do not fall into one of the three categories are considered "adultery," according to

Scripture. This exception to "one man, one woman," is common in our society and accepted by most mainstream churches today.

For tags, let's specify a particular remarriage, outside of the three Scriptural exceptions. Remarriage following a divorce because of an abusive spouse is a good example.

I have to tag this idea, that remarriage following abuse is considered ongoing sin, with exceptions today. I cannot find any exception in Scripture, and there does not appear to be a trajectory away from this rule in Scripture. In other words, in Scripture, remarriage following a divorce based on abuse, is adultery. It seems that many, perhaps most, churches today, do not hold to the idea that remarried couples are living in ongoing sin; thus, this idea simply no longer applies, as remarried couples are typically (appropriately, in my opinion), welcomed into mainstream churches.

Tithe

Many Christians tithe ten percent of their income to the Lord. The first recorded tithe in Scripture was prior to the Mosaic law, when Abraham gave ten percent of the spoils of battle to Melchizedek in Genesis 14:20. In the law, the Israelites were obligated to tithe ten percent of their harvest and remuneration for their work to the Levitical priesthood.

In the New Testament, Jesus mentioned the tithe to the Pharisees, noting that it was appropriate under the law. The author of Hebrews recounted that Abraham had tithed. (Hebrews 7:2) However, we do not see a scriptural mandate to tithe in the New Testament. There are promises within the New Testament about giving, but no particular mandate. In Luke 6:38, the Word states, "Give, and it will be given to you. A good measure, pressed down, shaken together and running over, will be poured into your lap." In II Corinthians 9, Paul reiterated that those who sow generously will reap generously. He stated that giving should not be under compulsion because God loves a cheerful giver.

The principle of tithing represents an honorable practice in the Scripture, one that, in my opinion, should be upheld by believers today. The bottom line is, there was a mandate in the Old Testament to tithe, but there is no mandate in the New Testament. Tags: trajectory in Scripture away from the original rule.

One Man, One Woman

Genesis 1:27 and 5:2, "male and female He created them."

Galatians 3:28: "There is neither Jew nor Gentile, neither slave nor free, nor is there male and female, for you are all one in Christ Jesus."

Paul actually issued a reversal of the distinction between male and female from the Genesis statement, using the same Greek letters and words in his text as he had read in the Greek translation of the Scriptures,[100] which he knew thoroughly:

- Genesis: Male and female He created them
- Galatians: Nor is there male and female, for you are all one in Christ Jesus

Christians understand that there is no distinction in Christ between Jews and Gentiles, nor is there any distinction in Christ between slave and free. Thus it continues, that there is no distinction in Christ between male and female. Therefore, the principle of one man, one woman is not absolute.

---

[100] The Septuagint

In other words, Paul reversed the very premise upon which the principle of male/female complementarity rests.

This Scripture (Galatians 3:28) represents one exception to the one man, one woman principle. Another exception is the declaration by God that He had given David many wives. God's plan for David was not one man, one woman. Jesus referred to a category of God's beautiful creation who would not fit within "one man, one woman," that is, eunuchs, some of whom were "born that way." Remarried couples represent another legitimate, accepted exception to "one man, one woman," as many remarried couples are allowed into traditional churches.

This principle, "one man, one woman," can be tagged with exceptions within Scripture as well as exceptions today in culture and within traditional churches. It is my firm belief, my entire premise, and the testimony of countless gay Christians, all fearfully and wonderfully made by their Creator, in His image, even without the capacity for heterosexuality, that gay Christians also represent exceptions today.

In Summary

These fifteen examples are provided as a means to understand that Scripture is interpreted by well-meaning Christians throughout centuries and millennia. We have been wrong about certain topics that were *clearly and unambiguously* addressed in Scripture.

How can Christians who recognize that we have been completely wrong in our interpretations of Scripture continue to reject people from our churches?

13

EATING DEFILED FOOD AND FORBIDDING PEOPLE TO MARRY

There is an important theme that Paul addresses throughout his writings, including in Romans, I Timothy, Titus, Galatians, and I Corinthians. He acknowledged that some believers are weak in their faith and find it reprehensible to eat meat that had been sacrificed to gods in the pagan temples in the community. Eating "defiled" food was an ongoing issue among the new Christians and had been addressed at the Council of Jerusalem, described in Acts 15. James, the head of the conservative church in Jerusalem, had declared at the meeting that the new Gentile converts to Christianity were not required to keep the law of Moses. The Council listed three rules that the new converts were to follow, one of which was to abstain from food sacrificed to idols.

However, Paul quickly dismissed that rule. Paul preached that an idol was nothing, (I Corinthians 10:19) and the Romans' "gods" were no gods at all. (Acts 19:26) He said multiple times that the meat was to be eaten without raising questions of conscience.

- Romans 14:20: "All food is clean."
- I Timothy 4:4: "For everything God created is good, and nothing is to be rejected if it is received with thanksgiving."
- I Corinthians 10:25: "Eat anything sold in the meat market without raising questions of conscience."
- Romans 14:14: "Nothing is unclean in itself."
- Titus 1:15: "To the pure, all things are pure, but to those who are corrupted and do not believe, nothing is pure. In fact, both their minds and consciences are corrupted."

In Romans 14, Paul explained that some people's faith allowed them to eat meat sacrificed to idols and that others with weaker faith abstained. Paul said,

> Therefore let us stop passing judgment on one another. Instead, make up your mind not to put any stumbling block or obstacle in the way of a brother or sister. I am convinced, being fully persuaded in the Lord Jesus, that nothing is unclean in itself. But if anyone regards something as unclean, then for that person it is unclean. (Romans 14:13-14)

Acts 15:28-29 records a portion of the letter from the Council of Jerusalem, written by the apostles and elders, to the churches. "It seemed good to the Holy Spirit and to us not to burden you with anything beyond the following requirements: You are to abstain from food sacrificed to idols...." Paul was present at that meeting. Let us consider why Paul allowed people to eat meat sacrificed to idols.

There were two potential issues with regard to eating food sacrificed to idols. One issue was the participation in the idol worship itself. Typically, animals would be sacrificed at the temple to the gods, and the meat would then be prepared for consumption. Eating meat as part of that ritual was a grave insult to God, not because the food itself was defiled, but because the person had participated in idol worship. Secondly, since the sacrifice of animals to idols was so common, the meat sold in the meat market typically came from the butcher at the local temple. Purchasing and eating this meat, while not having participated in the idol worship, was not offensive to God, according to Paul. However, many Christians had difficulty believing that God would not be offended by Christians purchasing and eating this meat that had been sacrificed to idols.

In the new covenant under Christ, the Holy Spirit states, "I will put My laws in their minds and write them on their hearts." (Hebrews 8:10b) Paul understood our freedom in Christ and that meat sacrificed to idols was not important to God. He taught that we could enjoy the food as we give thanks for it to God. However, he noted that some new believers would find it reprehensible to eat like their neighbors did, coming home from their temple, eating meals of food that had just been sacrificed to false gods. Who wouldn't expect that God might be offended? James recognized that some believers would assume it to be dishonorable to God, so he asked that all Christians abstain. Paul recognized that Christians are free in Christ, and that we are not required to abstain from this good food. But he acknowledged that if it offended his brother, he would not eat it in his brother's presence.

Importantly, "freedom in Christ" represents the freedom to live under the constant guidance of the Holy Spirit, freedom from condemnation, (Romans 8:1) freedom from the power of sin, (Romans 8:9) freedom from the law, (Romans 6:14) freedom from fear, (I John 4:18) freedom to live out a life to His purpose and pleasure, (Philippians 2:13) but never, under any circumstances, "freedom" to sin or to do anything that would bring dishonor to God. Sin and dishonor represent bondage, not freedom.

Paul stated in Romans 14 that some people observe special days, and that, as long as one does it, "fully convinced in his own mind," he does it to the Lord. But Paul noted in his letter to the Galatians, that some had "bewitched" the believers there, (Galatians 3:1) and that they had become enslaved again "to those weak and miserable principles" from before they knew God. (Galatians 4:8-9) He said that they had begun "observing special days and months and seasons and years!" There is freedom in Christ from observing special days and concern about meat sacrificed to idols, but believers were still bound to unnecessary rules by those who were erroneously teaching them according to the law, and not according to faith. (Galatians 3:2) Paul was very concerned about this situation: "I fear for you, that somehow I have wasted my efforts on you." (Galatians 4:11)

Eating meat sacrificed to idols and observing special days are two examples that Paul gave to underscore that we have freedom in Christ and are not bound by these rules. At the same time, he acknowledged that others would be "enslaved by them all over again," (Galatians 4:9) believing that they were not free.

He offered three reasons that Christians were unnecessarily in bondage to these rules.

1. Legalistic Judaizers, who were teaching adherence to the Law of Moses: In the example in Galatians, Christians were being led astray by false teachers who were "legalistic Judaizers," as noted in the NIV Study Bible.[101]
2. Weak faith: In the examples in Romans, Paul refers to those in bondage to the rules due to their weak faith.
3. Teachers who have followed deceiving spirits: In the example in I Timothy, Paul wrote that some people would "follow deceiving spirits and things taught by demons," which

[101] Barker, K. (1985). "Galatians 3:1." *The NIV Study Bible*. Grand Rapids, MI: Zondervan, page 1783.

were the teachings that would come from people whose "consciences have been seared as with a hot iron." Those teachers would "forbid people to marry and order them to abstain from certain foods." (I Timothy 4:3)

Consider the Parallel: Eating Defiled Food and Forbidding People to Marry

Eating food sacrificed to idols was a crucial issue in the New Testament Church that was deemed to be sinful by some and not sinful by others. One may want to immediately disregard this as a parallel issue to our argument, regarding gay Christians in the Church, by suggesting that eating cannot be remotely compared to sexual "sin." Sexual sin is egregious, and this is merely food. However, Paul did, more than once. For example, he wrote, "You say, 'Food for the stomach and the stomach for food, and God will destroy them both.' The body, however, is not meant for sexual immorality but for the Lord, and the Lord for the body." (I Corinthians 6:13) Furthermore, please consider the following carefully.

As noted above, there were two potential issues with eating meat sacrificed to idols:

1. Participation in idol worship and the feast that followed, and
2. Purchasing (or otherwise eating) meat sold in the market after an animal had been sacrificed to a god, which some deemed to be offensive to God.

Similarly, there are two potential issues under the umbrella of "homosexuality":

1. Same-gender sexual activity involving abuse, exploitation, idol worship, or rejection of the Creator, as described in Scripture, and
2. Gay Christians, or loving, monogamous, committed, same-gender partnerships, which some believe violate God's perfect design for humanity.

Regarding issue number 1 in both situations, no one would disagree with the sinfulness of the act. Regarding issue number 2 in both situations, there are valid disagreements among Christians, warranting this careful discussion.

Sin Requires Harm

Consider that the second issue in each case does no harm to anyone. In issue number 2, the sin involving eating food sacrificed to idols was deemed sinful only because it was believed that God may be offended by Christians eating the meat. That is the heart of the issue with committed, same-gender relationships. Non-affirming arguments suggest that a gay relationship offends "God's design." However, there is no promiscuity, adultery, or future spouse that would be harmed by the relationship. To be clear, regarding issue number 2 in the two situations, both do no harm to people; their perceived "sin" is that they are thought to be offensive to God.

I want to briefly re-examine a different New Testament situation that is not a good parallel to our argument. Recall that Paul, referring to the man who was sleeping with his father's wife, demanded that the church in Corinth "hand this man over to Satan." (I Corinthians 5:5) Non-affirming arguments attempt to equate this example with same-gender relationships, but the two situations are not comparable. The situation in Corinth was an egregious sin that caused harm to the man's father and his father's wife. However, Christ-centered, same-gender relationships that are consensual, not adulterous, and not harmful to anyone cannot be described by this picture of dishonorable adultery.

Romans 13:10a: "Love does no harm to a neighbor." The man who took his father's wife was not acting in love toward either of them. Gay couples and gay Christians do not violate this law. Adultery does do harm to a neighbor. And this man's action was especially harmful toward his own father, whom the man should honor.

Regarding "harm," I know that some readers immediately consider I Corinthians 6:18b, "whoever sins sexually, sins against their own body." However, please keep in mind that in order to use that Scripture, the premise that "homosexuality is a sin" must be demonstrated. If the premise is correct, that homosexuality is a sin, then it would indeed constitute a sin against one's own body. Yet we do not see in Scripture that homosexuality in general is a sin. We agree that abusive, exploitative forms of male sexual acts, as well as all same-gender sexual acts involving idol worship or rejection of God are sinful. We also recognize that "one man, one woman" is the appropriate marriage in the vast majority of cases. But Scripture does not condemn faithful, committed, same-gender partnerships, and Scripture does give affirmed exceptions to "one man, one woman." Thus, within the parameters of a fair argument, the non-affirming reader could not use I Corinthians 6:18b to suggest that the participants are harmed in a gay relationship, because the premise that "homosexuality is a sin" is in question. One could use that verse to refer to any agreed upon sinful acts, such as pederasty, adultery, promiscuity, prostitution, or abuse, for example. But using that verse against a same-gender, covenantal partnership presupposes a premise that is not established.

Promoting Homosexuality Among Children

Another "harm" suggested by non-affirming Christians is that of "promoting homosexuality." The idea is that an openly gay person or couple would encourage or promote homosexuality among children. I wonder if this is really the crux of the issue. Many adults can agree to live and let live, aware that a gay couple is not harming anyone. However, some suggest that the presence of an openly gay person or couple in the church would be harmful to children.

Anita Bryant, in her Save Our Children campaign in 1977, argued that gay people must "recruit" in order to maintain their numbers. This is simply a false statement, without logic, and with a faulty premise. Affirming Christians do not have any interest in attempts to entice people to "become homosexual." We do not even believe that to be possible. We simply advocate for the inclusion of gay people in our churches. There are, and will always be, more than enough LGBTQ people in the clubs who need to know that Jesus loves and accepts them. Each one of these people has been offered eternal life through the sacrifice of Christ on the cross, but they do not believe it because Christians have told them otherwise. We want them to be welcomed into church to hear the gospel. In no uncertain terms, we do not want someone's otherwise straight child to try to "become gay." The very idea is nonsensical.

Consider for a moment that a non-affirming Christian named Jon learns that his son reveals himself to be gay; then Jon would be faced with a very important decision. If Jon were to maintain the rejection of gay people with his hypothetical vote in the local church, his child would have limited options:

1. become *not gay* and not lose church and family—this is, without a doubt, Jon's preference,

2. pretend to be *not gay* and either maintain lifelong celibacy or enter into a (likely unfulfilling) mixed-orientation marriage—likely Jon's second choice,
3. leave the church and be welcomed into the clubs—this is the most common scenario,
4. try to find a Bible believing, LGBTQ affirming church, as this would allow for lifelong, Christ-centered, committed relationship—this is, I believe, God's heart and plan, and finally,
5. some see suicide as an option.

If Jon's answer is that many authors and people online have renounced homosexuality and have become heterosexual by the power of Christ, then recognize that Jon's answer is option 1. Please pay careful attention to the following chapter on ex-gay ministries, as this gives us a 40-year history of that option.

Does a gay Christian couple's presence negatively influence children? First of all, one simply cannot choose to be gay, regardless of how enticing a non-affirming parent may think it could be to their child. If it were a matter of choice, children would choose to be straight. Secondly, gay Christians want gay people to become Christian. We have no interest in people "becoming gay." Again, the idea itself is simply illogical. I only state this because I recognize that many Christians still believe the misinformation that the media and medical establishment presented in the last few decades.

Finally, Proverbs 22:6 (NKJV) reads, "Train up a child in the way he should go, and when he is old he will not depart from it." Parents influence their children as they see fit on many political and moral topics, racial issues, taxes, marijuana, guns, and abortion, for example. There are gay couples in society, online, and on television. Children cannot be completely shielded from the idea of gay couples.

Respectfully, let me reiterate: until churches accept gay people, when a child in church realizes he is gay, he will most likely hide it until he cannot hide it any longer, at which point, he will likely leave the church, and not long thereafter, the Christian faith. This is what the majority of gay people did in Andrew Marin's survey.[102] Most of those people who left the church (without the benefit of a survey, I suggest,) entered into the nightlife and the bars, because that is the only place where they felt welcomed. In a church where gay people are accepted, a gay Christian does not have to leave his faith, his church family, and his relationship with God. Keep in mind, parents, being gay will always be undesirable to a straight person. No one without the inclination would attempt to enter into a gay relationship. Exposure to a healthy model of a sober-minded, monogamous, kind, Christian, gay couple simply is not detrimental to children. If parents prefer that all examples of homosexuality be negative so that their children are not "enticed," I think this approach may backfire, as the younger generations are coming to realize that gay couples do not fit the exceedingly negative stereotypes that have been used against us.

This is reminiscent of the stigma attached to interracial couples decades ago. People feared the presence of an interracial couple in their church could negatively influence the children. However, as the sentiment changed regarding interracial couples, the Church revisited what they had believed the Scripture said about it.

It is my understanding and revelation in the Holy Spirit that my same-gender, covenantal partnership is blessed by God. My relationship is one of love, not of sin. Consider Romans 13:9. "The commandments, 'You shall not commit adultery,' 'You shall not murder,' 'You shall not steal,' 'You shall not covet,' and whatever other command there may be, are summed up in this one command:

---

[102] *Us versus Us*, chapter 1.

'Love your neighbor as yourself.'" One can understand that the listed commandments (adultery, theft, etc.) violate the directive to do no harm to a neighbor. Sexual relations outside of marriage harm the participants[103] and their spouses (current and future spouses). However, there is no harm done to a neighbor in a gay Christian seeking a committed relationship. Likewise, there is no harm done to a neighbor or the participants in a gay, Christian couple's relationship. Furthermore, there is no harm done to God. Countless same-gender, Christ-centered couples would testify honestly that they honor God and His Word as the highest authority in their lives. According to Romans 14:23b (NLT), "If you do anything you believe is not right, you are sinning." It would literally be a sin to dismantle the covenantal, same-gender relationships, which these Christians, myself included, humbly believe, under the leadership and guidance of the Holy Spirit, are continually blessed by God.

The Early Church Agreed to Disagree

Therefore, let us return to this reasonable parallel. James, the head of the church in Jerusalem, the conservative, "mother church," was unambiguous that the new Gentile converts to Christianity, although not required to keep the Law of Moses, would be required to completely abstain from food sacrificed to idols. Paul, the apostle to the Gentiles, knew this practice did not offend God and boldly declared that we are to eat meat sold in the market without concerning ourselves with its origin. This caused no small disagreement over something thought to be offensive to God, and Paul addressed this carefully. Meat eaters were to be respectful to those who abstained, understanding that it may be offensive to them, but not to God. Thus, Paul said he would not eat meat sacrificed to idols in the presence of his brothers and sisters in Christ who found

---

[103] I Corinthians 6:18b: "Whoever sins sexually, sins against their own body."

it reprehensible. The early Church was instructed to agree to disagree on this issue. And Paul demonstrated that this could be done out of respect for one another.

This may be a reasonable answer to our current problem in the Church. If there is any possibility in the minds of traditionalist Christians that there may be validity before God in a gay, Christian relationship, or in the simple suggestion that we should not reject gay people in our churches, then we could choose to agree to disagree as we continue to worship God together and seek His perfect guidance in the body of Christ on this issue. This would solve the problem of rejecting people in the church without requiring that a given church change its doctrine, theology, or definition of marriage. Jesus called us to unity. The Church is currently divided by this issue, but I believe that an arrangement to agree to disagree, as the early Church adopted with respect to eating meat sacrificed to idols, is an answer that would allow for unity in the Church, while we continue to ask God to bring us into an understanding and agreement with His heart on the matter.

Seared as with a Hot Iron

Paul told Timothy that in the last days, some, whose consciences had been seared as with a hot iron, would "forbid people to marry and order them to abstain from certain foods." (I Timothy 4:1-3) I find this phrase to be a beautiful, although anachronistic,[104] parallel. The parallel is beautiful because both issues have been thought to be offensive to God, but neither is offensive to God. It is anachronistic because eating food sacrificed to idols was an issue almost 2,000 years ago, and forbidding people to marry is an issue today.

---

[104] An anachronism refers to events incongruent with respect to time.

Consider the situation that gay Christians find ourselves in. Some people remain bound by the rule of law and believe that "man shall not lie with man," as was written in Leviticus, and they forbid gay couples to marry in the Church. However, others recognize the freedom in Christ, that "nor is there male and female" in Christ, and the understanding that Scripture does not condemn same-gender, covenantal partnerships, but rather exploitative sexual sin. There is no biblical reason to condemn same-gender couples or gay Christians in the Church. But many Christians, including gay Christians, remain in bondage to the teachings of people who do not understand these truths.

Everyone on the conservative side of the topic of homosexuality has the vast majority of Christianity supporting the idea that homosexuality is sinful. For decades now, well respected Christian leaders have concluded that homosexuality is a grievous sin against God. Christians were raised to believe that same-gender attraction is an abomination before God. This concept is ingrained in the minds of mainstream Christians. Even reading a book like this will make some non-affirming Christians very uncomfortable. (One evangelical Christian told me she could not, in good conscience, read beyond chapter 4, as she believes the translations to be inspired by the Holy Spirit.) Christians own NIV Bibles that clearly say, in black and white, that "those practicing homosexuality" are "ungodly and sinful."[105] Their Bibles actually read that homosexuals will never inherit the kingdom of God.[106] Male and female, He made them. For them, this is not an ambiguous or difficult topic. Some even suggest that to consider another point of view is heretical. This idea has been indelibly etched into the souls and minds of the vast majority of Christendom, including Bible translators. Many Christians cannot fathom that homosexuality, in any form, is not a grave sin. In other

---

[105] I Timothy 1:9-10
[106] I Corinthians 6:9-10

words, it has been *seared into our consciences as with a hot iron*. Some, in the name of Christ, go so far as to say, unapologetically, that God actually hates gay people.[107]

I Timothy 4:1-3: "The Spirit clearly says that in the later times some will abandon the faith and follow deceiving spirits and things taught by demons." Please consider that anything that is taught outside of God's plan and His heart for His creation will be taught by demons and deceiving spirits. That is, anything that we have been wrong about in the past would fall into this category. Continuing (verse 2), "Such teachings come through hypocritical liars, whose consciences have been seared as with a hot iron." I maintain that the latter part of this phrase includes most of Christendom with regard to gay Christians and gay Christian couples. Continuing (verse 3), "They forbid people to marry and order them to abstain from certain foods." Paul recognized that there are couples who should marry, but that some will wrongly prohibit them from marrying. He advocates for their marriage and the freedom to eat whatever they enjoy.

The non-affirming community may prefer to use this phrase in the following way: "Christians who are doing the wrong thing (like gay Christians) have been doing it for so long, they have come to determine that it's right. It is because their consciences have been seared as with a hot iron." The problem with attempting to use this phrase to describe gay people is the very next sentence: "They forbid people to marry." (I Timothy 4:2-3) In other words, it is the ones who oppose a certain type of marriage whose consciences have been seared as with a hot iron.

Paul, who understood freedom in Christ, exhorted believers to enjoy their daily meals, whether or not they included food sacrificed to idols. But he noted that those with weak faith (Romans 14:2) or a

---

107 Website: www.godhatesfags.com, the website for Westboro Baptist Church in Topeka, Kansas.

weak conscience, (I Corinthians 8:7-8) for example, may not realize this freedom in Christ. Similarly, I maintain that God honors same-gender, covenantal relationships and gay Christians, and that there is neither male nor female in Christ Jesus. Gay Christians are not living in sin in their committed relationship, or in their desire for relationship.

Given the deep divide on these issues, just as the New Testament Church handled the problem of eating meat sacrificed to idols, let us agree to disagree, and allow unmarried, gay Christians and monogamous, committed, gay couples to participate in our local churches, acknowledging that we disagree, but in love and respect for one another, holding the Scripture as the highest authority in our lives.

SECTION 3

· ·

HISTORY

Chapter 14: God Heals: Ex-Gay Ministries

Chapter 15: Therefore, Celibacy

Chapter 16: Where Did This Extreme Aversion to Gay People Come
From?

Chapter 17: Same-Gender Attraction Does Not Imply Pedophilia

14

GOD HEALS: EX-GAY MINISTRIES

Because of the belief that homosexuality is a grievous sin against God's design for humanity, traditionalists argue that gay Christians must wholeheartedly renounce homosexuality and seek to change their orientation. God is able to deliver and heal from sin and sickness. Therefore, the argument goes, since homosexuals are broken, then through faith in Christ, they can be completely freed from the brokenness and sin of homosexuality. In the most traditional sense of the argument, the goal is conversion to heterosexuality and heterosexual marriage. Lifelong celibacy because of an ongoing homosexual orientation is not the desired answer to homosexuality.[108]

There are many theories as to the causes of homosexuality, but there is no definitive understanding of it. Traditionalists typically point out that there is no "gay gene," and many deny that anyone is born homosexual. However, people within the gay community often relate that they do believe they were born gay.

---

[108] As noted by Baldock, "After all, imposed celibacy (as required of Catholic priests) was an idea straight from the devil [per] Martin Luther." Baldock, Kathy. (2019 August 7). "Where Does Christian Anti-LGBTQ Ideology Come From?" Retrieved December 2019 from www.CanyonWalkerConnections.com.

When Tony Campolo, an evangelical pastor in Pennsylvania and leader in the Red-Letter Christian movement, was still non-affirming of gay people,[109] he believed homosexuality was not chosen. In a talk he gave in 1996, he stated that in the 1960s and 70s, as a research project in sociology, he had interviewed hundreds of gay men. He said, "Out of the 300 male homosexuals that I interviewed, I never met a homosexual who chose to be one."[110]

Nevertheless, whether homosexuality was chosen or whether it was present at birth, traditionalists believe it to be a result of sin in the world. Thus, Christians who struggle with same-sex attraction can be healed and redeemed through Christ's triumph over sin and death.

Ex-Gay Ministries

Many gay people have agreed with this premise and have sought desperately to change their orientation. Ministries dedicated to helping people struggling with unwanted sexual attractions, called conversion or reparative therapies, were very popular until the last few years. More recently, there are groups advocating celibacy, but not denying same-gender attractions. (I will discuss this in the next chapter.) Some people, like Christian author Dr. David Kyle Foster, report great success with reparative therapy.[111] However, the leaders of the great majority of these (mostly now defunct) ministries report that almost no one actually changes orientation. I will discuss the

---

[109] In chapter 19, I present his change of opinion on this topic.

[110] Campolo, T. (1996 February 29). "Is the Homosexual My Neighbor?" Transcript of a talk given at North Park College Chapel. Retrieved December 2019 from http://WelcomingResources.org/Campolo.

[111] Foster, David K. (2018 April). "Homosexual-Turned-Pastor: What Gay Activists Refuse to Understand About My Ministry". Retrieved August 2018 from www.CharismaNews.com.

international ex-gay movement over the last 40 years and return to David Kyle Foster and stories like his in this chapter.

In the early 1970s, several Christian groups dedicated to conversion therapy were founded. Their mission was to convert homosexuals to heterosexuals, using the verse in I Corinthians 6:11 (NKJV), "and such were some of you," suggesting that God would heal Christians of their homosexuality. Importantly, that requires that "homosexuals" actually be the correct translation in I Corinthians 6:9, but new research[112] indicates that it is not. All of the ministries that I describe below, with the exception of two ministries, the Restored Hope Network and Hope for Wholeness, came to recognize the inefficacy and harm of this therapy, and are no longer in operation. It took approximately one generation (around 40 years) to realize the results of this well-intentioned plan.

Exodus International was a Christian ministry dedicated to providing "freedom from homosexuality through the power of Jesus Christ." It was an umbrella ministry with hundreds of member organizations. It began operating in 1976. In 1979, the co-founders Michael Bussee and Gary Cooper held their commitment ceremony, indicating that they had not converted to heterosexuality. In 2007, Bussee and other former Exodus leaders issued an apology for the harm done to those who heard their message and believed that something was inherently wrong with them. The letter asked current ex-gay ministries to "evaluate the fruit of their programs."[113]

In 2012, Alan Chambers, president of Exodus since 2001, stated, "The majority of people that I have met, and I would say that the

---

[112] The research from Baldock and Oxford's team is described in chapters 4 and 5.

[113] Bogle, Bussee, Marks, et al. (2007 June 27). "Apology from Former Ex-Gay Leaders". Retrieved September 2018 from http://www.BeyondExGay.com/article/apology.

majority, meaning 99.9 percent of them, have not experienced a change in their orientation."[114] Exodus International closed down in May 2013. In December 2018, Chambers wrote, "During my 22-year involvement in Exodus International I never met one person who changed their sexual orientation, including me."[115]

Love in Action was one of the first ex-gay ministries, established in 1973. In 2008, its executive director of 22 years, John Smid, resigned, saying he was homosexual and that he had "never met a man who experienced a change from homosexual to heterosexual."[116]

One of the founders of Love in Action, John Evans, left the ex-gay ministry after a friend committed suicide over his inability to experience a change in his orientation. In 1993, Evans told the Wall Street Journal, "They're destroying people's lives. They're living in a fantasy world."[117]

Love Won Out was an ex-gay ministry associated with Focus on the Family, an evangelical radio program founded by James Dobson. In 2009, Love Won Out was sold to Exodus International. John Paulk was its founder. He, at the time a professed former homosexual, and his wife, Anne Paulk, a self-identified former lesbian, together became the most visible faces of the ex-gay movement, declaring that "change is possible" all over the world. Together they wrote a book called *Love*

---

[114] Throckmorton, Warren (2012 January 9). "Alan Chambers: 99.9% have not experienced a change in their orientation". Retrieved August 2018 from www.WThrockmorton.com.

[115] Chambers, A. (2018 December 7). "Reflection on Conversion Therapy - Former Leaders". Retrieved November 5, 2019 from www.GraceRivers.com/exgayleaders/.

[116] Besen, Wayne (2011 October 12). "Former 'Ex-Gay' Activist Admits Gay People Don't Change". *FCNP*. Retrieved September 2018 from www.fcnp.com.

[117] Schlanger, Z. and Wolfson, E. (2014 May 1). "Ex-Ex-Gay Pride". Retrieved October 2018 from www.Newsweek.com.

Won Out: How God's Love Helped Two People Leave Homosexuality and Find Each Other. John Paulk, having been photographed going into a gay bar in 2000, renounced his claim to ex-gay status, denied that sexual orientation change is effective, and apologized for the harm he had caused in a formal apology in 2013.[118]

Exodus International closed down, and John and Anne Paulk eventually divorced. Anne Paulk is now the executive director of the ex-gay ministry, Restored Hope Network. In an interview, she revealed that she had considered herself a lesbian from ages 12 through 19, following multiple molestations at age 4. She stated that she had never had a romantic encounter with a woman.[119]

Courage was an ex-gay group affiliated with Exodus International in the United Kingdom. In 2002, following 15 years of ministry, Jeremy Marks, its leader, announced that he had never seen one client change orientation. The organization, re-named Courage UK, is now gay-affirming.[120]

The group New Directions was the Exodus International affiliate in Canada. In 2007, this group, under the leadership of Wendy Gritter, changed their stance, acknowledging that sexual orientation is not a choice.[121]

Other notable "ex-ex-gay" stories include the following.[122]

---

[118] Brydum, Sunnivie (2013 April 24). "John Paulk Formally Renounces, Apologizes for Harmful 'Ex-Gay' Movement". *The Advocate*. Retrieved September 2018 from www.Advocate.com.

[119] Smith, W. C. (2017 May 3). "Anne Paulk hasn't given up on ex-gay ministry". *World*. Retrieved September 2018 from World.wng.org.

[120] *Walking the Bridgeless Canyon*, page 300.

[121] Ibid, page 300.

[122] I do not know these people personally. Wikipedia contributors. (2018 November 24). Ex-ex-gay. In *Wikipedia, The Free Encyclopedia*. Retrieved October 6, 2018 from www.Wikipedia.org.

- Kori Ashton led the Christian band that worked with Exodus. She went to a Christian college and was involved romantically with women. "Wanting to please others," she repented of her sin and declared herself ex-gay. She started a band called Exit, which was affiliated with several ex-gay ministries. She was a featured speaker, and her band led worship at many ex-gay events. She stated that being busy and living her dream, "singing for Jesus and sharing God's love," allowed her to suppress her homosexual feelings. However, over time, she realized her hurt and loneliness despite the picture of a "perfect Christian" that she had created.[123] She is now "ex-ex-gay" and is happily married to a woman.[124]

- Günter Baum founded an ex-gay ministry in Germany. Later he formed Zwischenraum, which helps gay Christians to accept their sexuality and to reconcile it with their beliefs.

- Darlene Bogle, a leader in Exodus International until 1990, told Newsweek, "There were a lot of people in leadership positions who still felt they were gay but could not admit it." She stated, "We learned to lie." She was convinced that if she continued to declare heterosexuality and not have relations with a woman, she would be ex-gay.[125] In December 2018, she posted,

> I spent 10 years teaching conversion therapy in the 70s and 80s as an ExGay leader. These efforts never made any significant difference in changing the direction of sexual attraction in those whom I counseled, or in my

---

[123] Ashton, K. (undated). "Survivor Narrative". Retrieved September 2018 from https://BeyondExGay.com.

[124] Ashton, K. (2018). Retrieved November 2019 from www.AskKori.com/timeline/.

[125] Schlanger, Z. and Wolfson, E. (2014 May 1). "Ex-Ex-Gay Pride". Retrieved October 2018 from www.Newsweek.com.

own life. The despair and constant failure added shame and isolation to their journey. I found freedom from false expectations when I found a UCC church who accepted me and my wife into fellowship within the congregation! It was an amazing thing to loudly declare that the teaching of conversion therapy does more harm than good.[126]

- Ben Gresham is an Australian man who went through three years of ex-gay therapy starting at age sixteen. He has made media appearances regarding what he sees as the dangers and psychological harm associated with ex-gay programs. Gresham is also a part of "Freedom 2b," which offers support to LGBT people from church backgrounds.

- Peterson Toscano is an actor who was involved in the ex-gay movement for 17 years. He is known for performing a one-man satire titled *Doin' Time in the Homo No Mo Halfway House*, and with Christine Bakke (also ex-ex-gay) created Beyond Ex-Gay, a support website for people coming out of ex-gay experiences.

- Anthony Venn-Brown is a former evangelist in the Assemblies of God and an author whose book, *A Life of Unlearning*, describes his experience in Australia's first ex-gay program. Venn-Brown co-founded "Freedom 2b." Anthony Venn-Brown has been a leader in monitoring ex-gay activities in Australia, New Zealand, and Asia, countering the "ex-gay myth."

- In 2007, five Australian ex-gay leaders publicly apologized for their past actions.

- James Matheson, a practicing Mormon, ran a full-time conversion therapy practice in New Jersey. In January 2019,

---

[126] Bogle, D. (2018 December 7). "Reflection on Conversion Therapy - Former Leaders". Retrieved November 5, 2019 from www.GraceRivers.com/exgayleaders/.

he announced that he and his wife divorced and that he now identifies as gay.[127]

In my opinion, no one was more highly motivated to change than the leaders of these ministries and their clients. The faith movement places great emphasis on declaring healing and restoration and aligning one's words with the Word of God. Many did declare heterosexuality and took genuine steps of faith to live a life consistent with their belief that God did not want them to be gay. Some, like John Paulk, entered into heterosexual marriage, which was reasonable for many years. However, in many mixed-orientation marriages, at some point the gay spouse has to come to terms with never having lost homosexual attraction nor gained heterosexual attraction, as well as what has been denied the straight spouse, that is, a partner with genuine romantic and sexual attraction for the straight spouse.

Yvette Cantu Schneider[128] is an affirming Christian who was once an activist within the ex-gay movement, "working with just about every top anti-LGBT group." Schneider is happily heterosexually married with children. She was considered ex-gay because she had previously had relationships with women. As a Christian who supported the traditional view of marriage, she flourished in the "ex-gay" role for many years. However, over time she came to realize that she does affirm LGBTQ people. She does not identify as ex-gay, but stated,

---

[127] Wong, C. M. (2019 January 23). "Former Conversion Therapist Says He's 'Choosing To Pursue Life As A Gay Man'". Retrieved June 2019 from www. HuffPost.com.

[128] Schneider and Baldock together produced an excellent webinar series titled, "The History of Cultural and Religious Discrimination against the LGBT Community in America." The information presented is incredibly eye-opening, and I highly recommend it. It can be found at www. CanyonWalkerConnections.com.

"human sexuality, mine in particular, is more complicated than most labels can encompass."[129]

Beginning in the late 1990s, she worked with the Family Research Council, Exodus International, and Concerned Women for America, among many other anti-LGBT groups. In July 2014, in an interview with GLAAD (a pro-LGBTQ advocacy group), she explained that she "no longer wishes to identify with the 'ex-gay' or anti-LGBT movement; is sorry for the pain she caused as part of that world; is highly questioning of the idea of 'ex-gay' itself; and is now fully supportive of LGBT people."[130]

Yvette Cantu Schneider revealed that, as director of women's ministry for Exodus International, she spent her time "dealing with leaders in ex-gay ministries who were having sex with the people who were coming to them for help." She stated, "If the people who have been chosen to be leaders aren't changing, then no one is changing."[131]

Those who, after years of living a lie, could not continue in their ex-gay ministries did not have to besmirch the ministry. They could have maintained that their ministries had helped countless people. Instead, they stated that they had not seen anyone convert to heterosexuality. This was not a way to ease the pain of having been wrong. These Christian men and women are telling the truth. If anything, it would have been easier for them to lie or remain quiet on the subject. These people know more attempted converts

---

[129] Schneider, Y. (2018 June 13). "Finding My True Self". Retrieved December 2019 from www.Thrive.lgbt.

[130] Hooper, J. (2014 July 28). "Change is possible: Former 'ex-gay' activist Yvette Schneider 'celebrates the worthiness and equality of all people'". Retrieved November 5, 2019 from www.GLAAD.org.

[131] Besen, Wayne. (2019 June 10). "Ex-Ex-lesbian Yvette Cantu Schneider gives inside scoop on conversion therapy industry -- PART 1" *YouTube*. TruthWinsOut. Retrieved December 26, 2019 from www.YouTube.com.

than anyone else would know. The leaders of these ministries state in agreement that people, even highly motivated people who trust in the power of Christ, do not experience a change to heterosexuality.

Do Studies Prove that Change is Possible?

Dr. Robert Spitzer (born 1932) is considered by some to be the father of modern psychiatry. He published a study known as the "gay cure" in 2001, suggesting that reparative therapy is successful for highly motivated individuals. In 2012, at age 80, he referred to this study as his "only professional regret." He wrote, "the simple fact is that there was no way to determine if the subject's accounts of change were valid." Sadly, he admitted 11 years after its publication that he had made "unproven claims of the efficacy of reparative therapy." He apologized to anyone who was hurt by his study.[132]

In 2014, a scientific study was published regarding 1,618 same-sex attracted, former and current members of the Church of Jesus Christ of Latter-day Saints (also known as the Mormon Church). Of the 1,019 participants who had engaged in efforts to change their orientation, only one person reported to have been converted to heterosexuality.[133]

In 2007, Christian researchers Jones and Yarhouse published a book[134] with their findings of a study, funded by Exodus, of people

---

[132] Ralph, T. (2012 May 18). "Dr. Robert Spitzer, founder of the 'gay cure,' apologizes for his reparative therapy study". Retrieved December 2019 from www.Pri.org.

[133] Dehlin, Galliher, Bradshaw, Hyde, Crowell, "Sexual orientation change efforts among current or former LDS church members". *Journal of Counseling Psychology*, 62(2), (2014) page 95.

[134] Jones and Yarhouse. (2007). *Ex-Gays?: A Longitudinal Study of Religiously Mediated Change in Sexual Orientation*. Downers Grove, Illinois: IVP Academic.

involved in Exodus ex-gay ministries. The authors concluded that sexual orientation is changeable, but the results are complicated. As evangelical professor Dr. Warren Throckmorton explained,

> the final percentages being reported should... take into account the distinct possibility that many if not most of the [study] dropouts were not successful in their efforts to change. The study began with 98 participants and ended up with 65.[135]

One participant later reported that he had lied, stating that he had converted to heterosexuality, when he had not.[136]

As an aside, consider that as a Christian believing by prayer and faith in God for healing, if one states that he is not healed, then by definition, he does not have the faith to be healed. That is why ex-gay ministries lasted as long as they did.

One of the 11 conversion "successes" in the study continued to have unwanted homosexual desire; another one continued to have homosexual dreams, and a third recanted completely. There was another group of "successes," that is, those who had given up on hopes of conversion and embraced celibacy. "However, once again the actual desires and longings of the individuals remain homosexual."[137]

---

[135] Throckmorton, W. (2011 October 27). "The Jones and Yarhouse Study: What Does It Mean?" Retrieved December 2019 from www. WThrockmorton.com.

[136] Airhart, M. (2009 August 6). "Ex-Gay Researcher Mark Yarhouse Reacts to Repudiation by Psychologists". Retrieved December 2019 from www. TruthWinsOut.org.

[137] Chapman, P. (2007 November 2019). "A Critique of Jones And Yarhouse's 'Ex-gays?' – Part 2". Retrieved December 2019 from www.ExGayWatch.com.

Author Dr. Patrick Chapman reviewed this study and offered the following critique:

> [The authors] suggest the results demonstrate sexual orientation is changeable (pp. 42, 325), evidenced by 11 "Success: Conversion" cases out of the original 98. The conclusion is unwarranted because: 1) they acknowledge multiple anecdotal cases from previous "ex-gay" success stories who later recanted their "conversion" to heterosexuality (pp. 63-64, 72); 2) they freely acknowledge that people in ex-gay programs declare they are heterosexual even if they experience exclusive and powerful homosexual attractions (p. 220); 3) they admit that one of their 11 "Success: Conversion" cases recanted his claim of change, confessing his homosexual attraction was unchanged after the book manuscript neared completion (p. 285; Jones and Yarhouse did not remove his "success" from their data); and 4) the only way to determine if change actually occurred is through a long-term study, which this is not.[138]

Tony Campolo, in his aforementioned 1996 talk about his research project, explained that he interviewed ex-gays and asked if, "when [they] fantasize," did it continue to reflect a homosexual inclination. "I interviewed significant numbers of homosexuals who, quote unquote, claimed to be cured.... I always get the same answer. We fantasize homosexually."[139] He questioned the veracity of their claims to ex-gay status. As a non-affirming believer at the time, he stated

---

[138] Ibid.

[139] Campolo, T. (1996 February 29). "Is the Homosexual My Neighbor?" Transcript of a talk given at North Park College Chapel. Retrieved December 2019 from http://WelcomingResources.org/Campolo.

that homosexuality was not chosen, could not be cured, and was sinful.

Conservative Christian groups heralded "ex-gay" studies as "proof" that homosexuals could change their orientation. However, many within these ministries were devastated by the abysmal results. Regarding the final report by Jones and Yarhouse, Christian author Karen Keen wrote,

> Only 23 percent reported a shift after six years of trying, and most of the change was toward bisexuality or "complicated heterosexuality," as the authors put it. This percentage is likely optimistic, since several study participants dropped out before it was completed. In other words, even an optimistic view suggests that nearly 80 percent of gay people will not experience a change in sexual orientation despite years of actively attempting to do so.[140]

Given the utter failure of so many of these programs in Christians highly motivated to change their sexual orientation, would it not be reasonable to reconsider the premise? The success of the ex-gay movement absolutely requires that I Corinthians 6:9-11 and I Timothy 1:9-10 refer to homosexuals. A careful look at the Scriptures reveals that those passages refer to exploitative male sexual behavior, not relations within a covenantal partnership. If God lovingly, legitimately, purposefully creates some men and women with same-gender attraction, and if He does bless the covenantal relationships that are formed, then ex-gay ministries intent on conversion to heterosexuality are destined to fail.

At this point, every major medical organization opposes conversion therapy as harmful. This includes the American Medical Association,

---

[140] *Scripture, Ethics and the Possibility of Same-Sex Relationships,* pages 71-2.

American Psychiatric Association, American Psychoanalytic Association, American Psychological Association, American Academy of Pediatrics, among many others.[141] The harm done to children who undergo this treatment before the age of consent includes depression, anxiety, drug use, homelessness, and suicide.[142] As of early March 2020, twenty states and two territories, the District of Columbia and Puerto Rico, as well as multiple counties within the United States, ban conversion therapy for minors.[143]

Current Ex-Gay Ministries

Hope for Wholeness is a ministry currently operating which declares, "freedom from homosexuality through Jesus Christ." Its founder and former director, McKrae Game recently came out as a gay man.[144] In a social media post, he wrote, "I WAS WRONG! Please forgive me!" He expressed regret for harm caused by his ministry, including the slogan itself, which he called "a very misleading idea."[145]

---

[141] *Walking the Bridgeless Canyon*, page 303.

[142] The Human Rights Campaign. (2020). "The Lies and Dangers of Efforts to Change Sexual Orientation or Gender Identity". Retrieved March 3, 2020 from www.HRC.org.

[143] Wikipedia contributors. (2020, March 3). List of U.S. jurisdictions banning conversion therapy. In Wikipedia, The Free Encyclopedia. Retrieved 19:45, March 3, 2020, from https://en.wikipedia.org/w/index.php?title=List_of_U.S._jurisdictions_banning_conversion_therapy&oldid=943734606, as of March 3, 2020, per wikipedia.

[144] Iati, M. (2019 September 5). "Conversion therapy center founder who sought to turn LGBTQ Christians straight says he's gay, rejects 'cycle of self shame'". Retrieved September 22, 2019 from www.WashingtonPost.com.

[145] Game, M. (2019 August 25). "20 years in ex-gay ministry; I WAS WRONG! Please forgive me!" Facebook. Retrieved September 22, 2019 from https://www.facebook.com/mckrae/posts/10157639329596563.

Restored Hope Network (RHN) is a ministry that serves "those who desire to overcome sinful relational and sexual issues in their lives and those impacted by such behavior, particularly homosexuality." RHN formed as a reorganization of the ex-gay ministries associated with Exodus International as it was closing.

The harm in conversion therapy lies in the ongoing narrative that same-sex attraction can and must be fixed, instead of focusing on living a godly life within the boundaries of those attractions. I hope that these ministries will continue to exist to help those struggling with sexual immorality such as promiscuity, pornography, and prostitution, but that they will be open to Paul's offer that it is better to marry. Paul did not see mandatory celibacy as an answer to sexual immorality. He described relationship within the confines of a Christ-centered, covenantal commitment.

Inasmuch as this type of ministry brings healing and help to those like David Kyle Foster,[146] who was involved in prostitution, pornography, promiscuity, and cult worship, then it is beneficial. His story is remarkable. However, if the message continues to demand heterosexuality or celibacy from gay people, then many will remain in bondage by societal, church, and family pressures to either remain closeted and live a lie or leave the faith.

A new ex-LGBTQ movement is taking place, which is not affiliated with traditional conversion therapy, addressed above,[147] but does hold to the premise "homosexuality is a sin" and does promote conversion to heterosexuality and freedom from this "sin" by the power of Christ. On May 25, 2019, the second annual Freedom March

---

[146] Foster, David Kyle. (2014). *Love Hunger: A Harrowing Journey from Sexual Addiction to True Fulfillment*. Ada, MI: Chosen Books.

[147] Kuykendall, Aliya. (2019 May 29). "Ex-LGBT People Declare Freedom in Jesus at DC 'Freedom March'". Retrieved May 31, 2019 from www. Stream.org.

(organized by Jeffrey McCall, ex-gay founder of For Such a Time Ministry), was held in Washington, DC.[148] Somewhere between 70[149] and 200 former LGBT people and their allies participated in celebration of freedom in Christ from homosexuality and sin.

Luis Ruiz, one of the speakers at the event, stated, "It wasn't a 'gay to straight' thing; it was a 'lost to saved' thing." The speakers included survivors of the Pulse nightclub massacre (which took place in Orlando, Florida, on June 12, 2016) as well as several people who have entered into heterosexual marriage. Angel Colon, one of the survivors of the shooting, stated, "We have learned what true peace is. We have learned what true happiness is. We have learned what true love is in Jesus Christ, that our identity is not in our sexuality, but it is in Jesus."[150]

These people have come to know Christ and report freedom from bondage to sin. To see people come to Christ and live for Him is far more important than one's sexual identity. However, the message that this ministry proclaims, that *being gay* is a sin and must be corrected, has caused so much damage to the LGBTQ community. I have strong reservations about this new ex-gay ministry, but I thank God for bringing this group of people to Christ. I pray that He will bring all of us into agreement with His heart on this issue.

While I believe that this group remains under a false and dangerous premise, I recognize that they are reporting freedom in Christ from

[148] Christsforgiveness. "Ex-LGBTQ Pride March (Washington D.C)". *YouTube*. Live streamed May 25, 2019. Retrieved May 2019 from www.YouTube.com. (This is a recording of the Freedom March.)

[149] Villarreal, D. (2019 May 26). "Ex-ex-lesbian leader slams conversion therapy on eve of 'ex-gay' D.C. Freedom March". Retrieved May 2019 from www.LGBTQNation.com.

[150] Showalter, B. (2019 May 27). "Pulse nightclub shooting survivors: Move of Holy Spirit 'being birthed' among former LGBT persons". Retrieved May 31, 2019 from www.ChristianPost.com.

bondage to various types of sin. Some of the testimonies included freedom from prostitution, alcohol, drugs, and promiscuity.[151] This type of lifestyle can be overcome in Christ.

For these people who have been saved and are following Jesus, He may choose to lead them differently than He leads others. Some testimonies included promiscuity, which is not God's plan for anyone. If freedom from promiscuity means leaving the "homosexual lifestyle" for certain people, then I support it fully. I maintain that covenantal, same-gender relationships are not forbidden, but some LGBTQ Christians do not feel led by God at this point in their lives, and perhaps ever, into this type of relationship. Their focus is falling in love with Christ. Without any doubt, putting Christ first is the best way to live, as He will guide them step by step into the life He has planned for them, and for anyone who focuses on Him.

The bottom line is, we, gay Christians, seek Christ, whether it be from a position that Christians must renounce being gay, that they can be gay but must be celibate, or that they can express intimacy exclusively within a covenantal relationship. Every Christian who finds himself in one of these groups is a Christian first. Let us continue this conversation until Christ reveals His heart to all of us and brings us into agreement. In the meantime, I hope that we can disagree agreeably, and allow those with whom we disagree to be involved in our local churches.

---

[151] CBN News. (2019 April 29). "Jeffrey McCall: From Transgender to Transformed by God". Retrieved May 31, 2019 from www1.CBN.com.

15

THEREFORE, CELIBACY

As the ex-gay, conversion therapy movement crumbled, mainstream Christians came to realize that sexual orientation is exceedingly resistant to change, even in highly motivated, Bible-believing Christians. Thus, non-affirming Christians have suggested that, in the absence of heterosexual marriage, homosexuals must live a celibate life. Gay-affirming Christians have countered that if the church does not allow for marriage, then the church should provide the resources that one might expect from a marriage, including various kinds of support. However, this falls short as well.[152] A life of celibacy typically requires that one give up even the option of intimate companionship. It is not good for man to be alone. (Genesis 2:18) Nevertheless, some gay Christians may be called to and gifted with celibacy. Some may not have the gift of celibacy but believe that celibacy is the best option for them.

Celibate Gay Christians

Revoice is a group which aims to support and encourage same-sex attracted people "while observing the historic Christian doctrine

---

[152] Nancy Bartell, personal conversation, October 2018.

of marriage and sexuality."[153] They support the traditional view of marriage as only between one man and one woman. Some in this group prefer the term "same-sex attracted" rather than "gay" because they find the phrase "gay Christian" to be an oxymoron. These same-sex attracted Christians typically choose celibacy or mixed-orientation marriages rather than denying or attempting (or continuing attempts) to change their orientation.

Karen Keen described the origins of the modern celibacy movement. She wrote,

> In 2008, a small group of ex-gays and certain affiliated practitioners began to dialogue intentionally about better approaches to ministry (I [Keen] was part of this group). We were concerned about how the ex-gay movement was not being truthful about the lack of change. Too often people who attended ex-gay support groups became disillusioned and abandoned their faith when change did not transpire. While a small minority was able to achieve heterosexual functioning, we saw a need to minister to the majority that was neglected. Thus, the celibate gay movement was founded to promote greater integrity and effective ministry. It recognized that most gay Christians would face a life of celibacy and needed honest engagement and support given that reality.[154]

Despite this well-intentioned plan, there is fierce debate among traditional Christians who disagree with Revoice and the idea of celibate gay Christians. The Presbyterian Church in America (PCA)

---

[153] Revoice mission statement. Retrieved July 27, 2019 from https://revoice. us/about/our-mission-and-vision/.

[154] Keen, K. (2019 April 30). "In Defense of Revoice: A Response to Robert Gagnon". Retrieved May 4, 2019 from www.KarenKeen.com.

issued a 16-page statement rejecting the first Revoice conference, which took place in July 2018 in St. Louis, Missouri.[155] The Presbytery noted that speakers at the Revoice conference did not "reject those sexual desires outright." To be clear, Revoice believes that homosexual desires should not be acted upon. However, as an example, the report notes that one speaker, Ron Belgau, "stops short of affirming that the desires themselves are sinful."[156] They also criticized the (perhaps accidental) use of the phrase "gay Christian."

Revoice advocates "intimate friendships," which are non-sexual. They state, "We believe that the Christian tradition celebrates deep, committed relationships between believers that are marked by spiritual intimacy, emotional connection, and even chaste, non-sexual expressions of physical affection."[157] The PCA report rejected any "homosexual friendship that goes by different names and looks substantially different from the healthy friendships that all Christians should cultivate and enjoy."[158]

Clearly, both of these groups believe the traditionalists' premise that "homosexuality is a sin," which I reject. Although they both affirm that premise strongly, they still have very tedious, yet meaningful arguments within that context. In conclusion, the Presbytery does commend Revoice's "commitment to biblical marriage," but states, "we do not feel Revoice is a safe guide in helping Christians navigate questions of gender and sexuality."

---

[155] Gryboski, Michael. (2019 May 30). "PCA Presbytery rejects Revoice Conference, says it's not a 'safe guide' on gender, sex issues". Retrieved May 31, 2019 from www.ChristianPost.com.

[156] The Central Carolina Presbytery. (2019 May 28). *Central Carolina Presbytery: Study Committee Report on 2018 Revoice Conference*. [PDF file]. Retrieved May 31, 2019 from TheGospelCoalition.org.

[157] Revoice. "Statement on Sexual Ethics and Christian Obedience". Retrieved May 31, 2019 from www.Revoice.us.

[158] *Central Carolina Presbytery Study Committee Report on 2018 Revoice Conference*, page 13.

Both groups hold that gay Christians must be celibate or enter into heterosexual marriage. Consider where these groups diverge. Many straight, non-affirming Christians strongly believe that in order to be a Christian, one with same-sex attraction must definitively renounce homosexuality. However, for a same-sex attracted Christian who cannot become straight, to renounce homosexuality and claim to be not same-sex attracted seems like lying.

As noted by Keen above, the problem for those who have failed ex-gay attempts is the need to minister to others who have failed in this regard. For a group of same-sex attracted, traditionalists Christians who choose not to lie about their ongoing same-sex attraction, and to not enter into an unfulfilling heterosexual marriage, their *only* option is celibacy.

In Scripture, we see celibacy as a gift, but never a mandate. Matthew Vines, in his book, *God and the Gay Christian*, writes, "We can embrace gay relationships and maintain a traditional view of celibacy, or we can change our understanding of celibacy and keep a traditional view of Scripture. But we cannot do both."[159]

While we know that it is not good for man to be alone, the argument against celibacy for all gay Christians is not just a call for compassion. Consider Paul's words.

In I Corinthians chapter 7, a group of Christians had suggested that people should abstain from sexual relations. Paul countered by saying that "since there is sexual immorality," each person should have a spouse. He wrote, "it is good to remain unmarried, as I do, but if they cannot control themselves, they should marry, for it is better to marry than burn with passion." (I Corinthians 7:9) This verse demonstrates that celibacy is not to be imposed on someone. God calls us, not to celibacy if one could marry, but to monogamy.

---

[159] *God and the Gay Christian*, page 44.

A non-affirming response would be that marriage is only appropriate between one man and one woman. However, this would not alleviate the problem of "burning with passion" in the gay person. A mixed-orientation marriage does not satisfy Paul's intention that Christians avoid sexual immorality. For those who desire an intimate relationship, it is better to marry one with whom one desires an intimate relationship. Scripture does not promise that one will have alleviation and satisfaction of all one's desires. Certainly those who are single not by choice are required to remain chaste. Paul's exhortation is to marry and remain faithful, if the option is available, rather than engage in promiscuity. A mixed-orientation marriage would not address Paul's suggestion here, because the passion would be for someone other than the spouse.

Paul wrote to Timothy and said that, in the last days, some would become influenced by the hypocrisy of liars, and specifically, "they forbid people to marry." The Scripture does not agree with imposing celibacy on people.

Is Celibacy the Answer to Same-Sex Attraction?

For those who believe that celibacy is the answer to homosexuality, consider Jesus's sermon on the Mount in Matthew 5-7. Jesus expressed a standard of holiness that exceeded the law of Moses. He stated that not only would a murderer be subject to judgment, but "anyone who is angry with his brother will be subject to judgment." Likewise, Jesus said, "anyone who looks at a woman lustfully has already committed adultery with her in his heart." (Matthew 5:27-28)

If adultery is a sin, then adulterous desire is sin. If homosexuality is a sin, then homosexual desire is sin.

Thus, if one holds to the premise, "homosexuality is a sin," there is no Scriptural basis to support the view that gay Christians must commit to lifelong celibacy. In other words, one could not faithfully say, "only homosexual *behavior* is sin" if the preference, desire, and longing of an individual is for a "sinful" relationship.

The only answer, therefore, in the traditional teaching, is conversion to heterosexuality, and either heterosexual marriage or celibacy with no same-sex attraction. However, ridding oneself of same-sex attraction is simply not a viable option for the vast majority of gay people, as seen in the last chapter.

At this point, the only alternative is to reconsider the premise. The premise is wrong. Homosexuality is not a sin. Maintaining celibacy for gay people who choose to remain celibate is not a sin. Furthermore, expressing emotional, romantic, and physical intimacy within a loving, monogamous, Christ-centered, committed gay relationship is not a sin.

16

Where Did This Extreme Aversion to Gay People Come From?

In 1967, Mike Wallace hosted a CBS documentary titled, "The Homosexuals." In it, Wallace stated,

> The dilemma of the homosexual: told by the medical profession, he is sick, by the law that he's a criminal, shunned by employers, rejected by heterosexual society, incapable of a fulfilling relationship with a woman, or for that matter with a man. At the center of his life, he remains anonymous, a displaced person, an outsider.

Embarrassed by his part in the documentary, in the 1990s, Wallace said,

> I should have known better. That is, God help us, what our understanding was of the homosexual lifestyle a mere twenty-five years ago because nobody was out of the closet and because that's what we heard from doctors. That's what [the

popular psychoanalyst] Socarides told us; it was a matter of shame.[160]

Consider this carefully. In 1967 in America, virtually all homosexual couples were closeted. Society simply had no concept of a stable, consensual, committed, same-gender relationship.

The leading authority on homosexuality in America for decades was the American Psychoanalytic Association (APsaA).[161] This powerful group was responsible for many theories on the topic which sought to blame the parents, typically referring to an overbearing mother and a distant father, or some version of that dynamic. The "science" that came from this organization was based on small numbers of gay men who were in treatment for mental diseases, most commonly schizophrenia. In hindsight, we can easily say that ethical studies should have included gay people in society who were not in treatment for psychiatric diseases.

However, at the time, there were preconceived ideas about homosexuals, and studies were supporting those theories, but only because of the small number of participants, and most importantly, because they were in treatment for psychiatric diseases. The necessary ethical studies were rarely done, and when done, they were ignored

---

[160] Wikipedia contributors. (2019 January 16). The Homosexuals (CBS Reports). In *Wikipedia, The Free Encyclopedia*. Retrieved January 2019, from www.Wikipedia.org.

[161] Much of the information in this chapter is based on Kathy Baldock's extraordinary research. She uncovered an invaluable resource in Dr. Kenneth Lewes's book *Psychoanalysis and Male Homosexuality* (1988), as well as in conversations with him. When I reference his 1988 book in this chapter, it is often from information I learned in her book first. Baldock expounded upon his research with crucial cultural implications in her book, *Walking the Bridgeless Canyon* (2014). For a far more thorough review of this topic, I highly recommend her book as well as her soon-to-be-released second book, co-authored with Ed Oxford.

because of so much opposition to the idea that homosexuals could be normal, upstanding members of society. Based on the belief that homosexuality was a mental illness, the organization denied membership to any psychoanalyst who identified as gay until 2001.[162] As Baldock noted, "For ninety years there were no openly gay psychoanalysts in the primary policy-making organization in the United States dealing with the subject of homosexuality."[163]

Sigmund Freud (1856-1939), the father of psychoanalysis, called homosexuality a "mental illness," attributed to disrupted childhood psychosexual stages.[164] By the end of his life, he recanted, stating that homosexuality was not an illness, but a variation of human function.[165] Nevertheless, his original ideas persisted and fueled many similar theories.

Sandor Rado (1890-1972) was an influential psychoanalyst who produced work on the subject of homosexuality, based on his theories and work with small numbers of mentally ill people.[166] Rado taught that disrupted psychosexual stages were caused by a phobic avoidance by a child of the opposite sex parent.[167] Rado believed that if one could identify the missed developmental stage in one's life that had caused the homosexuality, then that person, with the help of a psychoanalyst, could be cured of homosexuality.

Edmund Bergler (1899-1962) was a leading psychoanalyst in the field of homosexuality in the 1950s. He published theories based

---

[162] *Walking the Bridgeless Canyon*, page 42.

[163] Ibid, page 42.

[164] Ibid, page 41.

[165] Freud, Sigmund, "Letter to an American mother", *American Journal of Psychiatry*, 107 (1951) page 787.

[166] *Walking the Bridgeless Canyon*, page 47.

[167] Drescher, Frank, "A History of Homosexuality and Organized Psychoanalysis," *The Journal of the American Academy of Psychoanalysis and Dynamic Psychiatry*, 36 (2008) page 447.

on a small number of his patients, that is, mentally ill patients who were both schizophrenic and homosexual. Bergler made statements about gay people without considering healthy gay people in the population. He referred in 1950 to gay people with the following words: swindlers, pseudologues (liars), forgers, lawbreakers of all sorts, drug purveyors, gamblers, pimps, spies, brothel owners. He declared them to be filled with "aggression, destruction, and self-deceit." He originated the false idea that gay people wanted to "recruit innocent children." He claimed that 99.9% of homosexuals could be "cured" using the principles he had created.[168] According to psychoanalyst Kenneth Lewes, by the end of Bergler's career, Bergler was an embarrassment to his profession.[169]

Alfred Kinsey (1894-1956) published findings of surveys and interviews that he had conducted about the sexual habits of Americans. It was a topic that was rarely discussed; therefore, the publication "helped dismantle the shroud of secrecy surrounding sex"[170] in America. While the numbers were skewed due to the high number of incarcerated participants, Kinsey's findings revealed homosexual activity in 10% of men. (The actual number of gay people in American society is now thought to be around 4.5% of the population.[171]) Kinsey's two books, *Sexual Behaviors in the Human Male* (1948) and *Sexual Behaviors in the Human Female* (1953), were very popular. People began to realize that their own children could possibly be homosexual.[172]

---

[168] *Walking the Bridgeless Canyon*, page 46.

[169] Lewes, Kennneth. (1995) *Psychoanalysis and Male Homosexuality.* Northvale, NJ: J. Aronson, page 141.

[170] *Walking the Bridgeless Canyon*, page 50.

[171] "In U.S., Estimate of LGBT Population Rises to 4.5%". Retrieved September 2018 from Gallup.com.

[172] *Walking the Bridgeless Canyon*, page 63.

Irving Bieber (1909-1991) was a psychoanalyst within the APsaA who published *A Psychoanalytical Study of Male Homosexuality* (1962). This book became the leading reference on the topic for two decades. As did his predecessors, Bieber studied a small number of patients (106) under care for mental illness. Bieber did not, as ethical science would require, consider a control group of healthy homosexual men, women, and couples in the community.[173] His information was gathered via questionnaires, the answers to which were provided by therapists, not the patients themselves.[174] He published findings on mentally ill patients as if representative of all homosexual people.[175] Among the patients in his studies, there were people suffering from schizophrenia, various types of neuroses, and people with "character disorders." Some even used circular arguments to then say that homosexuals were schizophrenic, neurotic, and had character disorders.[176] Bieber postulated that homosexuality was a mental illness caused by disruptions in family relationships, specifically,

> Though there are variations in the pattern, most such mothers are close, binding and intimate (CBI), sometimes in sexually inappropriate ways. This son is usually her favourite whom she openly prefers to her husband.... The fathers are hostile, competitive and do nothing to neutralize deleterious maternal influences. Patients' reports of their father are almost always negative. He is virtually non-existent, rejecting, hostile, harsh or brutal.

---

[173] Ibid, page 51.

[174] *Psychoanalysis and Male Homosexuality*, page 195.

[175] Bieber, I., & Bieber, T. B. "Male Homosexuality". *The Canadian Journal of Psychiatry*, 24(5), (1979) pages 409–421.

[176] *Psychoanalysis and Male Homosexuality*, page 191.

Bieber boasted "reversal estimates" from 30% "to an optimistic 50%." However, he noted that converts to heterosexuality would not necessarily lose homosexual interest.[177]

Lionel Ovesey (1915-1995) also published on the topic using data from his mentally ill patients without considering healthy gay people in the community.[178]

Charles Socarides (1922-2005) theorized that homosexuality was caused by a smothering mother and a rejecting father.[179] He practiced in New York City from 1954 to 2005. He reported that "about a third" of his patients became heterosexual after his treatment.[180]

I include these specific researchers and quotes because this is the cultural foundation of belief about homosexuality in this country. Many who came out as gay over the last generation, especially younger gay people, did not grow up in homes with "distant, weak fathers and smothering mothers." We know now that many gay people grew up in loving homes, and many were raised in church.[181] Because there were few gay people in the 1960s to address this information, society simply had no reason not to believe these ideas, disseminated by the professionals.

These post-Freudian theories influenced the inclusion of homosexuality into the Diagnostic and Statistical Manual of Mental Disorders (DSM), the handbook used by medical professionals for

---

[177] Bieber, I., & Bieber, T. B. "Male Homosexuality". *The Canadian Journal of Psychiatry.* 24(5), (1979) pages 409-421.

[178] *Walking the Bridgeless Canyon*, page 52.

[179] Ibid, page 52.

[180] Wikipedia contributors. (2018 July 27). Charles W. Socarides. In *Wikipedia, The Free Encyclopedia.* Retrieved October 6, 2018, from www. Wikipedia.org.

[181] *Us Versus Us*, chapter 1.

diagnosing and treating mental health disorders. The inclusion, therefore, prohibited any homosexual medical practitioners or researchers from joining the groups that were making these decisions.

There were professionals with opposing opinions, but the mainstream groups often simply did not acknowledge them. In 1957, Evelyn Hooker published a monumental study that revealed that the level of happiness and well-adjusted nature was not different between a group of healthy heterosexuals and a group of healthy homosexuals.[182] However, this study was largely ignored for many years.[183]

The National Security Act of 1947 allowed for the Central Intelligence Agency in the United States (CIA) to dismiss gay employees, calling them "security risks."[184] In 1953, President Eisenhower signed executive order 10450, which banned gay men and women from serving in the State Department. This ban affected all government jobs and the military. It was not until 1973 that a federal judge ruled that sexual orientation alone could not be the sole reason for termination of federal employment. The mass firings of gay people by the government of the United States is known as the Lavender Scare.[185]

By 1960, every state had anti-sodomy laws. These laws typically referred to any sexual act deemed to be unnatural or immoral. The State Liquor Authority in several states had the power to revoke the liquor license of any establishment that served gay people. It was

---

[182] Hooker, E. "The Adjustment of the Male Overt Homosexual". *Journal of Projective Techniques*, XXI (1957) pages 18–31.

[183] *Walking the Bridgeless Canyon*, page 85.

[184] Section 102c allowed the director of the CIA to, "in his discretion, terminate the employment of any[one]...he shall deem termination necessary or advisable in the interests of the [US]." https://www.cia.gov/library/readingroom/docs/1947-07-26.pdf.

[185] *Walking the Bridgeless Canyon*, page 68.

commonplace for police to raid establishments that catered to the gay community. In New York City, in 1969, gay people and those supporting gay rights held protests and uprisings against the regular police raids that had taken place in gay bars. This became known as the Stonewall riots, named after the bar in New York City where gay and transgender people gathered.

In the period following the Stonewall riots in New York City in 1969, a group of gay activists disrupted the American Psychiatric Association's annual meeting saying, "stop talking about us, and start talking to us." This opened the door for ongoing discussions with gay people in the community and the medical establishment.[186] In 1973, homosexuality as a mental disorder was removed from the classification of mental disorders, the DSM. It was replaced with "sexual orientation disturbance" for those people who were distressed by their orientation. In 1987, it was removed completely from the DSM.[187]

In 1969, *Everything You Always Wanted to Know About Sex but Were Afraid to Ask*, by psychiatrist David Reuben was a wildly popular book, read by over 100 million people in 51 countries.[188] The book suggested that all gay people were promiscuous and incapable of forming any satisfying relationships. This was accepted in the mainstream and believed by the majority of Americans.

In 1978, Pastor Tim LaHaye wrote *The Unhappy Gays: What Everyone Should Know About Homosexuality*. LaHaye listed "causes" of homosexuality from the neo-Freudian era, which had been completely debunked prior to the book's publication. LaHaye made unsubstantiated and outlandish claims that were truly absurd.

---

[186] Ibid, page 101.

[187] Ibid, pages 105-6.

[188] Allen, J. (1999 February 11). "Sex doctor David Reuben is back with some new advice". Retrieved September 2018 from www.CNN.com.

Among other things, he wrote that all homosexuals are angry, that they often have 2,000 partners, and that they want to recruit children. He wrote that "parents would prefer the death of their child to him adopting the unhappy wretchedness of homosexuality."[189] This book was considered the Christian view on homosexuality.

I would ask the reader to please stop and think about that for a moment. In many Christian circles, it was suggested that it may be preferable for one's child to be dead than to be gay. Gay kids heard it and understood it. Thankfully, today, there is far less hatred and vitriol, and some degree of understanding about people who are gay, even in the Christian community. In secular society, gay people are free to be open, and this has allowed for more people to get to know them. In the general public, all of the negative ideas surrounding gay people came from initially well-meaning people who simply did not know any gay people, and trusted the work of specialists in the field of psychoanalysis. People with same-gender attractions, understandably, did not let anyone know that they were gay. This created a cycle that allowed researchers to produce work that did not include healthy gay people in the community, since so few were known, and most lived their lives in oppressive secrecy. Gay people read these publications or heard from their parents and the media that homosexuals were broken, sick, and perverted, and decided that they would keep their secret hidden as long as they lived. However, over the decades, many realized that this burden was more than they could bear. As homosexuality has become accepted in the mainstream secular society, more gay people have felt the freedom to come out of the closet. However, in Christian circles, there remains extraordinary shame and fear in being gay.

The psychoanalysts, government mandates, and authors that I have noted above have barely scratched the surface of the foundation of

---

[189] LaHaye, Tim F. (1978) *The Unhappy Gays: What Everyone Should Know about Homosexuality*. Wheaton, IL: Tyndale House, page 157.

society's and many Christians' extreme aversion toward gay people. Further examples would include many television evangelists, Anita Bryant's campaign against gay people in the 1970s, my own pastor at a previous church who told the congregation at a Bible study that he was proud a member of his church had declined to pray for a gay woman who was sick, and the women's pastor who looked me in the eye and said, "I'll tell you what I would tell a Satan worshiper. I love you, but I hate what you do." (This approach does not actually convey a sense of love.)

On June 21, 2019, the American Psychoanalytic Association issued an apology for their "past views that pathologized homosexuality and transgender identities."[190] Dr. Lee Jaffe, president of the APsaA, stated,

> Regrettably, much of our past understanding of homosexuality as an illness can be attributed to the American psychoanalytic establishment. While our efforts in advocating for sexual and gender diversity since are worthy of pride, it is long past time to recognize and apologize for our role in the discrimination and trauma caused by our profession and say "we are sorry."[191]

On June 6, 2019, the Police Commissioner of the New York Police Department, James O'Neill, apologized for the police raids at Stonewall Inn. He stated, "The actions taken by the NYPD were wrong, plain and simple. The actions and laws were discriminatory and oppressive. And for that, I apologize."[192]

---

[190] Tene, W. (2019 June 21). "News: APsaA Issues Overdue Apology to LGBTQ Community". Retrieved June 22, 2019 from www.APSA.org.

[191] Trotta, D. (2019 June 21). "U.S. psychoanalysts apologize for labeling homosexuality an illness". Retrieved June 22, 2019 from www.Reuters.com.

[192] Drescher, F. (2019 June 21). "Stonewall's 50th Anniversary and an Overdue Apology". Retrieved June 22, 2019 from www.PsychologyToday.com.

17

SAME-GENDER ATTRACTION DOES NOT IMPLY PEDOPHILIA

In the 1970s, 70% of American respondents polled believed that homosexuals were sexually interested in children.[193] Although false, this was a foundation of the church's battle against gay people, most memorably during Anita Bryant's "Save Our Children" campaign in 1977. As noted previously, abuse of male children by an adult male has been termed "homosexual molestation," referring not to the abuser's orientation, but rather the gender of the child that was abused. However, frequent use of that term came to imply that homosexual men molested children.

The evidence reveals that homosexuals are less likely than heterosexuals to abuse children.

Groth and Birnbaum published their findings in 1978 of a sample of 175 male offenders who were convicted of child molestation.

---

[193] Klassen, A. D., Williams, C. J., & Levitt, E. E. (1989). *Sex and morality in the U.S.: An empirical enquiry under the auspices of the Kinsey Institute.* Middletown, CT: Wesleyan University Press.

All regressed offenders, whether their victims were male or female children, were heterosexual in their adult orientation. The possibility emerges that homosexuality and homosexual pedophilia may be mutually exclusive and that the adult heterosexual male constitutes a greater risk to the underage child than does the adult homosexual male.[194]

Dr. Carole Jenny collected data of 352 sexually abused children for one year (1991-1992) in a Denver Hospital. She found that the perpetrator was homosexual in only two cases. In 82% of cases, the molester was the heterosexual partner of a family member of the child.[195]

Dr. Nathaniel Conaghy published a review of the literature over a 30-year period. He wrote, "The man who offends against prepubertal or immediately postpubertal boys is typically not sexually interested in older men or in women."[196]

Dr. Gregory M. Herek has thoroughly researched this topic in his review article titled "Facts About Homosexuality and Child Molestation."[197] Based on his study of the literature, Dr. Herek writes that molesters of children are unlikely to be homosexuals, but are more frequently heterosexuals. In this article, Dr. Herek discusses a publication by the Family Research Council, written by Timothy J. Dailey. The Family Research Council does hold that

---

[194] Groth, A. N., & Birnbaum, H. J. "Adult sexual orientation and attraction to underage persons". *Archives of Sexual Behavior, 7*(3), (1978) pages 175-181.

[195] Jenny, C., Roesler, T. A., Poyer, K. "Are children at risk for sexual abuse by homosexuals?" *Pediatrics, 94*(1), (1994) pages 41-44.

[196] McConaghy, N. Paedophilia: A review of the evidence, *Australian and New Zealand Journal of Psychiatry*, 32:2, (1998) pages 252-265.

[197] Herek, G. "Facts About Homosexuality and Child Molestation". Retrieved December 22, 2018 from Psychology.ucdavis.edu. Http://psychology.ucdavis.edu/rainbow/html/facts_molestation.html#note2_text.

homosexuals are likely to be pedophiles. The article by Timothy Dailey, titled "Homosexuality and Child Abuse," is an "extensive attempt to document" the idea that homosexuality and pedophilia are linked.[198] Dr. Herek notes that Dailey used 76 footnotes, many of them referring to papers in scientific journals. Dr. Herek did the exhaustive work of researching the citations and presents findings that refute the Family Research Council's position.

To summarize, the Family Research Council, in an attempt to link homosexuality to pedophilia, has published an article with 76 scientific references which appear on the surface to support the Family Research Council's view that homosexuals abuse children. However, Dr. Herek has reviewed these 76 scientific papers and reports that they do not actually suggest a link between homosexuality and pedophilia, as the Family Research Council claims.

Consider this overview by Dr. Herek:

> In summary, the scientific sources cited by the FRC report do not support their argument. Most of the studies they referenced did not even assess the sexual orientation of abusers. Two studies explicitly concluded that sexual orientation and child molestation are unrelated. Notably, the FRC failed to cite the 1978 study by Groth and Birnbaum, which also contradicted their argument. Only one study (Erickson et al., 1988) might be interpreted as supporting the FRC argument, and it failed to detail its measurement procedures and did not differentiate bisexual from homosexual offenders.[199]

---

[198] Ibid.
[199] Ibid.

This issue is somewhat peripheral to our argument here, as we are discussing gay Christians who do not harm anyone. However, the idea that mainstream society believed that homosexuals molested children is very important to the cultural implications of the ongoing debate.

SECTION 4

••••••••••••••••••••••••••••

OPINIONS, POSITIONS, PROPOSITIONS

Chapter 18: Should Gay People Be Allowed to Serve in Our Churches?

Chapter 19: If This Is True, How Could We Have Gotten It So Wrong for So Long?

Chapter 20: The Two Main Non-Affirming Positions

Chapter 21: Addressing Other Non-Affirming Arguments

Chapter 22: Heart to Heart

Chapter 23: Summarizing the Premise: Is the Bible Clear That Homosexuality Is a Sin?

= 18 =

SHOULD GAY CHRISTIANS BE ALLOWED TO SERVE WITHIN OUR CHURCHES, OR SHOULD THEY REMAIN VISITORS?

There is a similar event in the Bible that we could consider. How did God show the Jews that Gentiles were allowed into the Church? The early Church following Christ's resurrection was strictly a Jewish phenomenon. For years, no one imagined the possibility that God would open up salvation to the Gentiles, although it was prophesied in Scripture.

Peter was given a vision in Acts 10 in which certain animals, which were forbidden as food, were lowered from the sky. In the vision, God said, "Get up, Peter. Kill and eat." Peter replied, "Surely not, Lord! I have never eaten anything impure or unclean." And God said, "Do not call anything impure that God has made clean." (Acts 10:15) Peter later explained, "God has shown me that I should not call *anyone* impure or unclean." (Acts 10:28b, emphasis mine)

This whole scene greatly perplexed Peter. It had never occurred to the Jews that God's dietary laws were allowed to be broken.[200] Forbidden foods were simply not questioned.

Then God instructed Peter that men were coming to the house, that he was to go with them. Meanwhile, Cornelius, a devout Gentile, had also heard from the Lord, "Cornelius, God has heard your prayer and remembered your gifts to the poor. Send to Joppa for Simon who is called Peter." (Acts 10:31b-32) So, Cornelius sent three men as God had instructed Cornelius, and Peter received the men as God had instructed Peter.

The men told Peter that Cornelius had sent for him, so Peter and some others went with them. This must have been an incredibly strange situation for Peter. He had likely never entered the home of a Gentile. There was no precedent for this. Jews were strictly forbidden from fellowshipping with Gentiles. As Cornelius awaited his guests, he invited family and friends to hear from the man that the Lord was sending.

Peter preached the gospel of Christ to Cornelius and his family and friends. As he was preaching, the Holy Spirit fell on them, and they were all baptized in the Holy Spirit and began to speak in tongues. This was an incredible, unprecedented, miraculous, shocking event. It had never occurred to the Jews that Christ's saving grace was intended for anyone outside of God's chosen Jewish people. But the Gentiles had received the Holy Spirit just as the new Jewish Christians had on the first Pentecost following the resurrection.

---

[200] However, in Mark 7:19, the author of the Gospel parenthetically noted that "Jesus declared all foods clean." Some suggest that the Gospel of Mark was heavily influenced by the Apostle Peter, and was written at least 2-3 decades after Peter's vision. I wonder if this realization that Jesus had declared all foods clean came to Peter long after the actual event during Jesus's lifetime, specifically, because of Peter's vision at Simon the tanner's house.

Following His resurrection, Jesus had told His disciples to wait for the promised Holy Spirit, that they would receive power when the Holy Spirit came on them. This is recorded in Acts 2, in the story of the upper room, where the Holy Spirit fell on the first believers, and they all began speaking in tongues, meaning, they spoke in other languages that they did not know.

Thus when Peter saw the same thing happening to the Gentiles in Cornelius's home, he was convinced that God had allowed even Gentiles into salvation through the death and resurrection of Christ.

When Peter returned to the conservative mother church in Jerusalem, the leaders argued with him (Acts 11:2, CEV) because he had entered a Gentile's home and visited with them. Peter recounted how the Holy Spirit had told him to have no hesitation about going with Cornelius's men. He relayed the story and explained,

> Then I remembered what the Lord had said: "John baptized with water, but you will be baptized with the Holy Spirit." So if God gave them the same gift He gave us who believed in the Lord Jesus Christ, who was I to think that I could stand in God's way? (Acts 11:16-17)

Scripture records, "When they [the Jewish leaders] heard this, they had no further objections and praised God, saying, 'So then, even to Gentiles God has granted repentance that leads to life.'" (Acts 11:18)

The baptism in the Holy Spirit remains an important tenet in many churches today and is often listed within a church's statement of beliefs. I have addressed this thoroughly in appendix B.

It is important to distinguish those gay people who reject God, and are appropriately represented by shocking videos from a gay pride parade,[201] from those sober-minded gay Christians who love and honor God, in the same way that Cornelius was different than other "sinful Gentiles." (Galatians 2:15) Remember, Cornelius and his family were "devout and God-fearing; he gave generously to those in need and prayed to God regularly." (Acts 10:2) When God made it known to the leaders of the Church that He accepted Gentiles, He demonstrated via a godly family.[202] Once it was recognized that Gentiles were allowed into the Church, then it became appropriate to invite people from the community in and teach them the gospel. One problem with non-affirming opinions is they typically consider all homosexuals to be described by the negative words in Romans 1, suggesting there are no godly gay people. However, this requires a misreading of Romans 1 and does not take into account the genuine evidence of faithful gay Christians among us.

In summary, the way that God made it clear to the Jews that Gentiles were allowed into His Church was that He baptized them in the Holy Spirit, just as He baptized the original Jewish believers in the Holy Spirit on the first Pentecost after Christ's resurrection. Knowing this, how can the Church exclude anyone who is baptized in the Holy Spirit, when this was God's specific sign that a group of people were to be included? Many gay Christians are baptized in the Holy Spirit and operate in the gifts of the Holy Spirit, as described in Scripture.

---

[201] *God's Gay Agenda*, page 11.

[202] I was introduced to this idea by Pastor Aaron Crowley-Guest during a sermon he gave at New Covenant Church of Atlanta in 2019.

19

IF THIS IS TRUE, HOW COULD WE HAVE GOTTEN IT SO WRONG FOR SO LONG?

Chapter 12 revealed many situations about which Christians had to change their minds over the decades and centuries. When and why did it become reasonable for women to speak in church? Both the culture and the church had to evolve with regard to interracial marriage, although their beliefs were firmly held at one point. Slaveholders were often devout Christians. Wearing jewelry in church, head coverings, greeting one another with a kiss are ideas that we can simply shrug off without much thought. Those were cultural norms which are not important to us today. But the churches held to those rules adamantly at one point.

Slavery in the Southern Baptist Theological Seminary

In December 2018, the Southern Baptist Theological Seminary released a report confronting the horrific reality of their history as it relates to slavery. In this section, we will carefully consider parallels in the way people used the Bible to argue points that were not reflective of God's heart on these issues. To be clear, I am not equating the issues. The horror suffered by so many African Americans in this country is difficult to fathom, and there was no escape for them. Often gay people have the option to hide, to live a lie, to enter into heterosexual marriage, and to appear completely normal in society. African Americans did not have this option. But these particular parallels that can be drawn are important. Christians believed that slaveholding was morally and biblically acceptable, and Christians believe that excluding gay people from membership in Christian churches, and thus, God's family, is morally and biblically acceptable.

Each of the Seminary's four founders owned slaves, more than fifty total, and they fought for their right to maintain their "property."[203] "The faculty believed that science had demonstrated African American inferiority. They were convinced of the superiority of white civilization and that this justified racial inequality."[204]

Just as Christian advocates of slavery and their descendants eventually re-examined their premise of white superiority and concluded that all people share the same right to freedom, it is time for non-affirming Christians to re-examine their premise and recognize that gay Christians are not broken, sick, or perverted, as was once honestly believed, even within the medical field.

In a letter introducing the report, Dr. R. Albert Mohler, the president of the seminary, wrote, "How could our founders, James P. Boyce, John Broadus, Basil Manly Jr., and William Williams, serve as such defenders of biblical truth, the gospel of Jesus Christ, and the confessional convictions of this Seminary, and at the same time own

---

[203] This, it was believed, was biblical. Exodus 21:21 refers to slaves as "property."

[204] The Southern Baptist Theological Seminary. (2018 December 12). *Report on Slavery and Racism in the History of the Southern Baptist Theological Seminary* [PDF file]. Retrieved December 15, 2018 from www.SBTS.edu.

human beings as slaves—based on an ideology of race—and defend American slavery as an institution?"[205]

Mohler wrote,

> The founding faculty of this school—all four of them—were deeply involved in slavery and deeply complicit in the defense of slavery. Many of their successors on this faculty, throughout the period of Reconstruction and well into the twentieth century, advocated segregation, the inferiority of African Americans, and openly embraced the ideology of the Lost Cause[206] of southern slavery.

He asked the question, "How can a school like Princeton University face the truth while we, holding to the truth of the gospel, would refuse to do the same?" Secular society has been able to confront this situation, while the Church has "been guilty of a sinful absence of historical curiosity."[207]

I believe that the Church is in a similar position today, and that future historical accounts will read similarly. While secular society embraces gay people, many mainstream churches continue to exclude them from membership, suggesting that they are not invited into the family of God.

---

[205] Ibid, page 3.

[206] Lost Cause was an ideology which held that despite the loss in the Civil War, the Confederacy's cause was just and heroic. Wikipedia contributors. (2019 February 24). Lost Cause of the Confederacy. In *Wikipedia, The Free Encyclopedia*. Retrieved February 24, 2019, from www.Wikipedia.org.

[207] The Southern Baptist Theological Seminary. (December 2018). *Report on Slavery and Racism in the History of the Southern Baptist Theological Seminary* [PDF file]. Page 2.

The report states,

> Southern Baptist defenders of slavery vindicated slavery as it existed in the South by appealing to an abstract form of slavery that hardly existed in fact. They generally described slavery in terms of what slavery should be, not according to how it was ordinarily practiced. Since slavery in practice did not measure up to its ideal, it was necessary to argue for slavery as an ideal construct and then insinuate that this ideal characterized slavery in actual practice. They instructed slaveholders regarding how they ought to treat their slaves, and then defended those instructions as if they represented the actual practice of slavery.[208]

Similarly, the church has constructed an evil view of gay Christians that simply is not true by maintaining for decades that gay people have an "agenda" that includes bringing harm to children and to heterosexual marriage.

The following statement was written by Pastor Ric Fritz:

> The focus of the LGBTQ [lesbian, gay, bisexual, transgender, queer] movement is nothing less than the utter destruction of the God-ordained equal, but distinct design of men and women; the corruption of the sanctity of marriage; and the obliteration of God's design of a family consisting of one man, one women [*sic*], joined together to have and raise Godly [*sic*] children. It also seeks to normalize

---

[208] Ibid, page 17.

sexual immorality. In short, it seeks to normalize and celebrate sin.[209]

This may be an effective way to motivate non-affirming Christians to continue their stand against gay people, but it simply is not reasonable. There certainly may be people, both straight and gay, about whom this shocking statement is true, but to suggest a blanket condemnation of all gay people like this is thoroughly inappropriate. For example, within the LGBTQ category, there are gay Christians, who have surrendered their lives to Christ, by definition. These are loving, God-fearing people who simply seek to live the abundant life that Jesus promised us and to bring Him glory and honor in our lives. Moreover, many gay people who do not know Christ, just like our straight unchurched friends and neighbors, are often kind, loving people. Pastor Fritz's statement is entirely unreasonable.

I ask the reader to consider again the parallel to the Church's previous firm stance on slavery and segregation. In declaring slavery to be something that it wasn't, there were factions in the church that continued to advocate for it even after society recognized its error. Similarly, in declaring lies about gay Christians, the non-affirming arguments continue to err in their condemnation and rejection of us.

"William Williams [founder of the Southern Baptist Theological Seminary] testified to his support of slavery in a New York newspaper in 1866. Before the war, he wrote, white southerners were nearly unanimous in their belief that slavery was just, and now that slavery was abolished, 'we still maintain that slaveholding is morally right.'"[210]

---

[209] Fritz, R. (2018 July 5). "The LGBTQ Movement and Christianity (Its Threat and Our Response): Part 1". Retrieved from www.Crosswalk.com.
[210] The Southern Baptist Theological Seminary. (December 2018). *Report on Slavery and Racism in the History of the Southern Baptist Theological Seminary* [PDF file]. Page 11.

If non-affirming Christians wonder how they could have been so wrong for so long on the topic of homosexuality, consider that the Southern Baptist Theological Seminary founders, faculty, donors, and students, that is, God-fearing, Bible-believing, Holy Spirit filled Christians, were undeniably wrong on the issue of slavery and "black inferiority" for a century.

The founders and thereafter the leaders of the Southern Baptist Theological Seminary were absolutely certain that slavery was an institution blessed by God, intended to be forever perpetuated by Him. I will present parallels to our current issue that appear remarkably similar to the types of arguments these Christians used to enslave African Americans.

The Southern Baptist Theological Seminary (SBTS): The founding fathers all owned slaves.[211]
Non-affirming churches: Openly affirming gay people are not allowed to join the church or participate in ministries. Homosexuals are not invited into the kingdom of God per I Corinthians 6:9-10.
Discussion: Slavery was accepted and believed to be scripturally sanctioned. Similarly, traditionalist Christians believe that Scripture is clear that homosexuality is a sin; therefore, gay people are excluded from God's family, and thus, churches.

SBTS: The Seminary's early faculty and trustees defended the "righteousness of slaveholding." They stated that "slavery was in the best interest of the slaves."[212] Slavery, it was argued, was "a God-ordained institution to be perpetuated.... Slavery was 'an institution of heaven,' essential to civil society."[213]

---

[211] Ibid, page 3.
[212] Ibid, page 5.
[213] Ibid, page 6.

Non-affirming churches: Make no mistake about it, any and all forms of homosexuality are sinful[214] in God's eyes. This is not a difficult or ambiguous subject.

Discussion: This defines the faulty premise in both cases. What were the assumptions that led to each false premise? Slaves were assumed to be biologically inferior to slaveholders and thus incapable of independence. Homosexuals were assumed to be broken, sick, and perverted, intent on living in willful rebellion against God.

SBTS: "The faculty taught white superiority and the inferiority of black capacities for civilization. They did so with the full confidence their views were the conclusions of empirical observation undergirded by leading scientific authorities."[215] There were innumerable scientific references at their disposal.

Non-affirming churches: The scientific and medical communities considered homosexuality to be a mental illness until 1973. Many in the Church continue to hold this view. Furthermore, evangelical Christians continue to suggest that homosexuals are pedophiles.

Discussion: "Scientific evidence" that homosexuals are broken, sick, and perverted stems from the long-debunked neo-Freudian theories, which traditionalists continue to use in their arguments. (I discuss this in chapter 16.) Timothy Daily published a report regarding the "scientific evidence" of a link between homosexuality and abuse of children. The report has been discussed and refuted by Dr. Gregory Herek. (I provided a detailed summary in chapter 17.)

---

[214] "Any and all forms of homosexuality are sinful." -a beloved pastor from a church I previously attended

[215] The Southern Baptist Theological Seminary. (December 2018). *Report on Slavery and Racism in the History of the Southern Baptist Theological Seminary* [PDF file]. Page 54.

SBTS: "Providence indicated that it was in accordance with God's will that blacks should be slaves. To oppose the enslavement of blacks was therefore to rebel against God's authority."[216]

Non-affirming churches: "Every single reference to homosexual practice in the Bible is categorically negative."[217]

Discussion: The same-sex practices referred to in the Bible involve idol worship, abuse, exploitation, and rejection of Christ; same-sex activity by gay Christians does not reflect the same-sex practices described in the Bible. Respectfully, every single biblical reference to women teaching men in any capacity is categorically negative, yet many women are gifted to be teachers today. To give another example from Scripture, every single reference to leadership positions in church are male, yet there are many leadership roles for women in churches today.

SBTS: "...I believe, sir, that it [slavery] is an institution of God, and that we have revealed to us in the Holy Bible clear and overwhelming evidence of its establishment by Him and of His intention to perpetuate it."[218]

Non-affirming churches: Homosexuality is wrong, period. Anyone who disagrees is disagreeing with the authority of Scripture.

Discussion: People believe their trusted leaders. When they hear "clear and overwhelming biblical evidence" from someone they trust, there is simply no need to study the Scripture further. This is the reason that Scripture records, "we who teach will be judged more strictly." (James 3:1)

---

[216] Ibid, page 14.

[217] Brown, M. (2018 December 10). "A Short Primer on the Bible and Homosexual Practice". Retrieved December 22, 2018 from www.CharismaNews.com.

[218] The Southern Baptist Theological Seminary. (December 2018). *Report on Slavery and Racism in the History of the Southern Baptist Theological Seminary* [PDF file]. Page 12.

Let's briefly review the "clear and overwhelming biblical evidence" for slavery. This is not hyperbole. In fact, the whole of the Bible actually presupposes the practice of slavery. There are strong biblical arguments that can be construed as defending this horrific institution. However, in order to accept the biblical arguments in favor of American slavery, one must assume that slaves were biologically inferior to slaveholders. The unraveling of that incorrect assumption was where the "biblical evidence" crumbled.

The Old Testament was written within a slaveholding context. Again, that is simply a tenet that one must accept as he reads the Scripture. The Jewish people had slaves, as God had instructed them. In the New Testament, not much had changed. Paul and Peter both wrote that slaves were to submit to and obey their masters.[219] In all of Scripture, Americans opposed to slaveholding did not have much to stand on. Galatians 3:28 was helpful: "There is neither Jew nor Gentile, neither slave nor free, nor is there male and female, for you are all one in Christ Jesus." Paul's letter to his friend Philemon was somewhat helpful, although problematic. Paul had requested that Philemon free a particular slave who had become a brother in Christ. However, as previously noted, Paul did not suggest that Philemon free his other slaves.

When one stood on the golden rule, "Do to others as you would have them do to you," (Luke 6:31) the response was that slaveholding was in the best interests of the slaves because they could never be educated or live independently. When abolitionists said, we are all free in Christ, Christian slaveholders agreed and stated that slaves could be Christians, but that they must remain enslaved, as the Scripture demonstrated. Slaveholders strongly believed and preached that opposition to the institution of slavery was "to rebel against God's authority."

---

[219] Colossians 3:22, Ephesians 6:5, I Peter 2:18

Similarly, many churches, teachers, and, importantly, Bible translators, have come into agreement that homosexuality is wrong and that homosexuals are broken, sick, and perverted. This leaves Christians with no real need to study the matter further. But I maintain that this has perpetuated a false argument, bringing condemnation to the innocent and keeping people in bondage by those "whose consciences have been seared as with a hot iron," who "forbid people to marry." (I Timothy 4:2b-3a)

Science appeared to demonstrate the inferiority of slaves (and the depravity of homosexuals). Church leaders proclaimed that the Bible had set forth the institution of slavery (and the sinfulness of all same-gender acts, not just abusive, idolatrous, exploitative same-gender acts, as depicted in Scripture). Proponents of slavery convinced the public of an institution which was actually the ideal, but not real in practice, that is, of benevolent treatment of their slaves, which was not the norm (not unlike the way some non-affirming arguments claim that homosexuals have an agenda which is the "utter destruction" of the heterosexual marriage).[220]

Some disagree that the Bible ever allowed for slavery, citing Exodus 21:16. That point is now irrelevant, since Christians no longer condone slavery. The important point for us today is obvious: for decades Christians erroneously believed that the Bible condoned American slavery.

Consider a quote from Dr. Mohler (the president of the seminary), referring to gay people. "The question is whether evangelicals will remain true to the teachings of Scripture and the unbroken teaching of the Christian church for over two thousand years on

---

[220] Fritz, R. (2018 July 5). "The LGBTQ Movement and Christianity (Its Threat and Our Response): Part 1". Retrieved from www.Crosswalk.com.

the morality of same-sex acts and the institution of marriage."[221] This statement is inaccurate. It was not until the late 1920s that the terms "homosexual" and "heterosexual" began to appear in common culture.[222] The translators didn't change the point of those Bible passages from abusive, exploitative sexual acts to "homosexuals" because a new word came to define the old understanding, as traditionalists assert. Translators introduced the word homosexuals in 1946 because they thought that all homosexual activity involved exploitation and abuse.[223] (Recall that in 1967, there was still no recognition in society of the idea of a gay couple. Love and monogamy within a homosexual relationship was inconceivable.[224])

Just as we now know that African Americans are every bit as capable of independence as any other group of people, so we also now know that homosexual people are not appropriately described by a term that refers to exploitative, abusive acts. American slavery was wrong, and the rejection of gay Christians in our churches is wrong. The Christian Church has had this "unbroken teaching" for less than one hundred years, not two thousand years, as Dr. Mohler suggests. Interestingly, one hundred years is approximately the amount of time that Dr. Mohler's seminary was wrong about the institution of American slavery, segregation, and "black inferiority."

---

[221] Mohler, A. (2014 April 22). "God, the Gospel, and the Gay Challenge—A Response to Matthew Vines". Retrieved January 13, 2020 from www.AlbertMohler.com.

[222] *Walking the Bridgeless Canyon*, page 36.

[223] This begs the question, why did translators continue to use the incorrect word "homosexuals" after it was changed by the team that originally used it? Sadly, in the time between the decision to remove the word "homosexuals" and the actual revision (more than 10 years), several new translations had copied the incorrect term. Baldock and Oxford have research and insight regarding other translations and will present this data in their highly anticipated, soon-to-be-published book, tentatively titled, *Forging a Sacred Weapon: How the Bible Became Anti-Gay.*

[224] The evidence for this is presented in the first paragraph of chapter 16.

Interracial Marriage

In 1912, there were so few interracial couples that the idea that the practice could be "forever prohibited" seemed reasonable to some, as a proposed constitutional amendment. However, over time, there were more interracial couples, and the sentiment in America and in the Church became more open and loving toward interracial couples. Christians no longer regard the "curse of Ham," the prohibition of intermarriage between the Israelites and Canaanites, or the boundaries referred to in Acts 17:26, as reasons to prohibit interracial marriage.

Discrimination of Marginalized People in Society

When there is discrimination against a marginalized group by the majority, it becomes easy to rely on trusted authorities in the church who have outspoken opinions. Unfortunately, with regard to gay people in general, the medical establishment got it wrong from the very beginning with work done only on small numbers of mentally ill gay patients. In hindsight, we recognize that it is not wise to make decisions about people without having relationships and discussions with those people. "Homosexuality" was an abstract idea for many mainstream Christians for decades. People held firm beliefs without ever knowing a gay person or discussing it with someone they knew. Gay people were forced into hiding and secrecy based on the painfully inaccurate information being disseminated and the laws that were written based on the erroneous findings.

Thus, Christians had no real need to question what was being taught. It seemed reasonable that if homosexuals were all the things that the scientific and medical community said they were, and if the Bible referred to same-sex acts in negative terms, and if it seemed possible that these homosexuals were really a threat to our children, as was described by the professional medical establishment and presented in the media, there was no reason to look into the matter more carefully.

In the 1970s, gay people began organizing and encouraging one another to come out to their friends and family, as this was the only way that a marginalized group could be recognized for who they were instead of for what was being said about them. However, the political and religious voices were so loud, and the rhetoric was so outrageous that gay people simply were not able to have an audience with mainstream Christians. Ex-gay ministries seemed the appropriate answer to the issue of homosexuality. It was only recently that we learned that the overwhelming result of those ministries (after 40 years) was failure to convert people to heterosexuality. Now the discussion has turned to celibacy. However, most traditionalists reject that celibacy is a solution, because if an act is sinful, the inclination toward that act is equally sinful as noted by Jesus in Matthew 5:27-28. In other words, the inclination, feeling, attraction, and desire for a sinful thing is sinful, even if celibate.

Bible Translations: "Helpful" Clarifications, Opinions, Objections, Errors

Traditionalists are beginning to concede that the Bible does not address loving, monogamous, gay couples, yet their belief in the premise, "homosexuality is a sin," remains immutable. The non-affirming focus has shifted to "one man, one woman." This represents "the whole of Scripture beginning in Genesis," referring to "male and female He created them" (Genesis 1:27) and "a man leaves his father and mother and is united to his wife." (Genesis 2:24) Increasingly, the foundation of the traditionalists' argument is "one man, one woman," *without exception*. Thus, the idea that all of the same-sex practices in the Bible are condemned is reinforcement of "complementarity," and no longer the primary argument.

We need to briefly consider the error in our Bible translations again. These errors are the foundation for the initial understanding that the Bible condemned gay people. In other words, for decades, the (erroneous) idea that "homosexuals will not inherit the kingdom of God" led to the understanding that "one man, one woman" was the only valid intimate, covenantal partnership. However, as noted throughout this book, in the Bible, we see exceptions to the "one man, one woman" tenet. The non-affirming focus shifted from the passages condemning same-sex acts to "complementarity" once it was realized that the translations were likely wrong. Now, with Baldock and Oxford's research, we have conclusive data that the head of the RSV translation team deemed the word "homosexuals" to be the incorrect translation. Thus, in order to maintain the non-affirming position, the focus must shift away from the passages.

To briefly summarize Baldock and Oxford's work, recall from chapter 4 that Baldock, Oxford, and their team searched the archives at Yale University and discovered an exchange between a young seminarian and the head of the Revised Standard Version (RSV) translation team, the first translation to use any form of the word "homosexuals" in the Bible. (Baldock and Oxford's book will be published soon. Until then, they are sharing information in blog posts and seminars.) Baldock writes, "As a result of the detailed challenge, the head of the team admitted making an error in using the word 'homosexual.' He assured the challenger that the team would correct the translation error in the RSV revision." However, by the time the term was changed to "perverts," which could represent anyone, straight or gay, several other translations had been published using the RSV as their base text. These new translations "duplicated [the] RSV wrong translation, and The Living Bible added homosexual(s), homosexuality in five more places."[225]

Job was Actually Impatient

Many Christians do not want to consider the enormous potential confusion in questioning their translations. Some want to believe that the translations are inspired by the Holy Spirit, as the original text is. However, unfortunately, this is actually not the case. As a simple example, recall the common phrase, "the patience of Job" from the King James Version, found in the book of James, the brother of Christ, in James 5:11. Just last year as I was reading Job, I noticed that twice Job referred to himself as impatient. (Job 6:11, 21:4) I learned that the original word in Greek (in James 5:11) could be translated as endurance or perseverance, which would be a better translation in this situation. Job was not patient, but he did persevere until he got an answer from God. Most modern versions of the Bible use the terms endurance or perseverance.

In fact, the NIV Study Bible addresses this explicitly in the note under this verse. It states, "Not 'patience.'"[226] I, and apparently the NIV team, believe that the KJV was mistaken in its choice of translation of that verse. I consider this of great importance because some groups declare the KJV to be inerrant. The New Independent Fundamental Baptist movement, which holds that all LGBTQ people in America should be executed by the government,[227] has

---

[225] Baldock, K. (2019 August 7). "Where Does Christian Anti-LGBTQ Ideology Come From?" Retrieved August 29, 2019 from www.CanyonWalkerConnections.com.

[226] Barker, K. (1985). "James 5:11". *The NIV Study Bible*. Grand Rapids, MI: Zondervan, page 1885.

[227] www.nifbcult.com.

this statement on their website: "The King James Version (KJV) of the Bible is the word of God without error."[228]

Some may wonder, if the translations could be wrong, can we believe anything we read in the Bible? For the vast majority of Scripture, the translations are agreed upon by scholars over the decades and centuries. Any controversial passage is readily researchable via numerous study tools available to us. The Blue Letter Bible (www. BlueLetterBible.com) is one example. Using this tool, one can easily find the (best known) original text within a portion of Scripture, any word of which can be examined, including its other occurrences in the Bible, its original Hebrew or Greek letters, and the Greek translation of the Hebrew text. Additionally, commentaries by multiple leading scholars are available and easy to find on virtually any verse in the Bible. We are very privileged and blessed to have this free online access to the agreed upon original Hebrew and Greek Scriptures right from our computers. These tools are invaluable for studying Scripture in depth.

On the website www.GotQuestions.org, the topic of translating the Bible was addressed. The author writes,

> Due to the faithful efforts of dedicated Christian translators (and of course the oversight of the Holy Spirit), the translations available today are superb and trustworthy. The fact that we cannot ascribe inerrancy to a translation should motivate us towards even closer study, and away from blind devotion towards any particular translation.[229]

---

[228] www.TheNewIFB.com.

[229] Houdmann, S. M. (2019 February 14). "How does the translation process impact the inspiration, inerrancy, and infallibility of the Bible?" Retrieved April 20, 2019 from www.GotQuestions.org.

Translators Find Jesus's Words Objectionable and "Correct" Them

Sometimes translators add words for clarification or change things from the original text. I was very surprised to discover[230] the following translation decision, made by the NIV team (and most other translations as well). In Matthew, Jesus is recorded as saying, "Two men will be in the field; one will be taken and the other left. Two women will be grinding with a hand mill; one will be taken and the other left." (Matthew 24:40-41) A similar statement was recorded by Luke as well, but the context was different. In Luke 17:34, Jesus said, in the original Greek, that, at night, two men would be in one bed; one would be taken, and the other would be left. In the following verse, he stated that two women would be grinding; one would be taken, and the other would be left.

In Luke's version, in the Greek, in the first sentence, "two" is gender-neutral, but "one" and "the other" are masculine. Similarly, in the next sentence, "two" is gender-neutral, but "one" and "the other" are feminine. It is well understood and agreed upon by scholars that in the two verses, Jesus was referring to two men and then to two women. One may expect that their Bible would simply translate Jesus's words from the original Greek. However, some translators[231] have *expressed objections* to the idea that two men would be in one bed at night.[232]

Therefore, instead of "two men," most translations used "two people" or "two" in Luke's Gospel. In the following sentence, most used "two women," which is the correct translation. Since those two women were "grinding," perhaps grinding grain, the translators added the

---

[230] Goetz, R. (2011 July 3). "Anti-homosexual Translator Bias". Retrieved August 6, 2019 from www.BibleThumpingLiberal.com.
[231] Ibid.
[232] Bratcher, R. (1982). *A Translator's Guide to the Gospel of Luke*. Swindon, England: United Bible Societies, page 287.

word "grain" and did not shy away from using "two women" as they did with the men in bed at night.

Let's look at Luke 17:34 specifically. It is clear from the passage that only one of the two men was condemned. If homosexuality is a sin, then the two men in bed at night should have both been condemned. Since one man was not condemned, translators considered this "a statement which could be objectionable."[233] Thus, to alleviate any incongruity between their assumptions about two men in one bed at night, and the idea that only one was condemned, they simply changed it, so that two people were in the bed together.

If Jesus had condemned both men, I think it is safe to say that the translators[234] would have translated the passage as "two men."

There are two important points to this discovery. First, Bible translators saw this statement by Jesus as affirming two men in one bed at night. Since this was incongruent with their beliefs, they altered an important detail so that the English speaking world might consider this a heterosexual couple. Secondly, Jesus Himself chose the level of detail that He wanted. He could have chosen two men in a boat fishing as Pastor Peterson did, in his The Message translation. But Jesus specifically referred to two men, one bed, at night, only one of whom was condemned.

Would it not be appropriate to keep the Word of God intact, and adjust one's belief rather than adjust the words of the Bible to fit one's belief? I consider this blatant mistranslation of Jesus's words to be misleading, and thus, egregious.

---

[233] Ibid, page 287.

[234] I consulted 33 translations. Only twelve of them rendered this appropriately, four of which were some version of the King James Bible.

It is important to understand that when reading our Bibles in English, one is sometimes reading a translation through a bit of an interpretive lens. Those interpretations are sometimes, unfortunately, incorrect. Similarly, in chapter 7, we saw that in Romans 1:29, the NIV and some other translation teams simply left out or failed to translate *porneia*, a very important word that has implications for this debate.

We now have invaluable research that reveals that the translations which converted condemnation of sinful, exploitative, male sexual acts into condemnation of all same-sex attracted people were in error. Graciously, some Bible translations have confirmed this in their footnotes, as described in chapter 5. Again, the focus of traditionalists has shifted to "the whole of the Bible beginning in Genesis," and "one man, one woman," in order to maintain the premise, "homosexuality is a sin." However, if these translations are wrong, I believe traditionalists need to carefully consider that the entire premise may be wrong.

It is Time to Reconsider the Premise

If the premise was wrong all along, and we can finally see that now, then now is the time for the Church to begin the healing process.

I am not angry at non-affirming people. Christians believe in the power of Christ to heal. Many gay Christians prayed earnestly, standing on the Word of God for healing from homosexuality. We understand what traditionalists have believed all this time and why. Some of us believed it too. Today is a new day, and God's mercies are new every morning. (Lamentations 3:22-23) I harbor no ill-will or judgment for all the erroneous assumptions that have been declared about us in the past. Let's agree to step back and consider the matter more closely.

In general, gay Christians, just like straight Christians, are not broken, sick, or perverted. We do not recruit. We do not harm anyone, neither children nor adults. We respect heterosexual marriage. We are thankful for straight couples and procreation. Our agenda is to honor God in absolutely every aspect of our lives. We have been chosen by God Himself. (Ephesians 1:4-6) We are not living in sin in our same-gender, covenantal relationships. We certainly sin just like everyone, and we are being sanctified just as our straight brothers and sisters are. But our covenantal relationships do not bring dishonor to God.

Three Traditionalist Pastors Extend Welcome to the LGBTQ Community

Tony Campolo (introduced in chapter 14) is the evangelical pastor who understood homosexuality to be sinful but recognized through his research that it was not a choice and it was not curable. For years, Pastor Campolo believed that homosexuals must commit to lifelong celibacy. In 2015, he changed his opinion and recommended "full acceptance of Christian gay couples into the Church." He wrote,

> I am old enough to remember when we in the Church made strong biblical cases for keeping women out of teaching roles in the Church, and when divorced and remarried people often were excluded from fellowship altogether on the basis of Scripture. Not long before that, some Christians even made biblical cases supporting slavery. Many of those people were sincere believers, but most of us now agree that they were wrong. I am afraid we

are making the same kind of mistake again, which
is why I am speaking out.[235]

Traditionalist Pastor Clay Peck, of Grace Place in Berthoud, Colorado, also welcomes LGBT Christians. He has a perspective that may appeal to non-affirming, traditional churches. He pastors a non-affirming, evangelical church. The website reads, "Grace Place affirms the Statement of Faith as adopted by the National Association of Evangelicals and the affirmations of the Evangelical Covenant Church." The church believes as follows: "Faithfulness in heterosexual marriage, celibacy in singleness—these constitute the Christian standard. When we fall short, we are invited to repent, receive the forgiveness of God, and amend our lives." On May 2, 2018, Pastor Peck presented from the pulpit an apology to LGBT people and their families, who had been hurt by the Church, and he issued an invitation, to be welcomed and loved in their church. He stated that his church would "agree to disagree." He presented the basic three positions. That is, 1.) Gay Christians must renounce and seek to change their orientation. 2.) Gay Christians can be gay, but they must be celibate. 3.) Gay Christians can be blessed by God within a covenantal, monogamous, same-gender relationship. He acknowledged that he strongly believes in the second position, that gay Christians must commit to lifelong celibacy. But he offered as an umbrella over all three positions, an invitation to belong to their local church and repentance for anyone who had been rejected in the past.[236]

---

[235] Campolo, T. (2015 June 8). "Tony Campolo: For the Record. Tony releases a new statement urging the Church to be more welcoming". Retrieved April 26, 2019 from www.TonyCampolo.org.

[236] Peck, Clay. (2018 May 2). *No Perfect People Allowed - Separation of Church and Hate.* [Video file]. Retrieved April 4, 2019 from https://vimeo.com/266337311.

On February 9, 2020, Pastor Dan Matlock of Eikon church in Kyle, Texas delivered a sermon during which he announced that their church would become "fully LGBTQ affirming without an asterisk." Per this decision by the elder board, the pastor and the church are thus no longer affiliated with the Assemblies of God.[237]

Let's Not Make This Mistake Again

I want to offer a simple encouragement to the reader beyond the topic of this book. Let us not continue to make this mistake. When dealing with people on the margins of society, let's get to know them, love them, and talk to them before making sweeping negative statements about them and about God's intention for them.

There is a social media meme that traditionalists post which states that your Creator has determined your gender; it was not assigned by a doctor. Indeed, God determines our gender. Surely we all agree, however, that doctors make mistakes. Consider a simple example. If a doctor incorrectly labeled a baby boy with ambiguous genitalia as a girl, and the genetic makeup was actually male, that girl may sense that she is male as she ages. Once this baby becomes a teenager (and in some cases, much sooner), she may determine that she is transgender, meaning, male, or, given her upbringing, she may feel that she is both female and male, or non-binary at all. If this person requests that they be referred to as "they/them" or "he/him," consider the possibility that it may be appropriate, merciful, kind, loving, gracious, compassionate, and good to do so. If you hesitate to accept that, recall that the premise in this scenario was that a male

---

[237] Matlock, Dan. (2020 February 9). *Clarity: Getting Clear.* [YouTube video file]. Retrieved February 27, 2020 from https://www.youtube.com/watch?v=X-k2G_culgM.

baby was incorrectly determined to be a girl by a doctor, and was thus raised as a girl.[238]

According to the Intersex Society of North America, approximately 1 in 1,500 to 1 in 2,000 babies is born with atypical genitalia.[239] Some of these babies have been raised in the wrong gender.

---

[238] See Baldock's research on this topic in *Walking the Bridgeless Canyon* (2014), chapter 8. This chapter, "The Myth of a Pink and Blue World" is available on her website as a free download. www.CanyonWalkerConnections.com.
[239] Intersex Society of North America. (2008). "How Common is Intersex?" Retrieved April 2019 from www.ISNA.org.

$\Longequal 20 \Longequal$

CONSIDER THE TWO MAIN NON-AFFIRMING POSITIONS

Let us review the two basic categories of the non-affirming position.[240]

1. One cannot be both gay and Christian. A follower of Christ must renounce his[241] same-sex attraction. He must commit to heterosexuality (or at least non-homosexuality[242]) as part of his identity in Christ, as outlined in the creation story and repeated by both Jesus and Paul. He must either enter into heterosexual marriage or commit to a life without an

---

[240] I should parenthetically note that there is a third position within this debate. The New Independent Fundamental Baptist movement (www. TheNewIFB.com) calls for government officials to execute all LGBTQ people. They believe that there is no hope of redemption for anyone who could be found by a judge to be LGBTQ. Thus, they could not agree with either of the two views above. This group sponsored the "Make America Straight Again" conference, in June 2019 in Florida. There are other groups who also hold this view.

[241] I will use he/him for simplicity, but this list refers to both men and women.

[242] "Non-homosexuality" is my attempt to include the position of those who recognize that conversion to heterosexuality is not typically an option for same-sex attracted (SSA) people. It basically includes those who renounce their same-sex attraction.

intimate partnership. He should not refer to himself as gay or same-sex attracted, as that would be a confession of sin as an identity. Friendships should be no more "intimate" than normal friendships that we all enjoy. "Gay Christian" is not an acceptable term. Homosexuality is a sin; thus, homosexual thoughts and desires are sinful and must be renounced.

2. A Christian who is gay can reveal his honest same-sex attractions as long as he commits to lifelong celibacy and the absence of covenantal partnership in life or enters into a heterosexual marriage. This person would be considered a celibate gay Christian or a celibate SSA (same-sex attracted) Christian or one involved in a mixed-orientation marriage.

Each of these views is held by well-respected, faithful Christians. I believe that neither of these honestly, faithfully reflects God's heart on this issue.

Non-affirming View 1: Gay Christians
Must Renounce Homosexuality

The first view, that gay Christians must renounce homosexuality, reject that they are gay, and seek to change their orientation, is held, for example, by Dr. Michael Brown (Christian author and radio talk show host), as well as the committee from the Presbyterian Church in America who published a rejection of Revoice (discussed in chapter 15). Dr. Albert Mohler, the aforementioned president of the Southern Baptist Theological Seminary agrees,[243] noting that "his 'biggest concern' about the [Revoice] conference is the event's apparent acceptance of the idea that sexual identity 'becomes a

---

[243] Mohler, A. (2018 August 2). "Torn Between Two Cultures? Revoice, LGBT Identity, and Biblical Christianity". Retrieved July 27, 2019 from www.AlbertMohler.com.

defining issue that isn't changed by the Gospel and isn't transformed by sanctification.'"[244] Dr. David Kyle Foster, noted in chapter 14, holds this view.[245]

If one believes that a person cannot be Christian and gay, then it looks like this: one who practices sin did not actually make Christ the Lord of his life; therefore, his confession of salvation and belief must not have been real, and his sins are not forgiven. Obviously, that view requires the premise, which I believe is false, that homosexuality is a sin. The view that someone cannot be a Christian if he is gay seems to disregard the grace of the gospel that simply requires belief and confession for salvation and the indwelling of the Holy Spirit. John 3:16 (KJV) states that *whosoever* believes will be saved. Christ said that He will by no means cast out anyone who comes to Him. (John 6:37, NKJV) Further, if salvation depends on one's behavior, then Christ died in vain. (Galatians 2:21, NKJV)

The response usually quotes I Corinthians 6:11 (KJV), "and such were some of you," which is to say that some people were once homosexual and were then washed, sanctified, and justified in the name of the Lord Jesus. The "such" in this Scripture would only apply to gay people if the Greek word *arsenokoitai* in verse 9 were accurately translated as "homosexuals." However, the research, including ancient translations, footnotes in modern Bibles, as well as Baldock and Oxford's research (reflecting Dr. Weigle's communication stating that the word "homosexuals" was a mistake) indicates that "homosexuals" is a mistranslation. The word *arsenokoitai* in verse 9 refers to exploitative male sexual acts. Thus, the "such" in verse 11 refers to the people who have been redeemed from bondage to

---

[244] Gryboski, M. (2018 July 31). "Revoice: LGBT Christian Conference Speaker Rejects Idea That Jesus Supports Gay Marriage". Retrieved May 31, 2019 from www.ChristianPost.com.

[245] The 23,000+ signers of the Nashville Statement also hold this view. https://cbmw.org/nashville-statement/.

abusive, sinful behavior. It does not address gay Christians or gay Christian couples who do not participate in these sins.

A non-affirming argument will quote Christ's words, "If you love Me, you will keep My commandments." (John 14:15, ESV) If a gay person has not "repented" of being gay, then ongoing, willful, sinful behavior precludes love of God, which is one of the most important commandments. My premise is that covenantal, same-gender relationships are not condemned in the Scripture, do not harm anyone, and thus do not involve ongoing, willful, sinful behavior. Nevertheless, does someone who holds the non-affirming argument still sin? If the non-affirming Christian holds grudges, gossips, smokes, overeats, or cheats on his taxes, for example, does he assume his ongoing sins are forgiven, but the gay Christian's "homosexuality" is not forgiven?

This is the "don't judge me because my sins are different than yours" argument. While I reject that homosexuality is a sin, I think this idea is worth considering for people diametrically opposed to each other on this topic. I would say that if my opponents in this debate confess Christ and His resurrection, then they are saved. Yet, I believe that rejecting LGBTQ people from membership and participation in mainstream churches is a tremendous sin. Many LGBTQ people believe that they are not allowed into the family of God because they are rejected by churches. Thus, anyone who stumbles in their walk with Jesus based on this incorrect teaching has been led astray by this ongoing, widespread belief. Again, I would still agree that my opponent is saved, despite this horrific sin. On the other hand, many traditionalists would say that even though I confess Christ, I am not saved because of my sin of homosexuality. Does that mean that they consider themselves sinless? *All* Christians have been made righteous by the sacrifice of Christ. (II Corinthians 5:21)

This particular non-affirming view would hold that a celibate 25-year-old man who trusts in Christ for salvation, but who knows he is a homosexual, is a Christian only if he renounces homosexuality. As Michael R. Saia wrote,

> If, no matter how pure [one man's] life is, he has to feel guilty for his attractions, then there is never any relief from guilt. "How would you feel," another man said, "if you had to feel guilty every time you became hungry?" Hunger is not gluttony, and preference is not homosexual sin.[246]

Nevertheless, someone with same-gender attraction simply hears that he can only be a Christian if he trusts in Christ and becomes *not gay*. To many gay people, being *not gay* was the goal from the moment they realized they were gay. But, becoming *not gay* has proved to be simply impossible. This is why people within the gay community commit suicide at rates much higher than the general population. Is it reasonable to suggest that anyone could be a Christian as long as they are not attracted to people of their same gender? In other words, salvation is only available for straight people? I think a faithful Christian has to agree that gay people can come to Christ and receive salvation.

Taking Up the Gay Christian's Cross

The non-affirming position is often compassionate, expressing sympathy for the pain and loneliness that gay Christians face if they are to be received in traditional Christian circles. Some non-affirming Christians state that they have actually cried tears for gay

---

[246] Saia, M. R. (1988). *Counseling the Homosexual*. Minneapolis, MN: Bethany House, p.23, as cited by Grenz, (1998) *Welcoming But Not Affirming*, p.122-32, as cited by Brownson, (2013) *Bible Gender Sexuality*, pages 173-4.

people. Salvation and inclusion in church, according to the non-affirming arguments, require faith in Christ and a renunciation of homosexuality. Thus, a person with same-gender attractions must receive salvation through Christ, as do heterosexual Christians. In addition, they must give up the hope of intimate companionship and live in a constant state of renunciation of a homosexual inclination. They are often strongly encouraged to enter into a mixed-orientation marriage. This is a very heavy burden to bear for gay people who want to live according to traditional Christian teaching. Thus, they are reminded by well-meaning Christians of Christ's words, "If anyone would come after me, let him deny himself and take up his cross and follow me." (Matthew 16:24b, ESV)

Indeed, gay Christians submit to Jesus's command to take up our cross daily, denying ourselves, denying the flesh, the desires that are ungodly, that harbor ill will, resentment, bitterness, dissatisfaction, complaining, fear. We submit daily to the will of God in our lives, focusing on the righteousness of Christ and the kingdom of God. We surrender to God's will, His pleasure, and His purpose. The non-affirming argument, however, suggests that for all gay Christians, to take up their cross means to daily reject any homosexual thoughts or inclinations and deny all hope of honest, fulfilling covenantal partnership.

Jesus did not say that the "cross" He wants gay people to take up is the ever-present denial of an *essential* part of themselves and the lifelong rejection of the idea of fulfilling covenantal partnership. But the non-affirming argument always concludes that this is Jesus's "cross" for gay people. Our cross is the same as the straight person's cross, the denial of self, of the flesh, of absolutely anything that doesn't bring God honor and glory in every aspect of our lives. However, our Christ-centered, covenantal partnerships do honor Him, as do many straight Christians' heterosexual marriages.

213

An Essential Part of Oneself

Many will suggest that sexuality should not be considered "an essential part" of oneself or one's identity because our identity is in Christ. If there is an unmarried person in the local church, what do friends and churchgoers love to do? We all have a desire to see people find love. We want to set our unmarried friends up for a coffee date or introduce them to potential suitors. A same-sex attracted person at church would not be interested in this. If one is same-sex attracted and observing the traditional view of marriage, he would likely come to events without a "plus one." He would turn down offers to meet someone's niece. This person likely does not date and spends weekends with friends but without an intimate companion. This is an entire *lifestyle* for a non-affirming, same-sex attracted Christian. It's not just a simple consideration or group of words. Furthermore, it is distinct from just being single. One's sexuality is actually an essential part of oneself, even if celibate. Nevertheless, our identity in Christ is far more important.

Advocating (Likely Unfulfilling) Mixed-Orientation Marriage

Many non-affirming Christians believe that heterosexual marriage, in other words, a mixed-orientation marriage, is the answer. However, there remain several issues even within a heterosexual marriage. The most obvious is that the person remains homosexual. Furthermore, the results have not been encouraging. Would a traditionalist Christian want his straight son or daughter to be involved in a mixed-orientation marriage, even in the hopes and faith of conversion to heterosexuality through prayer?

Nate Collins is the aforementioned president of Revoice, a ministry that advocates for the traditional Christian view of sexuality for same-sex attracted Christians. He is a gay man in a heterosexual marriage. The traditionalists typically reject his ministry on the grounds that "homosexuality is a sin," and thus, one cannot be both gay and Christian. Dr. Collins has entered into a "one man, one woman" marriage, which is the traditionalists' goal. However, he honestly and openly reveals that he continues to have a same-sex orientation. It seems that the more conservative traditionalists would prefer that Dr. Collins assume "ex-gay" status. Yet, how could he minister to others with same-sex attractions if he did not honestly refer to himself as having ongoing same-sex attractions?

Homosexuals Should Just Become Straight

When one desires to go into the field of medicine, he may imagine that he can achieve this if he undergoes the proper education and training. He may think, "I am willing to dedicate many years, do the hard work, and learn what I need to learn." This is what gay people have thought about the Church's idea that they can become straight. They have thought, "I'll do the work, join the ministry dedicated to converting me to heterosexuality, and I'll trust in the power of God that I'll come out on the other end straight," just as the one considering medical school would come out on the other end, a doctor.

However, 40 years of conversion therapy results reveal that people did not, typically, come out on the other end, straight. When one trusts that he can do "all things through Christ" Who strengthens him, he must recognize that this applies only within Christ's will for him. If God has not called people into conversion to heterosexuality, then they won't become straight, no matter how hard they try and how much they trust in God.

Homosexuality is Not Comparable to Adultery, Pedophilia, or Bestiality

The non-affirming position compares homosexuality to sins like adultery, pedophilia, and bestiality. However, none of these is a reasonable comparison. A gay Christian is not stealing one's spouse or harming anyone, as in adultery, and is not abusing anyone who cannot consent, as in the latter two, very poor analogies. Nonetheless, the non-affirming position would be that a homosexual must renounce his desire, just as an adulterer or pedophile must renounce his desires. Since no one is harmed in a gay Christian couple's relationship, these analogies are not only not comparable, but may be considered malicious, or at best, inappropriate.

A more appropriate comparison to homosexual desire between two uncommitted men may be a heterosexual man who experiences desire for a woman who is not his spouse. The goal in both situations would be to focus on the grace of our Lord Jesus, His atonement for sin, our righteousness in Christ, to reject the desire to sin, and ultimately, to not sin when tempted. This is why Paul suggested that, for those with desires for intimacy, "if they cannot control themselves, they should marry." (I Corinthians 7:9a)

Freedom from Bondage to Sin

The Holy Spirit guides the believer into His purpose for the Christian, to the extent that the Christian relies on the Holy Spirit and the Scripture in his life. But if the new Christian does not give the Holy Spirit reign in his life, he will continue in his life of sin.

It is true, unfortunately, that many Christians continue to live in sin, in addiction, in bondage, without knowing the freedom that is available in Christ. The gospel message is that anyone who professes their need for a Savior can come to Christ. All of us who trust in Christ continue to sin. Because of God's grace, Christ's blood has atoned for all sins. Some Christians will not live the abundant life that Jesus offers, and some will be saved, "only as one escaping through the flames." (I Corinthians 3:15) This is not optimal; it is not God's plan for His children. This is not how gay Christians should live. Affirming believers want all gay Christians to live with burning zeal and fire for the things of God. Unfortunately, however, many gay Christians cannot progress in their relationship with God because they are not convinced of God's acceptance of them. Many continue to live in bondage because they either have no church home or no Bible-believing, Holy Spirit filled community to guide them in their walk with God or help them learn the Scriptures.

If a pedophile or an idol worshiper from I Corinthians 6:9-10, came into a saving relationship with Christ, then the Holy Spirit in the new believer would guide him, by giving him the will and the ability to repent in his heart and actions from the molestation or idol worship. When the Lord washes, sanctifies, and justifies believers through Christ, we are changed. As Christians, we are new creations and reconciled to God in Christ. (II Corinthians 5:17-19) We thus begin to live life in harmony with God, in keeping with His purpose for our lives, inasmuch as we put our faith in Him daily. Those who were worshiping idols or harming children simply cannot go on sinning and maintain a relationship with Christ. As the new Christian faithfully trusts in Christ, he is changed and does not continue in the sin that he found himself in when he first believed. Again, this is the power of the blood of Christ to set believers free from slavery to sin. (Romans 6:22)

God was not concerned that people would not be able to live lives that were honorable to Him in the new covenant. He chose it this way: salvation first (while we were still sinners, Christ died for us, according to Romans 5:8), then redemption from destruction and guidance in day-to-day life by the indwelling of the Holy Spirit such that the believer is made holy, sanctified, and justified through Christ. Thus, anyone, gay or straight, who trusts in Christ's atoning work on Calvary and believes in his heart that Christ was raised from the dead can be saved.

Renouncing Presbyopia, Left-Handedness, Cancer, and Homosexuality

To a gay person, the idea of renouncing homosexuality seems like just denying something real in one's everyday life, or simply *lying*. Some would trust in God for perfect eyesight, even as they move into their fifties when a condition known as presbyopia requires most people to use reading glasses. To simply deny the existence of same-gender attraction is like spending years confessing perfect eyesight, denying presbyopia, refusing to purchase reading glasses, and eventually, being unable to read. Better than denying that same-gender attractions exist (and that opposite-gender attractions do not exist), may be, learning to live godly lives within appropriate boundaries. If one were to acknowledge in their 50s that they can no longer read, that person could wear reading glasses, and continue to live a normal life. Similarly, if we cease demanding that gay Christians renounce and deny their same-gender attraction, then they can have open discussions, and learn how to serve God within honest, appropriate, God-given parameters.

Someone with a new cancer diagnosis may renounce cancer and claim healing, or one who is left-handed renounce left-handedness and do most things with his right hand, or one who experiences presbyopia confess perfect eyesight and refuse to buy glasses. But if same-sex attraction is a sin, it is a far more serious situation to simply renounce it. If the cancer patient died of cancer, he would still have eternal salvation. If the left-handed person gave up and chopped onions with his left hand, he would still be saved. If the 58-year-old who could not read finally borrowed his wife's reading glasses, he would still be saved by the grace of the cross. But what if the same-sex attracted man confided to a friend that all these years he has had attractions to men? Confessing and owning this "sin" would then subject this man to the modern translations of I Corinthians 6:9-10, and render him ineligible for the kingdom of God. There is no room for open conversation within the view that gay people cannot be Christians. Nevertheless, whether gay people talk about it or not, they're still gay.

If one cannot be both gay and Christian, how does one become not gay so that he can become a Christian? The non-affirming argument will suggest that he is immediately *not gay* the moment he trusts in Christ because he is righteous in God's eyes through Christ. Gay no longer describes him. His identity is in Christ alone now. He will confess "holy sexuality"[247] and agree to remain chaste in singleness and faithful in (heterosexual) marriage. However, his preference that any intimate connection be with someone of the same gender remains. Is he thus, not actually saved? If one cannot be both saved and gay, how do traditionalists reconcile this?

- The non-affirming answer: one could be saved and same-sex attracted as long as he daily, continually renounces homosexuality and seeks conversion away from that sinfulness all of his life.

- A more gracious idea: let's allow the Christian to refer to himself as same-sex attracted so that he could be involved in a ministry like Revoice (introduced in chapter 15) that at least allows for open discussion and a commitment to serve God.

- The affirming Christian's response: chastity in singleness and faithfulness in the marriage that God has for him,

---

[247] Yuan, Christopher (2018). *Holy Sexuality and the Gospel: Sex, Desire, and Relationships Shaped by God's Grand Story*. Portland, OR: Multnomah, chapter 6.

which may be a gay marriage. There is no reason to deny one's same-sex orientation. He must get involved in an affirming, Bible-believing church so that he can grow in his walk with God.[248]

To consider it from another angle, a straight person becomes a Christian the moment he trusts in Christ. At what point does a person who does not have opposite-gender attraction become a Christian, after he trusts in Christ? What if he regards his same-sex attractions as unwanted, but does not deny that he continues to experience a same-sex orientation?

On the question of salvation, I do not think that even the most conservative Christian can faithfully assume that God's mercy does not allow for gay people to come into a saving relationship with Christ. Even as the gay person (or anyone) has ongoing sin in his life, the gospel never requires someone to become sin-free before the Holy Spirit is deposited into the new believer's spirit and eternal salvation is given. The whole point of the gospel is that we could not earn salvation. Thus, anyone, absolutely anyone, who trusts in Christ's atoning work on Calvary and believes in his heart that Christ was raised from the dead can be saved. That is the gospel.

If the view that all gay people must renounce homosexuality and achieve heterosexuality, or die trying, in order to be a Christian, may be in error, then let's consider the other non-affirming view.

---

[248] If a Bible-believing, affirming church is not available, I recommend an affirming internet church (www.NewCovenantAtlanta.com) and participation in a friendly Bible-believing local church.

Non-affirming view 2: Christians Can Be Gay but
Must Be Celibate or Heterosexually Married

The second view, that gay Christians can be gay, but must commit to celibacy or a mixed-orientation marriage, is held by many non-affirming Christians including those from Revoice, as well as Pastor Clay Peck (noted toward the end of the previous chapter).

I have found that some who hold the first view sometimes give in to the second view. In other words, it is difficult to maintain the idea that someone cannot be a Christian if he is gay. For example, Dr. Michael Brown said the following in 2015: "I know some fine Christians who still have same-sex attractions, but they just don't act on them. They don't give themselves to it. They don't act on it, and they're celibate and blessed."[249] However, he is opposed to the message of Revoice, specifically their willingness to identify as people with same-sex attractions. Dr. Brown states, "nothing 'queer' will enter [the heavenly city]."[250] Even the most conservative, non-affirming position seems to, at times, agree that one cannot be excluded from Christianity just because one is gay.

Many non-affirming Christians feel that this view, that one may be gay but must be celibate, is a reasonable way to not reject gay Christians outright, as if it provides an answer to the issue. However, many gay people realize that they are simply not gifted with celibacy, or the capacity to live life without an intimate companion, and thus cannot consider the God of the people who demand that of them. Since these two views together make up the vast majority of opinions within the non-affirming world, for a gay person who

---

[249] Slife, J., (2015 April 28). "Professor, author discusses the question: Can you be gay and Christian?". Retrieved August 1, 2019 from World.wng.org.
[250] Brown, M. (2018 July 30). "The Revoice Conference and the Danger of a Big Theological Tent". Retrieved August 1, 2019 from www.TheChristianPost.com.

genuinely wants a relationship with Christ and with a local church, the two options are to commit to remaining single for life, which is a painfully lonely idea, or to become *not gay*, which seems impossible. (If your first thought is that all things are possible with God, please see chapter 14 again.) Neither of these options is tenable for many gay people. Thus, gay people feel they cannot come to church, and they lose the opportunity to fellowship and grow in Christ with other believers. Sadly, many simply walk away from the faith.

Many Christians believe that celibate, gay Christians can be saved, but gay Christians in a monogamous, committed relationship are not saved because they are practicing sin. According to this line of thinking, in order to be a Christian, one must trust in Christ and never act on his gay feelings, suggesting that if one did act on his gay feelings and did not repent, if he married a man, for example, he may lose his salvation. However, one must consider homosexuality an *unforgivable* sin to hold that belief. To settle this conflict, many Christians must choose to believe the gay man was not saved in the first place. Is it appropriate for people to be making these judgments? God will judge; our job is to love.[251]

Scripture demonstrates that anyone, gay or straight, who trusts in Jesus and accepts His atoning sacrifice receives forgiveness for all sins, past, present, and future. (Colossians 2:13b) Christ offered one sacrifice (Hebrews 10:12-14) for sin, and in fact, atoned for the sins of all mankind, (I John 2:2) so that anyone who receives Him, (John 1:12) believes in and confesses His Lordship and resurrection (Romans 10:9-10) will be saved, and thus receive in his heart the deposit of the Holy Spirit, (II Corinthians 1:21-22) guaranteeing what is to come for God's children. I maintain that the hypothetical Christian in a same-gender relationship is not living in sin in his

---

[251] "It is the Holy Spirit's job to convict, God's job to judge, and my job to love." - Billy Graham

marriage, but is one of a very small minority of exceptions to "one man, one woman."

In the New Covenant, the Holy Spirit Guides Us From Within

The new covenant was brought in as God had found fault with the old covenant (Hebrews 8:7-8) because we simply were not able to keep the law. We needed a Savior from our own inability to live lives which bring honor to our holy God. The new covenant includes forgiveness for all sins, as all sin was atoned for on the cross, (Colossians 2:13) the indwelling of the Holy Spirit, (Ephesians 1:13-14) and guidance of the Holy Spirit, as God puts in us to will and to do for His good pleasure. (Philippians 2:13) The non-affirming Christian does not believe that the Holy Spirit is *unable* to lead a faithful, gay Christian in the right way. Thus the non-affirming Christian must conclude that the gay person is either 1.) blind, and has believed lies, or 2.) living in willful rebellion.

Regarding the first line of thinking, the Holy Spirit Himself leads the believer in all truth. (John 16:13) Furthermore, the affirming gay Christian who is in fellowship and communion with God holds the Word of God as the highest authority in his life. He wants to honor God in every aspect of his life, meaning he would live a life of celibacy if that were God's call on his life. And celibacy may be God's call in the lives of some gay Christians. But in others, the Holy Spirit and Scripture do not bear witness that either celibacy or dismantling the relationship is appropriate.

This leaves the non-affirming Christian only one answer if he maintains that a gay Christian couple is living in sin; that is, that they are living in willful rebellion. However, a faithful gay Christian, by definition, is not living in rebellion, but with an open heart before God saying, "Show me Your ways, Lord, teach me Your paths. Guide me in Your truth and teach me, for You are God my Savior, and my hope is in You all day long." (Psalm 25:4-5)

Comparing Homosexuality to a Non-Practicing Pedophile, Anorexia, and Singleness

Affirming Christians reject the call for mandatory celibacy for same-sex attracted Christians. The non-affirming response would be, someone who is attracted to children must remain celibate. A pedophile is not allowed to marry the object of his attraction. This is correct, but the pedophile would be harming someone, who cannot and does not consent. In a Christ-centered, covenantal relationship, there is consent, and there is no harm. Again, one cannot honestly equate exploitative, non-consensual relations with monogamous, consenting, same-gender relationships. This is the exact mistake that the Bible translators have made, erroneously referring to a sinful, exploitative male sexual act as all people with a homosexual orientation.

Another non-affirming argument compares homosexuality to anorexia. An anorexic girl, for example, would wrongly believe herself to be fat and thus starve herself. Her family members would seek to help her by demonstrating that she is believing lies, and getting her help from therapists and doctors to correct this wrong thinking. The difference between the anorexic girl and the gay Christian is that the girl is harming her body, the temple of the Holy Spirit. There is no harm done to God, to a neighbor, or to the participants in a same-gender, Christ-centered, covenantal relationship.

Another non-affirming response would be that single heterosexual people must be celibate. Thus, gay Christians should be celibate. The Bible does call for single people, gay or straight, to be abstinent. However, most single people are allowed the hope of the possibility of dating and marriage. This is in stark contrast to the non-affirming position that suggests that single gay Christians must not be allowed even the possibility of marriage and companionship within a Christ-centered, covenantal relationship.

It is true that homosexual couples are not the only couples excluded from membership in churches. The exception is heterosexual couples who live together without the commitment of marriage. These couples are allowed to come to church but often cannot become members until they are married. But there is no path to membership for gay couples.

We Will All Stand Before Him

The affirming gay Christian responds, God knows my heart. I want to bring honor and glory to God in every aspect of my life. My life is His; my relationships are His; my career is His. There is nothing I would not give up or change if He called me. If someone were to suggest that I should end my Christ-centered, same-gender, covenantal relationship, I would direct them to Paul's statement, addressing Christians in Rome, some of whom enjoyed their freedom in Christ (from fear of offending God by the food that they ate), and some of whom with "weak faith" could not enjoy such freedom. Paul wrote, "You, then, why do you judge your brother or sister? Or why do you treat them with contempt? For we will all stand before God's judgment seat." (Romans 14:10) Paul stated, "Who are you to judge someone else's servant? To their own Master, servants stand or fall. And they will stand; for the Lord is able to make them stand." (Romans 14:4)

The Scripture states that the Lord is able to make gay Christians stand and not fall. We trust in Him. We trust in His Word. We trust in His guidance in our lives.

If it were God's will that a particular relationship should be dismantled, then His Holy Spirit is well able to lead and guide the believer in that direction. If He wanted me to live a life of celibacy, the Holy Spirit would bear witness in my spirit. The question becomes, how can the non-affirming Christian continue to maintain that celibacy is God's will for someone when the Holy Spirit has not borne witness of this plan in the spirit of the gay believer? One of us is wrong. God is able to lead faithful Christians out of sin.

Perhaps Only Homosexual Behavior is Sinful

We cannot get far in this discussion without again noting that celibacy is not the traditionalists' goal. The traditional argument requires that people simply *not be gay.* The foundation of the traditionalists' criticism of the celibacy movement is very simple: if homosexuality is a sin, then homosexual longings, thoughts, or desires are sinful. A gay person who longs for even emotional or romantic connection to another gay person of his same gender, would be sinning, even if he were celibate. In an effort to be accommodating, however, many kindly suggest that only homosexual *behavior* is sinful.

What would constitute homosexual behavior, at a minimum? If one man's heart skipped a beat at the possibility of sitting close to someone, what if their thighs barely touched as the two sat together on the couch? Would this represent sinful homosexual behavior in two celibate, mutually-attracted gay men? What if they actually held hands?

As the staunch traditionalists point out, declaring celibacy is not the answer, because if the premise is correct, and homosexuality is a sin, then the desires are also sinful. Specifically, thighs touching on the couch, even if possibly inadvertently, is sinful. We have come full circle. The traditionalists' only answer is conversion to heterosexuality. For those who recognize that conversion to heterosexuality is not an option, the recommendation is to be, not heterosexual, but rather, not homosexual. In other words, rather than advocate that people become heterosexual, they recommend that people just not be homosexual.

Where does this leave the honest 35-year-old, same-sex attracted man who spent ten years in ex-gay therapy but continues to experience unwanted same-sex attraction? This is a reasonable example of a member of Revoice. His only options are celibacy or a (likely unfulfilling) mixed-orientation marriage, which is the message of Revoice. The traditionalists reject Revoice. Nevertheless, who can argue that celibacy is this 35-year-old gentleman's only option? He wants to maintain what he believes is a biblical approach to sexuality, but he cannot quit having unwanted same-sex attraction, despite his prayers and desires to be straight.

It appears that the only option that would appease the traditionalists would be for this man to claim ex-gay status and remain celibate.[252] That would solve the problem for any given gay Christian who does not mind keeping this secret to himself. It does appear that many "ex-gay" people continue to have same-sex attraction and may fit this description. Again, one problem with claiming to be ex-gay while still experiencing same-sex attractions, however, is that it prevents ministry to others who find it impossible to lose their unwanted same-sex attractions. Furthermore, many people are just not willing to live a lie when there is opportunity for ministry and connection with other like-minded Christians within ministries dedicated to observing the traditional view of sexuality for same-sex attracted Christians.

---

[252] The premise in this example is that the man cannot achieve heterosexuality, despite his efforts. Obviously, someone who has successfully achieved ex-gay status would not fit into this hypothetical example.

As with this hypothetical gentleman, would a traditionalist concede that a significant number (if not tens or hundreds of thousands[253]) of real people with real testimonies were never converted to heterosexuality despite years of therapy, counseling, and faith-filled prayers? If the traditionalist realizes that, then the idea that one must renounce homosexuality and convert to heterosexuality is indefensible.

If one cannot become heterosexual, and cannot be accepted as a celibate homosexual, where does that leave us? The affirming argument will conclude that the premise is wrong, and the non-affirming argument will conclude that we must continue efforts to convert to heterosexuality. To be clear, I do not consider the premise wrong because I cannot find a more pleasant solution. There is no suitable pastoral answer to the "problem" because there is no problem. The premise is actually wrong. God calls gay Christians to lifelong monogamy or chastity, but not heterosexuality or forced celibacy.

---

[253] Mallory, C., Brown, T., Conron, K. (2018 January) "Conversion Therapy and LGBT Youth". The Williams Institute UCLA School of Law. Retrieved December 2019 from www.WilliansInstitute.law.ucla.edu.

=21=

ADDRESSING OTHER NON-AFFIRMING ARGUMENTS

The non-affirming argument routinely, convincingly, and very confidently offers the following typical sentiments. "The Bible is not ambiguous on this," and "there is no question as to what these words mean" (referring to the Greek words that became translated as "homosexuals"), as well as, "there is no new data...that changes what we always thought the Bible said on this."[254] These quotes are taken from a talk by Dr. Michael Brown[255] in 2015.

Dr. Brown states, "There is no question they [the two Greek words] speak of those who practice homosexuality, not just abusive man-boy relationships, not just prostitution."[256] However, as noted previously, there is legitimate debate about what the word *arsenokoitai* means. Recall that *arsenokoitai* and *malakos* were combined and rendered

---

[254] Brown, M. (2015 February 15). "Can You Be Gay and Christian? Dr. Michael Brown". *YouTube*. Retrieved September 18, 2019 from www. YouTube.com.

[255] Dr. Michael Brown hosts a daily podcast called *Line of Fire* which I typically enjoy, despite our differences on this topic.

[256] Brown, M. (2015 February 15). "Can You Be Gay and Christian? Dr. Michael Brown". *YouTube*. Retrieved September 18, 2019 from www.YouTube. com. This sentence can be found within minute 51 of the video.

"homosexuals" the first time that word ever appeared in a Bible, which was in 1946. Translations now refer to *arsenokoitai* alone as "homosexuals." The ancient translations, including the Luther Bible, and the others as noted in chapter 4, as well as the footnotes in the modern translations, refer to *arsenokoitai* as abuse and exploitation, not committed gay couples. Furthermore, Dr. Weigle, who led the committee that added "homosexuals" to the Bible the very first time, believed that the translation was in error.[257]

What the Bible is actually not ambiguous on, is its condemnation of abusive, exploitative, male sexual acts, as well as all same-gender idolatrous acts. One cannot *faithfully* convert this condemnation to all gay Christians. Specifically, Dr. Brown's statement is not true: in fact, there are very legitimate questions around the modern translation of *arsenokoitai*. Consider two simple examples. Before 1946, the word referred to a particular sinful act, not to a specific segment of the population. Secondly, no one has ever questioned that *arsenokoitai* refers to males, but modern translations have added females.

Dr. Brown states that there is "no new data," as follows:

> I can tell you that there is no new data that has been discovered that changes what we always thought the Bible was saying about this. No new texts... No new manuscripts of the Bible... no new linguistic data, no new archaeological data. In other words, the reason that people are questioning what the Bible says is not because the Bible is unclear and not because there's new information, rather because of what we're experiencing in our society around us.[258]

---

[257] Baldock, K. (2019 March 26). "How the Bible Became Anti-Gay: Forging a Sacred Weapon". Retrieved May 2019 from CanyonWalkerConnections.com.
[258] Ibid. This begins at 10:55 into the YouTube video.

Since that talk (in 2015), there is new data that the church must address. Specifically, the new information which is coming from Baldock, Oxford, and their team[259] which coincides with the ancient texts and modern footnotes. To suggest that the Greek words translated homosexuals "always" meant homosexuals is not accurate. Ancient translations referred to exploitative male sexual acts, not homosexuality. In fact, the passage in I Corinthians 6:9-10 was not thought to refer to homosexual people until the mistranslation was printed in 1946. It was only then that Bibles began condemning homosexuality instead of exploitative, abusive sexual acts. At the time, it was honestly, erroneously believed that homosexuals committed those acts.

Dr. Brown states that we're questioning this issue "because of what we're experiencing in our society around us," as if that is problematic. However, every time we have realized that we were wrong on what we thought Scripture said, it was exactly because of what we were experiencing in our society. Consider interracial marriage, remarried couples, slavery, and every other topic from chapter 12. The "traditional view" of Scripture at one time forbade interracial marriage. A woman and a man with different skin tones were once going against scriptural authority to be a couple. What makes traditionalists so certain that it's appropriate to reject gay people in our churches when we look back and recognize that we have been wrong in the past? The stakes are too high. We have to stop rejecting people.

Eunuchs Who Were Born That Way

Traditionalists believe that their most persuasive argument is the story of creation. When appealing to the creation story to suggest

---

[259] This was addressed in chapter 4 and summarized in chapter 19. Their book is expected to be published in Spring 2020.

that all people must be heterosexual, one *must* recognize Jesus's discussion of eunuchs who were "born that way." (Matthew 19:12) I think that a natural-born eunuch today would be someone within the LGBTQ community. However, the only thing we can say for certain from Scripture is that eunuchs were the sexual minority of Jesus's day. When reading about eunuchs from non-affirming arguments, there is a presumption, without evidence, that eunuchs are "not created for marriage."[260] This is the only way for the non-affirming case to hold merit. However, there is no evidence and no reason to assume that all eunuchs were required to live without covenantal partnership.

Non-affirming, same-sex attracted author and Bible teacher, Dr. Christopher Yuan states that Jesus was only speaking in metaphors[261] and not about actual people. Again, this line of thinking is crucial to the non-affirming argument. If natural-born eunuchs were real people, then rejection of LGBTQ people is indefensible.

In fact, they were real people. There are five natural-born eunuchs in Scripture. Recall that in Deuteronomy 23:1, God prohibited eunuchs who had been cut from entering the temple. Thus, any eunuch who was involved in work in the temple was a natural-born eunuch. Sandra Turnbull has presented this fascinating scholarship in her book, *God's Gay Agenda*.[262]

Jesus said that some eunuchs were born that way; thus, this does not refer to one born into lifelong singleness because everyone was born into singleness. Furthermore, someone "born" is unlikely to be a metaphor. And, emphatically, there is no evidence that natural-born

---

[260] McCall, J. (2019 August 22). "Prophetic Word: Eunuchs Trapped in LGBT Community Will Overthrow Jezebel". Retrieved August 26, 2019 from www.CharismaNews.com.

[261] *Holy Sexuality and the Gospel*, chapter 13.

[262] *God's Gay Agenda*, chapter 5.

eunuchs are asexual and uninterested in marriage, as the non-affirming arguments conveniently assert, without evidence, as if obvious.

Importantly, a eunuch from birth was not born with the capacity for heterosexuality. I believe that people who determine that Jesus was only speaking metaphorically, or that He was only speaking about the state of being single, which all humans experience, and not about real, distinct people, are exactly the people "who cannot accept this word." (Matthew 19:11) If Jesus might have been talking about real people, and not metaphorically, does it not seem reasonable to assume that position, when the lives of real people are at stake?

Let's Talk About a Slippery Slope

Another typical non-affirming argument considers this issue a "slippery slope," suggesting that allowing for same-gender relationships within the Church opens the door to all manner of sexual immorality, including pedophilia, bestiality, incest, and polygamy. Dr. Brown stated, "If you say Leviticus 18 does not apply to us today, then where is the prohibition for incest? On what biblical basis do we say incest is forbidden?"[263] This argument is irrelevant; it is simply a distraction beyond the topic.

Nevertheless, if one takes this idea to its logical conclusion, as Pastor Grayson Fritts of All Scripture Baptist Church in Knoxville, Tennessee does, then it is not appropriate to exclude Leviticus 20. Pastor Fritts states,

---

[263] Brown, M. (2015 February 15). "Can You Be Gay and Christian? Dr. Michael Brown". *YouTube*. Retrieved September 18, 2019 from www.YouTube.com. This begins at 33:51 into the video.

God has instilled the power of civil government to send the police in 2019 out to these LGBT freaks and arrest them and have a trial for them, and if they are convicted, then they are to be put to death... Leviticus 20:13 should be a law that is enforced by our government.[264]

In other words, if one holds that Leviticus 18 should inform Christians with regard to certain behaviors, then it would be appropriate to support enforcing the penalty for breaking those laws, as these people in the New Independent Fundamental Baptist churches do. To be clear, the penalty was death. As noted previously, the death penalty was also applied to "a stubborn and rebellious son who does not obey his father and mother." (Deuteronomy 21:18-21) Calling for the executions of all LGBTQ people in this country is the result of a *slippery slope* of erroneous condemnation and rejection of LGBTQ people that began decades ago.

As a general rule, just like straight Christians, LGBTQ Christians do not participate in incest, polygamy, bestiality, or pedophilia. We advocate for faithful, consensual monogamy inside a committed, until-death-do-us-part, covenantal relationship, whether straight or gay, and celibacy outside of a monogamous, covenantal partnership (aka, marriage).

---

[264] Fritts, G. (2019 June 2). "Why Leviticus 20:13 Should Still Be Enforced". Retrieved September 2019 from www.AllScriptureBaptist.com. This begins at 27:05 into the audio file.

Answers to Dr. Michael Brown's Questions

There are two questions put forth by Dr. Brown, who represents the non-affirming position. I will address them here.[265]

1. "Can you give me a single, unambiguous biblical example of a God-blessed homosexual relationship?"

   Almost. In Luke 17:34 (KJV), Jesus stated that two men would be in a bed at night, and that one would be taken and one left. (However, be aware that only a few translations render this verse appropriately, as described toward the end of chapter 19.) I would not call this couple blessed, as only one of the men is saved. However, since only one of the two men is condemned, it is clear that their relationship is not the determining issue of their salvation. Nevertheless, since only one of the two men knows Christ, I believe they are not completely blessed by God as a couple.

   A traditionalist will immediately say that these three pieces of the story:
   - Two men
   - One bed
   - At night
   do not constitute a gay couple.

   Since traditionalists will reject that those two men were involved romantically, I will answer this question in another way as well. If one suggests that there are no unambiguous examples of blessed homosexual relationships in Scripture, then allow me to list several examples of other things that

---

[265] Brown, M. L. (2015 July 10). "Dr. Michael Brown Has 40 Answers and 2 Questions for 'Gay' Christian Matthew Vines". Retrieved December 2019 from www.AskDrBrown.org.

are not addressed or blessed in Scripture, which we know God blesses. Consider this list:

o   People who stole slave owners' "property"—for example, Harriet Tubman, who risked her life to free slaves,

o   women in teaching roles including at the college level,

o   remarried couples,

o   women asking a question in church instead of asking their husbands at home,

o   internet church for those who cannot attend,

o   female church elders,

o   civil rights activists,

o   a family's love for its pet,

o   interracial couples,

o   ultrasounds offered to those considering termination of pregnancy,

o   pearls and gold jewelry,

o   fertility treatments, including in-vitro fertilization.

2.   "Do you agree that every reference to homosexual practice in the Bible is decidedly negative?"

No, the only thing negative about the Luke 17:34 passage is that one man did not know Christ. While that is eternally negative for the man, the point is, the relationship was not condemned, or both men would have been condemned.

I will also answer the question in another way, as I did above.

Every other biblical reference to homosexual practice involved gang rape, exploitation, pederasty, abuse, and idolatrous promiscuity. Every time those acts are referenced with regard to heterosexuality, they are also decidedly negative. Other things in Scripture which are decidedly negative should be considered here as well: seven of the twelve bullet points above are decidedly negative in Scripture, yet, we uphold these today as blessed by God.

Dr. Brown's questions are worth asking, but this is not a firm enough foundation to support continued rejection of gay Christians from our churches, and by extension, LGBTQ people in the community from God's family.

Hundreds of Thousands of Person-Years of Experience

In summary, if the premise is correct, that homosexuality is a sin, then a Christian cannot be a homosexual. If a Christian does actually experience same-sex attraction, and is thus, by definition, homosexual, and if he cannot become heterosexual, then he could at least be celibate. However, Scripture holds that if an action is sinful, then the desire for that action is sinful. Thus, a commitment to lifelong celibacy as a same-sex attracted Christian is not the answer. Conversion to heterosexuality is the only answer if homosexuality is a sin.

However, conversion to heterosexuality does not appear to be a viable option. Hundreds of thousands of person-years of experience[266] in worldwide ex-gay ministries have left us with one absolutely unchallenged[267] result: the majority[268] of people who seek to change their orientation, even those who trust in Christ and His Word

---

[266] Over 40 years (1970s -2010s) it is estimated that 698,000 people (from the Mallory paper) underwent conversion therapy.

[267] Brown, M. L. (2015 July 10). "Dr. Michael Brown Has 40 Answers and 2 Questions for 'Gay' Christian Matthew Vines". Retrieved December 2019 from www.AskDrBrown.org.

[268] Some would say the *vast* majority. See chapter 14. Many ex-gay leaders suggested that they saw almost no one change.

for healing and redemption, will not experience conversion to heterosexuality.

The affirming argument will conclude that the premise is wrong. The non-affirming argument will conclude that we must continue conversion efforts.

Brown: Have We Tried Hard Enough to Convert People to Heterosexuality?

Matthew Vines asked the question, "Do you accept that sexual orientation is highly resistant to attempts to change it?" In 2015, Michael Brown responded,

> Again, using your definition, in the majority of cases, certainly. However, we must not downplay the many successful stories of change through counseling and, more importantly, the possibility of change through the gospel. Cannot Almighty God change a homosexual into a heterosexual if it so pleases Him? Has the church really devoted itself to seeking God to help men and women who struggle with same-sex attractions?[269]

They want to double down on conversion efforts. This is the non-affirming argument's *only* solution.

---

[269] Brown, M. L. (2015 July 10). "Dr. Michael Brown Has 40 Answers and 2 Questions for 'Gay' Christian Matthew Vines". Retrieved December 2019 from www.AskDrBrown.org.

I would like to repeat Dr. Brown's rhetorical question: "Cannot Almighty God change a homosexual into a heterosexual if it so pleases Him?"[270]

Absolutely. Shouldn't that tell us something?

Holy Sexuality

Bible professor and author Dr. Christopher Yuan, a non-affirming, same-sex attracted Christian, advocates "holy sexuality," which he defines as "chastity in singleness and faithfulness in marriage."[271] While this term does not address Dr. Yuan's view that same-sex attraction is sinful, this phrase is the general understanding of a Christian view of marriage. Affirming Christians, including LGBTQ Christians and their allies, also hold to the idea of chastity in singleness and faithfulness in marriage.

Dr. Yuan recognizes the problems with calling for conversion to heterosexuality for all same-sex attracted Christians. At the same time, he opposes the message of Revoice,[272] which advocates celibacy or mixed-orientation marriage, but allows for one to identify as same-sex attracted. The distinction is that Dr. Yuan believes same-sex attraction is sinful and is not merely a temptation.

Dr. Yuan states that he does not think that heterosexuality is the goal, nor that celibacy is the answer. He states that same-sex attracted

---

[270] Ibid.

[271] *Holy Sexuality and the Gospel*, chapter 6.

[272] (Last names unknown), Jake and Matt (co-hosts). (2019 March 31). *Holy Sexuality with Christopher Yuan* [Audiovisual podcast]. *Coffee and Cream*. Retrieved January 10, 2020 from www.CoffeeandCreamPodcast.com.

Christians should embrace "singleness" instead of celibacy.[273] He does not rule out the possibility of mixed-orientation marriage.[274]

Dr. Yuan expresses the importance that same-sex attracted Christians be involved in their local church. I agree that it is vital for any Christian to be involved with other Christians in a local church community. In many churches, these same-sex attracted Christians may not be allowed into membership and ministry. Perhaps the local church would allow non-affirming gay Christians to be members, but not affirming gay Christians. One may then wonder, is that reasonable?

Could We Agree to Disagree?

We have to understand God's heart on this topic. He may not be calling us to come into agreement on our doctrine right now. It may be that He is calling us to unite, to reconcile, to accept and love one another, and work together despite our differences without changing our core theology. The question is, is it God's pleasure that gay Christians and straight Christians worship separately? Or, consider the possibility that God is honored by the majority in His evangelical and mainstream churches accepting the minority, loving them, encouraging their gifts within the body of Christ, as we all faithfully seek God's purpose in our lives and in the Church together.

It seems evident to me that once very firmly held, non-affirming beliefs about gay Christians and Christ-centered, same-gender, covenantal relationships, simply are not faithfully supported in

---

[273] Renoe, E. (2019 January 16). Homosexuality and the Bible with Christopher Yuan. [Audio podcast.] *Abscond* with Ethan Renoe. Retrieved January 10, 2020 from www.AbscondPodcast.com.
[274] Ibid.

Scripture. The non-affirming phrases, heralded for decades, like this one: "The Bible is crystal clear that homosexuality is wrong," could only faithfully be stated as follows: "The Bible is crystal clear that idolatrous, abusive, exploitative same-sex acts are wrong."

The Bible is actually not crystal clear on the topic of "homosexuality" in general. There were sinful same-sex practices that took place, but Christ-centered, same-gender, monogamous, covenantal partnerships were not explicitly addressed. The Author of the Bible is omniscient, however, and Scripture is living and active. It can be applied to absolutely every situation in life, through the guidance of the Holy Spirit. Scripture is crystal clear on the gospel of Jesus Christ, and the salvation that is available for anyone who by grace through faith accepts Christ's atoning work on the cross, believing in His sinless life, death, burial, and resurrection, and the indwelling of the Holy Spirit, such that He guides us from faith to faith.

The Church is terrified of "condoning sin," which is honorable. But the Church must re-examine its premise on this issue. Why is the Church not terrified of excluding people? Will God not hold the Church accountable for rejecting gay people and not seeking to bring them into His family and not allowing their gifts to be used as members within their local churches? Many non-Christian LGBTQ people actually believe that they are not qualified to come into the family of God. The narrative that homosexuality, or homosexual behavior, is sinful turns countless LGBTQ people away from pursuing a relationship with Jesus.

If the idea of agreeing to disagree seems dangerous, as if we may be allowing or promoting sin, consider a perspective that Dr. James Brownson presented recently.[275] Recall the parable of the sower

---

[275] Brownson, J. "What Do We Mean by an Affirming Church?" Plenary Session of The Reformation Project annual conference. Seattle, WA, November 9, 2019. I have used my handwritten notes to recall the content.

and the weeds. Jesus described in Matthew 13:24-30 that weeds had been sown among the good seeds in a field. The owner of the field said, let the two grow together, lest by removing a weed, one might inadvertently remove good wheat. The separation occurs at the harvest. The weeds will be gathered and thrown into the fire, and the wheat will be brought into the barn.

If traditionalists fear allowing sin into the community by allowing gay people to participate in church, then consider this: the kingdom of God is a mixed community in many parables. The Church is not expected to weed out all of the sinners. God will judge by His standard. This does not suggest any softening of ethics. God's standard is perfection. (Matthew 5:48, ESV: "You therefore must be perfect.") Let us allow gay Christians to freely worship in our churches and participate in ministry. We can trust that God will sort it all out at the judgment.

I ask that my reader consider that the traditional, non-affirming position may have been wrong. If so, maybe the confession of our local churches should be something like this: We believe that the appropriate Christian marriage in the vast majority of cases is between one man and one woman; however, we recognize that there may be exceptions to this tenet. Another potential idea is as follows: We believe that the appropriate Christian marriage is between one man and one woman. We accept those Christians who believe that monogamous, covenantal, Christ-centered, same-gender relationships are blessed by God while maintaining that we disagree with gay relationships. We agree to disagree on this issue, and we welcome our LGBTQ brothers and sisters into our local church, as we all strive to pursue God's call on our lives and in our church body.

If one could possibly be wrong one way or the other, would we not rather invite gay people into the local church, allow them to get to know Christ-followers and the Lord Jesus, to learn how to walk under His guidance and influence? In other words, what would be worse, wrongly inviting someone into the church, or wrongly rejecting them? If our focus were to bring gay people to Jesus and allow them into our local churches, we could trust the Holy Spirit to lead them out of a sinful lifestyle, just as we would with someone with opposite-gender attraction, and into a commitment to celibacy or monogamous, covenantal relationship if that is His intention. Can we lead them to Jesus, first and foremost, as we all seek to fall in love with Jesus and live out His purpose for our lives?

=≡ 22 ≡=

HEART TO HEART

A wise woman once said to her mother, "If you were wrong about all of this, would you want to know?"

For years I stood on two Scriptures that said God knew the hairs of my head (Luke 12:7) and that if I asked anything in His Name, He would do it, that the Father may be glorified in the Son. (John 14:13) With those two Scriptures, in great faith, I asked God to double the number of hairs on my head. After a decade or so, it occurred to me that even though I had very thin hair, and this was a reasonable request that I asked in faith, I was not getting this prayer answered. I have certainly seen miracles in my life. Just this year, I was dramatically healed during a church service of a concerning skin condition that had plagued me for two months. I know that God works miracles. God is able and willing to heal and bring about miracles in people through faith in Christ Jesus.

When I did not see healing in my hair problem, I recognized that my premise was wrong. There was nothing wrong with my thin hair, and I now express gratitude for it. When a generation of leaders in gay conversion therapy all over the world declare that they saw no one change, it is reasonable to reconsider our premise.

Again, I know that God has caused miracles of hair growth in some people and that He has given some people opposite-gender attraction or removed same-gender attraction. But the overwhelming evidence suggests that conversion to heterosexuality is not the answer for people with same-gender attraction.

Given the failure of conversion therapy, the call to celibacy has thus been the answer. The Church has held up celibate gay Christians as "admirable examples of how to live a self-sacrificial life."[276] The problem with demanding celibacy of people is twofold: it will not work for most people because it is not good for man to be alone, and mandating celibacy is not scriptural.

The appropriate answer in the setting of gay Christians who wholeheartedly seek to follow Christ is, just as with straight men and women, intimate relations only within the confines of a monogamous, committed relationship. The one man, one woman principle has exceptions within Scripture and within the body of Christ today.

My Statement of Faith

To my non-affirming brother or sister in Christ, one of us is wrong. Let us trust in God to open our eyes, to allow the two opposed camps of this debate to see and come into agreement with God's heart on this topic. One of these two sets of arguments has set itself up against the knowledge of God, (II Corinthians 10:5) resulting in terrible bondage by the enemy, bringing immeasurable harm to countless people, including those within the traditional church, as well as the LGBTQ community and their allies.

---

[276] *Scripture, Ethics & the Possibility of Same-Sex Relationships*, page 11.

Innumerable LGBTQ Christians could testify to Christ's redemption in their lives. Here is the testimony of just one. Consider whether you believe I am saved, based on your understanding of Scripture.

I am a gay woman in a same-gender, monogamous, committed, Christ-centered relationship. I trust in the gospel, the exceedingly good news that Christ, who was both fully God and fully human, a member of the holy Trinity, the only begotten Son of the almighty God, lived a sinless life on earth, became the propitiation for the sins of the whole world on the cross on Calvary, died, was buried, and after three days, rose again from the dead. He presented Himself as the risen Christ to more than 500 believers to attest to His resurrection. He promised His disciples the gift of the Holy Spirit before He departed earth for heaven, and thereafter ascended into heaven to sit at the right hand of God the Father and intercede on behalf of the saints.

To those, myself included, who confess with their mouths His Lordship and believe in their hearts that God has raised Him from the dead, there is eternal salvation. I am saved by grace through faith, and I recognize that, apart from His grace, I am a sinner, unable to come before God, Who is holy. I repent of my sin and trust in Christ's atoning work on my behalf.

Thus, God sees me through the righteousness of His sinless, perfect Son. I am therefore included in Christ, and God's Holy Spirit, the third Member of the Trinity, lives in me. I no longer conform to this world and its priorities, but I am transformed by the renewing of my mind as I study the Word of God. I am guided by the Holy Spirit daily from faith to faith. Specifically, God works in me to will and to do for His good pleasure, according to Philippians 2:13. That is, He makes me want to, and makes me able to live out His purpose for my life. And He is well able to guide me forward and correct me when necessary.

The fruit of His work in my life is profound, including freedom from addiction to cigarettes and alcohol, as well as provision of peace, health, harmony, joy, and energy, among others. He removed bitterness and unforgiveness from me, like the weight of a piano off my back one beautiful day in September 2012, just as I stepped out of church into the light of the sun. I actually looked behind me, because the feeling of a burden off my back was so real, so powerful. Just like that, it was gone in the wind and has never returned.

Having experienced the power of Christ as a believer, having been counted "dead to sin but alive to God in Christ Jesus," (Romans 6:11) I want to share this freedom and joy with others, and I want to live out the life that God has planned for me. Through the Holy Spirit in me, I am God's workmanship, created in Christ Jesus to do good works. I endeavor every day to live out His purpose and His pleasure through the works He has prepared for me to do. (Ephesians 2:10) People who know me can attest to the many positive changes in me that are solely attributable to His ongoing presence in my life.

Am I Saved?

Is there anyone who would say at this point that I am not saved? In fact, many non-affirming Christians would maintain that I am not saved unless I repent of "homosexuality." Consider Dr. Michael Brown's answer to a woman with a similar statement of faith:

> If they have rejected God's mercy, if they have lived in disobedience to His commands, they're lost. If they have received His grace and mercy and lived a new life, they're saved. So what it would mean explicitly, as much as you're devoted to your spouse and believe you're scripturally right, if you do not repent of that and turn to the Lord in obedience, I

> would fear that you would be lost.... This is not my
> opinion. The question is what does Scripture say,
> and I believe that Scripture is clear on that.[277]

I do not believe Scripture holds that only heterosexuals can be saved, but I am aware that many people would believe, despite my statement of faith, that I am not saved. (However, no one has ever said this to me personally.)

No Division in The Body

Some readers will agree that this confession, belief, repentance, and fruit constitute salvation. If that is the case, then I am a member of the body of Christ. Paul discussed the body of Christ in his letter to the church in Corinth.

> For we were all baptized by one Spirit so as to form
> one body... Those parts of the body that seem to
> be weaker are indispensable, and the parts that
> we think are less honorable we treat with special
> honor.... But God has put the body together, giving
> greater honor to the parts that lacked it, so that there
> should be no division in the body, but that its parts
> should have equal concern for each other. If one
> part suffers, every part suffers with it; if one part is
> honored, every part rejoices with it. (I Corinthians
> 12:13-14, 22-26)

If gay Christians are members of the body of Christ, and if there should be "no division in the body," and if the remainder of the

---

[277] Brown, M. (2018 September 24). "DEBATE: Is Homosexuality Consistent with New Testament Obedience?" *YouTube*. AskDrBrown. Retrieved September 22, 2019 from www.YouTube.com. (1:11:30 - 1:12:47 in the video).

body of Christ should have "equal concern" for us, then perhaps gay Christians should be allowed membership in the local church.

He has given us gifts. Many people appreciate the gay interior designer, artist, gym coach, and hairdresser. God intended our gifts to also be used in His kingdom. As a general rule, we have faced marginalization and rejection, often by our families and our churches. Just as God said to Israel that they were not to mistreat people, and "remember that you were slaves in Egypt," (Deuteronomy 15:15) gay Christians typically have a heart of compassion for those on the margins. Among us are very kind, loving, talented people. God intended for our gifts and blessings to be used in the body of Christ.[278]

Inconsistencies in the Non-Affirming Argument

If one maintains that gay people are living in sexual sin, then why does the church not shun them? Paul wrote, "I am writing to you that you must not associate with anyone who claims to be a brother or sister but is sexually immoral... do not even eat with such people." (I Corinthians 5:11) I find that many kind, well-meaning, non-affirming Christians seem ambivalent when speaking with gay people, but at the same time, firmly believe that "homosexuality is a sin" and that anyone who disagrees is "twisting Scripture."

Although the non-affirming Christians who will discuss the topic with me believe that Romans 1 is describing "homosexuality," no one has agreed that any of the thirty descriptors in Romans 1:29-32 ("full of wickedness, evil, greed, depravity...") describe gay Christians. It seems strikingly obvious to me that if one holds that Paul is discussing "homosexuality" in Romans 1, then his descriptors

---

[278] This idea was beautifully articulated by James Martin in his book, *Building a Bridge*, 2017.

of those people will accurately describe "homosexuals." In fact, those words do not generally describe gay Christians (any more than they describe all of us at one time or another), and non-affirming Christians agree with that.

Furthermore, despite claiming that they believe that "homosexuals will never enter the kingdom of God," non-affirming Christians routinely tell me that they believe I am a Christian, that I am saved, and that I will go to heaven, based on my confession and belief in Christ's crucifixion and His resurrection. One pastor stated that he believed I was saved, yet would not allow me to be baptized in his church. In my opinion, these conflicting sentiments reveal that the premise, "homosexuality is a sin" is in error, or, at the very least, suggest the very real need for the Church to re-examine this premise carefully.

Does the reader think that the "sin" of gay relationships is equivalent to the sin of unmarried people living together? I would argue that both relationships can be honorable to God, only as committed, monogamous, covenantal, until-death-do-us-part relationships. God did not intend for intimate, one flesh kinship to be pursued for any relationship other than a committed, monogamous relationship. Sexual relationships outside of this type of commitment harm the participants as well as their future spouses.

Gay Christians either are or are not allowed in the kingdom of God. If the translations that we have read and trusted for decades, which read that homosexuals will never enter the kingdom of God, actually refer, not to homosexuals, but to abusive and exploitative sexual sin, then perhaps gay Christians are allowed in the kingdom of God.

If you consider that the Bible translations may have been wrong on this issue, would you not rather practice love and acceptance, rather than rejection? We have to practice "speaking the truth in love," (Ephesians 4:15) as my pastor has beautifully taught us. If we love people, but there is no truth, then it does not benefit them substantially to be loved without being told about Christ, for example. If there is truth, but no love, there is no relationship, no influence, and this does not honor God. If there is both truth and love in our relationships with one another, this is honorable. What if the Church's "truth" that homosexuality is a sin against God, representing sexual immorality, may not be true, in the setting of committed, gay couples or in the lives of single, gay Christians?

Is Christianity's Rejection of Gay People to Blame for the Decline in Numbers?

I once asked a gay friend of mine if he was a Christian. He said, "Are you kidding? I would love to be if they would let me!"

Imagine a well-adjusted, intelligent gay adult who is not a Christian. He has known he was gay since his teenage years. He understands from Christian teaching that he does not qualify to be a Christian. However, he did not choose to be gay. To suggest that Christians can determine that their God calls homosexuality a sin means nothing different to him than if those same people were to suggest that being left-handed is a sin. LGBTQ issues affect an increasing percentage of Americans, and this is the reason, in my opinion, that people in America are decreasingly identifying as Christian.[279] Some people do not want to be associated with a group who suggests to this gay man that he is disqualified from a relationship with God because he is gay.

If one believes that all gay people must renounce same-sex attraction in order to be a Christian, then how can that person ever share the

---

[279] Dimock, M. (2019 October 17). "In U.S., Decline of Christianity Continues at Rapid Pace: An update on America's changing religious landscape". Retrieved October 18, 2019 from www.PewForum.org.

gospel with someone in the LGBTQ community? The traditional argument *needs* to tell gay people that being gay is inconsistent with their modern Bible translations. To not do so feels like caving to worldly pressures and not upholding one's core belief.

I, too, once believed that homosexuality was a sin. Had I continued with that stance, I can imagine the gut-wrenching prospect of falling on my face before God and begging Him, *not primarily to forgive me*, but go back to them, to save them, to make sure that they know the truth, despite what they heard from me. And then pouring out my repentance before Him, with the agonizing thought that some gay people never came into faith in God because I steered them away. God forbid!

Consider the words of Joshua Harris (author of *I Kissed Dating Goodbye* and previous pastor of a megachurch in Maryland), who recently announced that he and his wife are separating and that he no longer identifies as a Christian. He wrote on social media,

> To the LGBTQ+ community, I want to say that I am sorry for the views that I taught in my books and as a pastor regarding sexuality. I regret standing against marriage equality, for not affirming you and your place in the church, and for any ways that my writing and speaking contributed to a culture of exclusion and bigotry. I hope you can forgive me.[280]

Christians are distraught over the recent news that several United Kingdom venues canceled Reverend Franklin Graham's planned

---

[280] Barnhart, M. (2019 July 27). "Joshua Harris falling away from faith: 'I am not a Christian'". Retrieved August 1, 2019 from www.TheChristianPost.com.

2020 tour.[281] The "LGBTQ agenda" and the "sexual revolutionaries," (as the LGBTQ community is sometimes called[282]) have expressed concerns that Reverend Graham's opinion that homosexuality "should be repented of" is damaging to the LGBTQ community. This is a painfully real fight on both sides. Reverend Graham rightly responded, "The Gospel is inclusive. I'm not coming out of hate, I'm coming out of love."

While I support the spreading of the gospel, even by non-affirming preachers, I recognize the issue. Traditionalists have not yet come to terms with the idea that the LGBTQ community cannot be referred to as a sin, but that they should be recognized as people. Even as traditionalists reject that being LGBTQ is anything other than a sin against God, they may soon have to be willing to recognize that LGBTQ people are, even though they self-identify, they are, in fact, *people*, with the same rights to life, liberty, commerce, education, marriage, and any other right that any other person has.

The traditionalist responds that the LGBTQ community and their allies are intolerant of the non-affirming beliefs. We are indeed intolerant of each others' beliefs. Gay affirming people reject traditionalists' claim, for example, that being gay is something "that should be repented of." Being gay is not something someone chooses. Traditionalists reject the LGBTQ community as people who have chosen a sinful path. Traditionalists even consider sinful those who know they are gay, even if they choose lifelong celibacy. How do we reconcile this? Can we find common ground? How about our love for and devotion to Christ above all else? If traditionalists and gay Christians can find common ground in Jesus, then is rejection of gay Christians appropriate?

---

[281] Taylor, D.B. (2020 February 7). "Franklin Graham, Dropped by U.K. Venues, Says He Will Proceed With Tour". *The New York Times*. Retrieved February 13, 2020 from www.NYTimes.com.

[282] Dr. Albert Mohler uses these terms often in his daily podcast, *The Briefing*.

Consider that if one continues to reject gay people from participation in church and from discussions of salvation, then that person bears some responsibility for the gay people who never come to Christ because they heard that homosexuality is a sin and knew that homosexuals are disqualified. Nevermind that if the traditionalist could sit them down, he would explain justification and sanctification and "such were some of you." That's not even an option if he never invites them into his life, his church, his dinner table. If he does invite a gay person to his office, as a pastor once did to me, and reads the mistranslation in I Corinthians 6:9-11 to them, they may not pursue or continue in a relationship with Christ. I thank God for His mercy, that I did not leave the faith. But I have seen countless LGBTQ people who have left the faith because of this rejection by God's non-affirming Christian children.

Suicide Among Gay Youth and Groups Who Combat It

Consider the suicide rates among gay and transgender youth, which are much higher than those within society as a whole. According to a study in the journal *Pediatrics*, "LGB youth who come from highly rejecting families are 8.4 times as likely to have attempted suicide as LGB peers who reported no or low levels of family rejection."[283]

The non-affirming argument suggests that this "evil" (homosexuality) within our society is killing our children and must be rooted out. However, when this faulty logic prevails, gay Christian youth commit suicide because they are rejected by their families and churches and do not see a way out of their problem. They can see only two options: become *not gay* and maintain family and church approval, or lose this approval and experience painful rejection by those they love.

---

[283] Quoted from www.TheTrevorProject.org. Ryan, C, Huebner, D., et.al. (2009). "Family rejection as a predictor of negative health outcomes in white and Latino lesbian, gay, and bisexual young adults". *Pediatrics.* 123(1), 346-52.

They recognize the potential impossibility of becoming *not gay*, and cannot imagine facing a life of rejection. The non-affirming idea suggests that otherwise straight children can be "recruited" into homosexuality, and then become at risk for suicide. However, gay youth are not taught to be gay just as straight youth are not taught to be straight. Same-gender attraction, or the feeling that a romantic relationship could only genuinely be felt with someone of the same gender, cannot be manufactured or chosen. If so, rather than committing suicide, these youth would simply choose to be straight.

The Trevor Project is an organization that offers support for LGBTQ youth via their 24-hour crisis and suicide prevention helpline. The Trevor Project provides availability via text, chat, and phone. Their digital crisis counselors and volunteers undergo 40 hours of training before beginning their work.[284] One volunteer, Kelly Erin, has spent over 6,200 minutes on the phone with young people who were experiencing despair, hopelessness, and suicidality due to the belief that homosexuality is a sin. In 2019, over 100,000 LGBTQ youths, many of them desperate, were provided with counseling and affirmation of their personhood and worth as beautiful people created by God in His image.

Isn't it stunning to realize that a traditional, non-affirming church could not offer this service to LGBTQ people? Sadly (and erroneously), the church needs to tell them that they can be set free, they can be changed, they can be redeemed, but never, that they are simply loved, as they are. The church says to straight kids, "you are beautiful; you are loved; you are accepted just as you are." With the best of intentions, the church says to LGBTQ people, "yes, you are beautiful, and you are loved, but we are all sinners." That "but" has cost this community so much despair and so many suicides.

---

[284] TheTrevorProject.org.

The Tyler Clementi Foundation is an organization whose purpose is to end bullying through inclusion and assertion of dignity and acceptance. They have initiated the Million Upstander Movement, which is an agreement to put an end to bullying. They have over 698,000 upstanders who have agreed to not "use insulting or demeaning language, slurs, gestures, facial expressions, or jokes about anyone's sexuality, size, gender, race, any kind of disability, religion, class, politics, or other differences, in person or while using technology," and to speak up for people who are being bullied. They speak out specifically against "religion-based bullying." In 2017, they joined forces with Faith in America, an advocacy group founded in 2006 to end "faith-based discrimination."[285]

Thank God for these organizations who have stepped in to help combat the despair and suicidality caused by the view that being gay is a sin.

Our Identity is in Christ

Traditionalists are correct when they point out that a sinful action cannot be a label for a Christian. There is no adulterous Christian or greedy Christian. Rather than identify as something he deems sinful, Dr. Yuan, who is described as having same-sex attractions, states that he is neither gay, ex-gay, nor heterosexual.[286]

Christians recognize the profound power of words. The power of life and death are in the tongue. (Proverbs 18:21) Christians declare what the Word of God says about us. We are children of God, wonderfully and fearfully created in His image, forgiven, healed, crowned with

---

[285] www.TylerClementi.org.

[286] Stonestreet, J. and Morris, S. (2019 April 14). "Christopher Yuan on holy sexuality: Your desires don't define you". Retrieved January 14, 2020 from www.ChristianPost.com.

mercy and compassion, redeemed from destruction, satisfied, renewed, made new, guided by Him. We are the righteousness of God in Christ.[287] We are who God says we are!

Thus, affirming Christians understand why those who believe homosexuality is a sin must insist that no one label himself that way. However, affirming Christians do not believe that it is, in any way, sinful to *be gay*. To gay-affirming people, it is no different than being left-handed. (I would never label myself as something sinful.) We use a term like "gay Christian" only for the purposes of communicating. Our identity is in Christ, first and foremost.

Someone may say, "I experience same-gender attraction and do not experience opposite-gender attraction. But that is not who I am. It merely describes my experiences and how I feel. My identity is in Christ." Amen! Affirming Christians wholeheartedly respect this statement. We find "gay Christian" to be shorter and more appealing because it eliminates the unnecessarily descriptive language.

Discrimination versus Religious Freedom: Are Gay People Really Gay, or Are They Confused Straight People?

While I believe that continued LGBTQ discrimination in society is untenable, I recognize the fear of the loss of religious freedoms for those who see the LGBTQ community as a group of sinners actively engaged in and promoting sin. There are two cases currently before the Supreme Court to determine if the Civil Rights Act of 1964 covers LGBTQ people.[288] It's a gut-wrenching fight. Both

---

[287] John 1:12, Psalm 139:14, Psalm 103:3-5, Romans 12:2, II Corinthians 5:17, Philippians 2:13, II Corinthians 5:21.

[288] Law, T. (2019 October 8). "9 Landmark Supreme Court Cases That Shaped LGBTQ Rights in America". Retrieved December 2019 from www.Time.com.

sides honestly hold their views as if straight from God, but they are diametrically opposed. As Dr. Mohler[289] often points out, the "LGBTQ agenda" will not stop until all of their demands are met. This is true, because the LGBTQ community and their allies do not believe that we are the sin ascribed to us by the traditional Christian teaching. If LGBTQ non-discrimination is not decided in the fall of 2020, it will be eventually.

Secular society recognizes and celebrates the LGBTQ community. Just recently, two large banks pulled funding for Florida's school voucher program because the Christian schools deny entrance to students who identify as LGBTQ.[290] The Christian community unapologetically upholds this rule as necessary, assuming that all homosexual behavior and identity is sinful. Thus, one cannot belong to a Christian school and be labeled as LGBTQ. The ever present problem is becoming more and more obvious.

These are just people, just different kinds of people. All of secular society recognizes it. Even kids who know that they are different, that they are not straight, may want to be involved in Christian activities, including Christian school. In the eyes of secular society, denying these families access to Christian schools is discrimination against LGBTQ people, plain and simple. How does the church justify it?

They say, there is no gay gene; there is no biomarker for being LGBTQ; there is no scientifically determinable, immutable characteristic of these people that allows them to claim that they are

---

[289] Dr. Mohler is the president of the Southern Baptist Theological Seminary. I typically enjoy his daily podcast titled *The Briefing* which is "a daily analysis of news and events from a Christian worldview," again (as with Dr. Brown's podcast), despite our differences on this topic.

[290] Sopelsa, B and Ruggiero, R. (2020 January 29) "Wells Fargo pulls Florida voucher donations over anti-gay school policies". Retrieved January 31, 2020 from www.NBCNews.com.

different. The problem is that this is completely unsustainable. There *are* gay people; there are LGBTQ people; there are people who are different from straight people. Even as left-handed people and right-handed people are different, gay people are different than straight people. The only way for ongoing discrimination against gay people to hold any merit in the church is for the Christian community to believe that all LGBTQ people are not really LGBTQ, and that they are either confused or are blatantly sinning against God.

When Dr. Michael Brown responds to Matthew Vines's questions, Dr. Brown refers to Vines as "'gay' Christian," with "gay" in quotes, as if Vines really is not gay but only claims to be gay or perhaps, only thinks he is gay. If the church wants to say that gay people are not gay, what does the church want to call people who experience ongoing physical, emotional, or romantic same-sex attraction comparable to the way straight people experience ongoing opposite-sex attraction (and do not typically experience opposite-sex attraction the same way straight people do not typically experience same-sex attraction)? The church's suggestion is that these are all actually straight people with sinful inclinations.

Even as we agree that the church does not see things as the world does, the church is going to have to recognize that some people are actually gay. If the church's entire ability to discriminate against gay people comes down to just suggesting that people are not gay, then is this honest? Is this sustainable?

If there are no actual gay people, if LGBTQ people are only confused straight people, then the church is condemning only willful, sinful, or confused behavior, and is thus, correct in their discernment and rejection of people who engage in that behavior.

Are there different kinds of people, or are we all the same? We're all sinners in need of a savior. Amen. But are some people different in terms of sexuality? We are who God says we are. Amen. But are some people actually, legitimately born different?

I have the answer, straight from Jesus's mouth in Matthew 19:12. "For some are eunuchs because they were born that way."

Some people who are different in terms of sexuality were born that way. Church, we cannot continue to reject them.

Accept One Another, Then

People often say, "don't judge me," referring to Jesus's words, "do not judge, or you too will be judged." (Matthew 7:1) Many suggest that "this charge [is typically] levied from those seeking to justify aberrant and ungodly behaviors."[291] There is good scriptural evidence for carefully discerning biblical truths and standards in the lives of our brothers and sisters in Christ, as well as restoring those who have strayed from the faith. This is especially true for leaders within the local churches.

Here are some instances in Scripture when this approach is exemplified.

- I Corinthians 5:11-13:
    > But now I am writing to you that you must not associate with anyone who claims to be a brother or sister but is sexually immoral or greedy, an idolater or slanderer, a drunkard or swindler. Do not even eat with such people. What business is it of mine to judge those outside the church? Are you not to judge those inside? God will

---

[291] Jackson, Wayne. (2019). "Don't Judge Me!" *ChristianCourier.com.* Retrieved July 16, 2019 from www.ChristianCourier.com.

judge those outside. "Expel the wicked person from among you."

This is the aforementioned example in Scripture of a man from the Corinthian church who was living in adultery with his father's wife.

- Galatians 6:1a: "Brothers and sisters, if someone is caught in a sin, you who live by the Spirit should restore that person gently."

- John 7:24: "Stop judging by mere appearances, but instead judge correctly."

- Galatians 2:11: "When [Peter] came to Antioch, I opposed him to his face, because he stood condemned." This was Paul writing. The conservative Jewish Christians had visited the church in Antioch, which was mostly Gentile Christians. Peter had withdrawn from the Gentiles in the presence of the Jewish Christians. Paul denounced Peter's hypocrisy, as he was inappropriately concerned with what the Jewish leaders thought of him. Paul stated that Peter was "not acting in line with the truth of the gospel," (Galatians 2:14) which is that we are justified by faith in Christ and not by observing the law. (Galatians 2:16)

- I Timothy 1:20: "Among them are Hymenaeus and Alexander, whom I have handed over to Satan to be taught not to blaspheme." These men were teaching that the resurrection had already occurred. (II Timothy 2:18)

- II Timothy 2:25-26:

  Opponents [of the Lord's servants] must be gently instructed, in the hope that God will grant them repentance leading them to a knowledge of the truth, and that they will come to their senses and escape from the trap of the devil, who has taken them captive to do his will.

- II Timothy 4:2b: "correct, rebuke, and encourage—with great patience and careful instruction."
- James 5:20: "Remember this: Whoever turns a sinner from the error of their way will save them from death and cover a multitude of sins."

Obviously, we should be very careful that we are guided by the Holy Spirit in any condemnation or restoration that we bring to a brother or sister in Christ, or to a debate stage. We must never forget the "clear and overwhelming biblical evidence" in support of slavery. Let's consider the other side of speaking "the truth in love." Imagine, reader, that you hold the responsibility to vote on the inclusion or exclusion of certain people within your local church while reading these passages.

- Romans 2:1: "You, therefore, have no excuse, you who pass judgment on someone else, for at whatever point you judge another, you are condemning yourself, because you who pass judgment do the same things."
- Romans 14:4: "Who are you to judge someone else's servant? To their own master, servants stand or fall. And they will stand, for the Lord is able to make them stand."
- Matthew 7:1: "Do not judge, or you too will be judged."
- Romans 15:5-7:
  > May the God who gives endurance and encouragement give you the same attitude of mind toward each other that Christ Jesus had, so that with one mind and one voice you may glorify the God and Father of our Lord Jesus Christ. Accept one another, then, just as Christ accepted you, in order to bring praise to God.
- Romans 14:10-14a:
  > You, then, why do you judge your brother or sister? Or why do you treat them with contempt? For we will all stand before God's judgment seat. It is written: "'As

surely as I live,' says the Lord, 'every knee will bow before me; every tongue will acknowledge God.'" So then, each of us will give an account of ourselves to God. Therefore let us stop passing judgment on one another.

- I Corinthians 10:29b-30: "For why is my freedom being judged by another's conscience? If I take part in the meal with thankfulness, why am I denounced because of something I thank God for?"
- Romans 8:1: "Therefore, there is now no condemnation for those who are in Christ Jesus."
- Acts 10:28b: "God has shown me that I should not call anyone impure or unclean."
- James 2:12-13: "Speak and act as those who are going to be judged by the law that gives freedom, because judgment without mercy will be shown to anyone who has not been merciful. Mercy triumphs over judgment."
- James 4:11-12:

   Brothers and sisters, do not slander one another. Anyone who speaks against a brother or sister or judges them speaks against the law and judges it. When you judge the law, you are not keeping it, but sitting in judgment on it. There is only one Lawgiver and Judge, the one who is able to save and destroy. But you—who are you to judge your neighbor?

- John 8:7b: "Let any one of you who is without sin be the first to throw a stone at her."

I believe that this topic is coming before the churches, and ultimately, within (the second third of) my lifetime,[292] churches will become inclusive of gay Christians. The Church will reconsider its stance on gay people, just as it did about slavery and interracial marriage.

---

[292] I was born in 1972.

Christian professor Dr. David Gushee wrote that, at any given Christian college around the country, there might very soon be an "eruption over its LGBTQ policy." He stated, "It's a case of the irresistible force meeting the immovable object." The irresistible force is generational change. He pointed out that gay marriage was legalized "all the way back in 2015. For a 20-year-old, that's ancient history."[293] The immovable object, of course, is "traditionalist understandings of sexuality."

My heart grieves for those who believe that the Bible truly states that homosexuals will never enter the kingdom of God. It doesn't. Neither does Romans 1 refer to or, in any way, describe Christian gay couples. This misunderstanding has held families and churches in bondage. Many relationships have been destroyed by the incorrect belief that Christians had to choose between God's Word and their loved ones. What joy this has brought our common enemy!

If being left-handed were a sin, forcing a left-handed person to write with his right hand might appear to solve the problem, but in fact, that person remains left-handed. And yet, even within the environment of gay-friendly churches, some people and some Bible translations state that an attraction to people of the same gender is a sin. This idea is utterly nonsensical. Sometimes I wonder if the affirming group and the non-affirming group are speaking two different languages.

"Homosexual" is the non-affirming group's preferred term, but it seems demeaning to many gay Christians. Do non-affirming people realize that being gay is not even about sex for some people? Non-affirming arguments seem to want to reduce gay people to an assumed sex act. Some gay people refer to themselves as homo-emotional.

---

[293] Gushee, D. (2019 December 3). "Christian higher ed can't win the LGBTQ debate unless it transforms". Retrieved December 8, 2019 from www.ReligionNews.com.

"Gay" is the affirming group's preferred term, but the non-affirming group prefers not to use such a pleasant word to describe us. Many gay Christians don't see any need for a descriptive term that includes the word "sex." There is simply no reason to assume *anything* about any gay couple in their bedroom. God knows us intimately and will judge perfectly.

Someone is currently thinking, "Why do I need to know that someone in my church is gay? I don't go around telling people that I am straight." A gay person often cannot carry on a simple, even perfunctory conversation without revealing this basic fact in their life. "We went fishing this weekend" immediately begs the question, who is "we." A couple cannot pretend they are not a couple without being deceptive. Most gay people are just not willing to lie or be deceptive in order to prevent other people from feeling uncomfortable. If straight people prefer that we not let them know we're gay, it's just a sign that we're not welcome.

Some people simply do not have the capacity for heterosexuality, including those born eunuchs, of whom Jesus spoke. Once we have acknowledged that a small minority of people do not have the capacity for heterosexuality, is it appropriate to accept them only if they are closeted and celibate? The reality is that these people can enter into monogamous, Christ-centered, covenantal partnerships, and have been doing so for decades and probably centuries.

The Bible absolutely forbids molestation of children and exploitative male sexual activity as well as all same-sex idolatrous acts. After centuries of translation, publishers of the Bible came to call those forbidden acts "homosexuality." However, the Bible does not condemn same-gender attraction, and it does not condemn faithful, same-gender, Christian, committed relationships.

Churches Led by Gay Christians

Imagine, reader, if you attended a gay Christian service, like the one described in chapter 2. You would likely be confronted with Christians who take the Word of God very seriously and worship Him in spirit and in truth. If your church operates in the gifts of the Spirit, such as prophecy or tongues and interpretation, you may find that a word manifest even in a gay congregation is not different than the spiritual gifts that are manifest in your own church. If you saw undeniable evidence that God was honored and glorified and responded to the worship and prayers of gay people and gay couples, would you reconsider your long-held beliefs that homosexuality is a sin? If you would concede that God was honored in a situation like that and that He responded to the praise of His people, do you think that all gay people should only worship together and that our straight brothers and sisters should continue to exclude gay Christians from membership in their churches and participation in their ministries?

If you cannot imagine a Spirit-filled atmosphere like the one I describe among gay people, I invite you to look up New Covenant Church of Atlanta. This is a dynamic, Bible-believing, Holy Spirit filled church, operating in the gifts of the Spirit and the five-fold ministry, per Ephesians 4:11. They post every sermon on their website, www. NewCovenantAtlanta.com. The pastor and his husband founded the church and the Covenant Network (a network of affirming, Bible-based churches) in 2000. The vast majority of the congregants are gay Christians, including gay married couples. If you really want to see if the Lord is at work in a large group of LGBTQ Christians, consider attending the Immersed Conference (described in chapter 2), in Atlanta, Georgia (www.theImmersedConference.com), or see their videos online.

Non-Affirming Same-Sex Attracted Christians

I believe that many same-sex attracted Christians do not realize that the Church's rejection of gay Christians stems from a misunderstanding and mistranslation of the Scripture, and they live in bondage and condemnation. To my non-affirming, same-sex attracted Christian brothers and sisters, I encourage you to consider what Paul said to the churches in Galatia in chapter 3 of Galatians. There were "legalistic Judaizers"[294] who believed that Christians must remain under the law of Moses, leaving them in bondage. Those people in Paul's day did not understand the new covenant, that since Christ's atoning work on the cross, they were (and we are) filled with the Holy Spirit, Who provides His guidance from within the believer. "I will put My laws in their hearts, and I will write them on their minds." (Hebrews 10:16b) They believed the Mosaic law was still necessary as a "guide." Paul said in Galatians 3:23-25 that the law is no longer our guide. Some today still use the law as a "guide," prohibiting "homosexuality" as part of what they deem "the moral law." Those people also typically believe the mistranslations of the Bible, that "homosexuals will never enter the kingdom of God."

I encourage my non-affirming same-sex attracted brothers and sisters to reconsider this carefully. More information is now available to us. Paul wrote to the believers in Galatia who were being fooled, (Galatians 3:1) "do you wish to be enslaved by them all over again?" (Galatians 4:9b) Many of you faithfully trust in Christ's atoning work on Calvary and just do not know how to navigate this enormous, controversial topic on your own and simply wait to hear from God.

I would ask my same-sex attracted friends, is it a sin to *be gay*? Likely, most of you will answer this as if I had asked if it were a sin to be left-handed. I hope that my gay Christian brothers and sisters will reject

---

[294] Barker, K. (1985). "Galatians 3:1." *The NIV Study Bible*. Grand Rapids, MI: Zondervan, page 1783.

what appears to be the traditionalists desire that gay people pretend or claim in faith to be not gay. We are all, gay and straight alike, fearfully and wonderfully created in God's image. If you believe God's call in your life is to celibacy, then embrace it. If you study this issue and over time believe that God allows for monogamy, then I encourage you to remain open to the option that God has a covenantal partner for you.

I pray that God makes His truth known to all of us, affirming and non-affirming Christians alike, so that, just as Christ prayed before His arrest, we may all be one in Him.

> I pray also for those who will believe in Me through their message, that all of them may be one. Father, just as You are in Me, and I am in You, may they also be in Us so that the world may believe that You have sent Me. I have given them the glory that You gave me, that they may be one as We are one—I in them, and You in Me—so that they may be brought to complete unity. Then the world will know that You sent Me and have loved them even as You have loved Me. (John 17:20b-23)

As Christians, Christ does not want us to have factions among us.

Various Analogies

Is there another example to which we could compare this issue? Is there another "sin" that the faithful Christian completely rejects as sin and thanks God for, as if it were a gift? Imagine the Christian who smokes a pack of cigarettes daily. With every cigarette, he senses in his spirit and soul that the practice of smoking is not honorable before God. If the believer maintains that he is redeemed from destruction (Psalm 103:4, KJV) by the power of the blood of Christ and confesses that the Holy Spirit puts in him, the believer, to will and to do for God's good purpose, (Philippians 2:13) then if he chooses, that believer will have the power to overcome the habit of smoking. But there is not a time when this faithful Christian would say that God blesses him with a pack of cigarettes to smoke every day. He may defiantly declare that he'll never give up smoking, but in his heart, the Christian realizes that the practice is not entirely honorable before God and that it would be preferable to not smoke cigarettes daily.

However, my same-gender, covenantal partnership does bring glory and honor to God. My partner is His gift to me, and our relationship is centered on Christ and His will for our lives. We do not defiantly declare that we are not leaving our partnership. Rather, we recognize His handiwork in our lives, and we seek to honor Him in every aspect of our relationship.

Consider another example. A man whose marriage is failing may be flirting with another man's wife. The faithful Christian does not express gratitude to God for the potential to destroy another marriage. Rather, he sees this as a grievous sin against God. He cannot continue to be faithful in his walk with God and continue to flirt with the woman. One of those things will not proceed.

Is there any example the non-affirming argument could supply which shows an honest, faithful Christian who is living happily in ongoing sin without realizing it? This simply is not possible. One may suggest that Christians could sin without knowing it, for example, by holding grudges or having a negative attitude. However, those are not activities that the Christian thanks God for. The Holy Spirit addresses those thoughts, words, and actions in our lives that do not bring honor to God. We repent of those sins and seek the Holy Spirit's guidance and pray for freedom from those sins. We recognize that the blood of Christ has atoned for those sins, and, in fact, all sin in our lives.

Simply put, light cannot have fellowship with darkness. (II Corinthians 6:14) The faithful Christian cannot live in sin and continue in a close relationship with God. Again, I maintain that the premise held within the non-affirming argument therefore must be wrong. There is simply no sin, either to God, to the participants, or to a neighbor in a same-gender, covenantal relationship.

Let's consider an analogy that traditionalist Christians may accept. Imagine a remarried couple, both of whom are divorced. Their former spouses are each happily remarried, and there is no bitterness among either of the previous or new spouses. In our hypothetical situation, both couples divorced one year into their first marriages in their early 20s because they simply did not get along with their first spouse. In other words, neither divorce fell within the biblical exceptions for remarriage, which are sexual immorality (Matthew 19:9) and an unbeliever who wishes to leave the marriage. (I Corinthians 7:15) I think a non-affirming Christian may find this remarriage to be a reasonable parallel to a Christ-centered, monogamous, committed gay couple.

There is no harm done to the participants or to others. There is no spouse who is harmed, as would be the case if one participant were still married (or if the ex-spouse were unhappy about the divorce), and no future spouse to be harmed since it is a monogamous, covenantal relationship. The non-affirming argument believes that a covenantal gay relationship brings dishonor to God's view of marriage, as "one man, one woman." Wouldn't a faithful, consistent application of these situations, applying the premise that "homosexuality is a sin," consider these two situations analogous? In other words, the Scripture records that this remarriage would qualify as "living in adultery," yet we would all agree that no one is harmed.

Similarly, the non-affirming position would recognize a gay, covenantal relationship to be one that dishonors "God's design of one man, one woman," while not harming anyone. Would the non-affirming reader agree that the remarried couple would be allowed in the local church, but that the gay couple would typically be rejected from membership and participation in ministries? Would Paul's admonition (Romans 14:10-13a) not apply to the church in both scenarios:

> You, then, why do you judge your brother or sister? Or why do you treat them with contempt? For we will all stand before God's judgment seat. It is written: "'As surely as I live,' says the Lord, 'every knee will bow before me; every tongue will acknowledge God.'" So then, each of us will give an account of ourselves to God. Therefore let us stop passing judgment on one another.

The Affirming Church's Answer to Gay Christians

This is what I believe should be the Church's answer to gay Christians: God did create some people with same-gender attraction who are blessed and loved by God as they are. Each gay person was knit together by God in their mother's womb. Just as was the eunuch (of whom Jesus spoke in Matthew 19:12), each and every gay person is fearfully and wonderfully made. (Psalm 139:13-14) Make meaningful friendships with other faithful, committed Christians. The dating scene must be approached carefully under the guidance of the Holy Spirit. Flee from sexual immorality. Sexual activity is only appropriate within a monogamous, committed, until-death-do-us-part, covenantal relationship. Date only like-minded Christians, who trust in the Lord and hold God's Word as the highest authority in their lives. Find a Bible-based church that is at least friendly, if there is not yet an affirming Bible-based church in your area, and get involved in an affirming church online. Submit your life to the Lordship of Christ, understanding that the Holy Spirit within you is well able to guide and direct you through this life.

23

SUMMARIZING THE PREMISE: IS SCRIPTURE CRYSTAL CLEAR THAT HOMOSEXUALITY IS A SIN?

The traditional non-affirming premise holds that all forms of homosexuality are sinful based on two arguments:

1. The passages in the Bible referring to same-sex acts, and
2. The idea that God created marriage as one man and one woman for everyone.

With regard to "all forms of homosexuality," I again ask the reader to make a distinction between sober-minded, upstanding, gay Christians who behave as Romans 13:13 describes, "decently, as in the daytime," as opposed to those people who have no regard for the heart of God or His will and purpose in their lives. (Consider this compassionately: many gay people who fit the latter description, who have no regard for the heart of God, have heard that God refers to them as an "abomination." I want to reach them and tell them the truth. I want to be able to invite them to a Bible-believing church that does not reject them.)

The Bible Passages that Address Same-Sex Activity

- Sodom and Gomorrah: That story is about gang rape. That simply has nothing to do with gay couples or gay Christians. There is a strikingly similar story in Judges 19, but the sexual sins committed involved heterosexual rape. Both heterosexual and homosexual rape are condemned in Scripture. This passage simply does not address "homosexuality" in general, or, better said, gay people.

- Levitical prohibitions: We do not keep the law under Christ. Christ canceled the written code, "nailing it to the cross." (Colossians 2:14, 1984) It was an abomination to eat shellfish, (Leviticus 11:9-11, KJV) and anyone who did not obey his parents was to be put to death. (Deuteronomy 21:18-21) These types of prohibitions and punishments are no longer held. Ancient translations of the Levitical prohibitions refer to pederasty. The sins were egregious in a patriarchal society, just as it was appropriate to offer one's daughters to rapists to save the dignity of male guests. Prohibitions grounded in that culture are not relevant today, just as the prohibition of sex during a woman's monthly menses is no longer applicable today. In fact, the entirety of the law is considered to be "obsolete." (Hebrews 8:13) The righteous requirements of the law have fully been met in us through Christ alone, (Romans 8:4) not in attempts to keep the law. (Galatians 3:10-11) Those who attempt to keep the law are "cursed." (Galatians 3:10)

- Romans 1: Paul describes activities of people who worshiped idols and rejected God. They engaged in shameful and unnatural, same-gender, sexual acts. Just as with the Sodom and Gomorrah story, traditionalists use the word "they" in this passage interchangeably with the word "homosexuals." This is a fallacy. "They" refers to idol worshipers, not homosexuals. Furthermore the people in the passage were heterosexual. Gay Christians glorify God and give thanks to Him; thus, they cannot be described as people who "neither glorified Him as God nor gave thanks to Him." If gay Christians could be described by this passage, then the 30 descriptors, including "God-haters," would apply. However, gay Christians love God.

- I Corinthians 6:9-11 & I Timothy 1:9-10: Unfortunately, in the 1940s, translators referred to abusive, exploitative male sexual acts as "homosexuals." Sadly, this mistranslation has been repeated ever since then.

Those cover the "clobber passages," all the passages that involve same-gender sexual activity. The condemned activities in those passages represent abuse, exploitation, idolatry, and rejection of God. Christians who are gay have nothing whatsoever to do with those activities.

One Man, One Woman and the Whole of Scripture, Beginning in Genesis

Marriage between one man and one woman is indisputably the appropriate Christian marriage in the vast majority of cases. However, there are exceptions. In King David's case, the Scripture records the exception in first person, that is, in the voice of God Himself. (II Samuel 12:8) Jesus noted, in contrast to the creation story of marriage, that there are actually eunuchs who were "born that way," implying that "one man, one woman" would not be appropriate for that small minority of people. Another exception is seen in Paul's statement that in Christ Jesus, we are all one; "there is no longer male and female." God sees us all, including his gay children, through the sinlessness and righteousness of His Son, the Lord Jesus, as neither Jew nor Gentile, neither slave nor free, and neither male nor female. Remarried couples are yet another exception to "one man, one woman," one that is affirmed by most mainstream churches today.

The overall non-affirming argument summarizes that the whole of Scripture "presupposes" heterosexuality. Gay-affirming Christians agree wholeheartedly with this. There is no reason that Scripture should not presuppose heterosexuality. It is, without any doubt, the appropriate marriage for the vast majority of Christians. For example, all humans come from a mother and father (even if not raised by them), and we are instructed to love and honor them. Paul addressed husbands and wives because the vast majority of Christendom is composed of husbands and wives. These are scriptural, incontrovertible truths. One would not expect Scripture to spend much time on the exception to a rule. Regarding women being deacons, the whole of Scripture presupposes the rule that deacons are men. Yet there is one small exception in one verse in the Bible. All of Scripture presupposes heterosexuality, yet there are two rarely quoted statements by Jesus, one about eunuchs who were born that way and one about two men in one bed at night. The whole of Scripture also presupposes that women do not teach men, that slaves are to obey their masters, that polygamy is perfectly acceptable at times, and that the sun rises and the sun sets.

Historical and Cultural Misconceptions

Researchers in the fields of science and medicine, unfortunately, mischaracterized gay people decades ago as broken, sick, and perverted. For many Christians, there is no hesitation about trusting in the work of Christ on the cross for healing. Thus, we believed that conversion from what we thought was a sickness to heterosexuality through faith in Christ was the answer. However, after 40 years of attempts to convert people by faith, leaders of these ministries worldwide came into agreement that sexual orientation is simply not changed in most people. It turns out, our premise was wrong. I Corinthians 6:9 was not referring to homosexuals. That's the reason that the vast majority of attempted converts were not "healed;" they weren't sick in the first place.

When Paul referred negatively to those who "forbid people to marry," I believe the Holy Spirit was referring to our modern-day, non-affirming churches. Paul implied that they should allow couples to marry.

But Isn't Homosexual Activity Unnatural?

One might, at this point, suggest that all the arguments bring some degree of doubt to the premise that homosexuality is a sin. However, many remain stuck on one idea. Returning to Romans 1, does Paul not suggest that homosexual activity is unnatural? Paul *did not* say that all same-gender activity is unnatural. He said that certain people who were actually heterosexual rejected God and served idols, and therefore, God gave them over to shameful lusts. In other words, God gave them over, not to monogamy within a loving, covenantal relationship, but rather, to shameful lusts. These idol worshipers who had been given over to the sinful desires of their hearts committed the most shameful and unnatural acts that one can imagine. They even committed same-sex acts, which were contrary to their own nature, and shameful. They were not honorable, natural acts, as would be seen within a covenantal, monogamous relationship.

Again, the passage refers to heterosexual people, as noted by "the men" and "their women." Furthermore, the vast majority of the population would not even have attraction to people of the same gender. The same-sex orgies of straight idol worshipers who participated in all manner of sexual immorality simply cannot faithfully be applied to people who advocate "chastity in singleness and faithfulness in marriage," whether gay or straight.

The traditional thinking was reasonable for a time. We thought homosexuals were broken, sick, and perverted. We just made a mistake. Let's consider that maybe the gay Christians in our churches are not living in sin. Perhaps the gay people in our communities could be welcomed into our churches, and taught that there is a path that allows them to know Christ, to live the abundant life that He offered, without asking that they do something that intrinsically they know they can't do, which is, not be gay.

The Holy Spirit Guides the Believer From Within

As a gay Christian, a member of the body of Christ, I am promised in the Word of God that He has put His laws in my mind and written them on my heart. (Hebrews 8:10) The Scripture states that the Holy Spirit will guide me in all truth (John 16:13) and that He works in me to will and to act according to His good pleasure. (Philippians 2:13) God disciplines and corrects me. (Hebrews 12:6) He is Lord of my life. There is nothing I wouldn't give up or change to be in alignment with God's Word and God's purpose in my life. I believe, in no uncertain terms, that God has blessed my covenantal relationship and those of countless gay Christian couples in the world today. Importantly, despite the traditional arguments that I know very well, after years of study, I find not only that there is literally nothing in Scripture that condemns monogamous, loving, covenantal, Christ-centered, gay relationships, but also that God is honored and glorified by gay Christians and within these relationships.

As we carefully submit ourselves to the Holy Spirit and read Scripture under His guidance, our understanding of God's heart, His purpose, and His pleasure is revealed to us as Christians. Faithful Christians have made mistakes in the past. Let us continue this conversation until we come into agreement with His heart on this topic. Until then, let us accept one another in love, as we are all included in Christ.

APPENDIX A

WHERE DO YOU STAND?

Please email me (IamIncludedinChrist@gmail.com), post on my website (www.IncludedinChrist.net), or just consider your answers to the following questions:

1. Which of the following, a through g, best describes your view today?

   a. Affirming of gay Christians: I believe that gay Christians can be blessed by God in their expression of romantic intimacy within monogamous, committed, permanent, Christ-centered, same-gender relationships.

   b. Possibly affirming of gay Christians: I believe the possibility exists that God blesses romantic intimacy within some same-gender relationships.

   c. Unsure on gay couples: I believe that gay people can be Christians. I am unsure as to whether or not committed, same-gender couples are living in sin.

   d. Accepting but not affirming: I believe that God designed marriage and covenantal relationships to be for one man and one woman only. However, I accept and welcome those who believe that same-gender partnerships could be blessed by God. Specifically, I would agree to allow gay Christians and same-gender couples into my local church, to be members, and to participate in ministries within the church.

e. Non-affirming of gay Christians: Gay people can be Christians. However, same-gender intimacy is not acceptable under any circumstances. All forms of homosexual expression are sinful. Gay Christians can honestly admit that they are gay, but they must remain celibate or enter into heterosexual marriage.

f. Non-affirming of gay people: Gay people cannot be Christians unless they believe that their same-gender attractions are wrong. They must renounce and seek to change their orientation. Salvation is available through Christ, having renounced and repented of same-gender desires. Terms such as "gay Christian" are unacceptable, just as "adulterous Christian" would be unacceptable.

g. There is no hope of redemption for anyone who is LGBTQ. These people do not belong in any Bible-believing Christian church.

2. Is it justifiable to reject gay people from participation in membership and ministries of the local church, or is rejection of people dishonorable to God?

3. Has your view changed within the last year? What was it previously? Why was there a change in your opinion?

4. Do you belong to a church as either a member or regular visitor? Is the church affirming or non-affirming of openly gay people, or is it unclear?

5. Imagine that the issue has come before your local church and that you are obligated to vote. Would you vote to ask the gay Christians and gay Christian couples to leave the church, or would you vote to allow them to stay, and be offered membership, assuming they are respectful and non-confrontational?

6. Would you vote to allow gay couples committed to celibacy to become members?

7. Would you vote to allow openly gay Christians in your church to participate in various ministries such as the worship team or the children's ministry, assuming they are very well qualified?

8. Would you leave your church if gay couples were allowed to remain as visitors? Would you leave if they were allowed to become members?

9. Do you believe the presence of gay Christians and gay couples is harmful to children?

10. Would you feel comfortable encouraging an openly gay Christian in your church to bring his friends, who may be gay, to church?

11. Which would be worse, to reject people and later find out you were wrong, or invite people into the church and later find out you were wrong?

12. Would you vote that the church post publicly on its website its exact stance on openly gay Christians and couples, whether they are allowed to be visitors, whether they could be members, or whether they could participate in ministries in the church?

13. Could you envision an "agree to disagree" arrangement? All parties would recognize that this is an enormously controversial topic. The affirming Christians would respect that the vast majority of marriage is defined by "one man, one woman," and that most within the congregation believe that remarriage is the only appropriate exception to "one man, one woman." This "agree to disagree" arrangement would respect the core, foundational theology of the church and its definition of marriage, with the one caveat that we simply agree not to reject gay Christians from our local church family, as we continue to ask God to bring us into agreement on the topic. We will heed Paul's advice to accept one another, just as Christ has accepted us. (Romans 15:7)

14. If you find yourself firmly in category e, f, or g, non-affirming (and possibly non-accepting) of gay Christians, what if you are wrong? Many advocates of slavery held firmly to very popular positions; their legacies are shameful to their families and the institutions they represented. If even the mere possibility exists that just one same-gender relationship is blessed by God, then would you want to be on the side of rejecting gay Christians?

Christ has not rejected us; why should His Church? I firmly believe that it is God's heart that the local churches open wide their doors and ministries to gay Christians and openly renounce the rejection of this group of God's beloved children.

A word of the Lord, spoken by a brother at our church on March 21, 2019:

> Rise, rise up, see what you're doing here on the earth. This is a house where the Lord is already intricately positioning those I've launched out of darkness into My marvelous light. I'm strategically aligning you. Understand that which I am doing. It's the Lord's doing. It's not of the enemy. It's the Lord's doing. I am building. I am constructing. I am shutting the mouth of the lion. I am dispensing with the accuser of the brethren. It is I that's doing it, says the Lord. It is the Lord's doing. And there is coming a season in this house where a united people of God shall shout in one voice, it is marvelous in our sight. It is the Lord's doing. It is marvelous. He desires to passionately hover upon His people, and draw us, draw us, into a oneness and a uniqueness that cannot be broken. A house divided against itself cannot stand. But there is a uniting coming

in this house that the enemies will see and fear, and trust in the song of the Lord that's rising out of this house. I'm building homes today. I'm restoring families today. I am the God Who is able to do exceedingly, above all that you ask or believe. He is able. Trust in the Lord your God and enter into the beauty that is of your God and see, come and see, that the Lord desires to passionately do it in this season.

APPENDIX B

THE BAPTISM IN THE HOLY SPIRIT

1. What is the baptism in the Holy Spirit?
   a. You will receive power when the Holy Spirit comes upon you.
   b. Tongues, a prayer language
2. Every believer receives the Holy Spirit the moment the believer puts his trust in Christ.
3. The baptism in the Holy Spirit is different than the infilling of the Holy Spirit at salvation.
   a. The believers in Ephesus in Acts 19
   b. The believers in Samaria in Acts 8
   c. Apollos in Acts 18
4. Why tongues?
   a. The Holy Spirit's perfect prayer
   b. Evidence of the baptism in the Holy Spirit
5. Diversity of tongues
   a. Tongues as a sign for unbelievers, as was seen on the day of Pentecost
   b. Tongues in the assembly of believers, one of the nine gifts of the Holy Spirit
   c. Prayer language, which is available to all believers

6. Why would I want to be baptized in the Holy Spirit and speak in tongues?
   a. Benefits of using one's prayer language
   b. Twelve scriptural reasons to pray in the Spirit regularly
7. Can I receive the baptism in the Holy Spirit and not speak in tongues?
8. Tongues as a message for the assembly of believers
   a. Tongues and interpretation in the church service
   b. This is distinct from one's prayer language.
9. Anticipated objections
   a. Tongues went out with the apostles.
   b. My mind is unfruitful.
   c. Tongues is a sign for unbelievers.
   d. Do all speak with tongues?
   e. I am new in the faith, and this is for mature Christians.
   f. Speaking in tongues simply means knowing a foreign language.
10. How to receive the baptism in the Holy Spirit
11. Interesting study
    a. Published by researchers at the University of Pennsylvania
    b. Titled, Speaking in Tongues: Medical Study Proves Holy Spirit Praying
12. My testimony

1. What is the baptism in the Holy Spirit?

The baptism in the Holy Spirit is a gift, freely given to Christian believers who choose to receive it. Jesus told His disciples, "you will receive power when the Holy Spirit comes on you." (Acts 1:8) This word *power* in the Greek is *dunamis*; it is the root from which we get the word "dynamite." It is the same word in this phrase from Ephesians 3:20: "Now to Him Who is able to do immeasurably more than all we ask or imagine, according to His power [*dunamis*] that is at work within us...." His power at work within us comes through the Holy Spirit.

The baptism in the Holy Spirit is also accompanied by a "prayer language" or the ability to pray in tongues, as the Holy Spirit gives utterance. In other words, the Holy Spirit puts in the believer the utterance, and the believer thus speaks an unknown language, from his spirit, fully surrendering to the will of the Holy Spirit. The believer can thus pray God's perfect prayer, not his own, often flawed, prayer. "For we do not know what we ought to pray for, but the Spirit Himself intercedes for us...." (Romans 8:26)

The baptism in the Holy Spirit is different than water baptism. In Acts 1:5, the risen Christ said to the disciples, "For John baptized with water, but in a few days you will be baptized with the Holy Spirit."

On the day of Pentecost (50 days after Passover, which occurred the weekend of Christ's crucifixion), suddenly a sound like the blowing of a violent wind came from heaven and filled the whole house. What appeared to be tongues of fire came to rest on each of those present. All of them were filled with the Holy Spirit and began to speak in other languages, as the Spirit enabled them. There were God-fearing Jews there in Jerusalem from all over the known world for the festival of Pentecost. They heard the Galileans, who wouldn't know other languages, speaking in their native languages. (Acts 2:1-6)

In Matthew 3:11, John the Baptist said, "I baptize you with water for repentance. But after me comes One Who is more powerful than I, Whose sandals I am not worthy to carry. He will baptize you with the Holy Spirit and fire."

Baptism in water is done by man; baptism in the Holy Spirit is done by God. In the Bible, it is often seen following the laying on of hands of the apostles. However, that is not always the case. Cornelius and his family received the baptism in the Holy Spirit without the laying on of hands, for example.

In Acts 19:1-7, Paul came across some believers in Ephesus; they were Christians. Paul asked them, "have you received the Holy Spirit?" The people said, no, that they had not heard of the Holy Spirit. Paul said, "what baptism did you receive?" They said that they had received John's baptism of repentance. When Paul laid his hands on them, the Holy Spirit came on them, and they began to speak in tongues.

2. Every believer receives the Holy Spirit the moment the believer puts his trust in Christ.

To put one's trust in Christ is to believe and receive the gospel, "that Christ died for our sins... that He was buried... and that He was raised on the third day...." (I Corinthians 15:3-4) Every believer receives the Holy Spirit when they become a Christian, regardless of whether that person ever experiences the baptism in the Holy Spirit or ever prays in an unknown tongue.

At the moment of salvation, the Holy Spirit is deposited into the believer's spirit. We are thus guided from within, by the Holy Spirit, to the extent that we allow His guidance in our everyday lives. This is how we live out our lives, being guided and supported by the Holy Spirit, such that we are continually being sanctified. This is true for every believer, whether someone is baptized in the Holy Spirit or whether they have a prayer language or not. (Again, it is important to realize that this guidance comes only to the extent that we surrender every aspect of our lives to the will of God.)

Ephesians 1:13b-14 says, "When you believed, you were marked in Him with a seal, the promised Holy Spirit, Who is a deposit guaranteeing our inheritance until the redemption of those who are God's possession--to the praise of His glory."

I John 2:27 (The Living Bible, 1971): "But you have received the Holy Spirit, and He lives within you, in your hearts, so that you don't need anyone to teach you what is right. For He teaches you all things, and He is the Truth, and no liar."

In John 14:26, Jesus said, "But the Advocate, the Holy Spirit, whom the Father will send in My Name, will teach you all things and will remind you of everything I have said to you."

3. The baptism in the Holy Spirit is different than the infilling of the Holy Spirit at salvation.

We saw this with Paul and the believers in Ephesus, noted above, in Acts 19. They were believers in the gospel but had not yet experienced the baptism in the Holy Spirit until Paul preached it to them.

Another example is in Acts 8:14-19.

> When the apostles in Jerusalem heard that Samaria had accepted the Word of God, they sent Peter and John to Samaria. When they arrived, they prayed for the new believers there that they might receive the Holy Spirit, because the Holy Spirit had not yet come on any of them; they had simply been baptized in the name of the Lord Jesus. Then Peter and John placed their hands on them, and they received the Holy Spirit.

It was obvious to Simon the sorcerer that they had received the Holy Spirit, because he offered them money for the power to lay hands on people. What was the sign that they had received the Holy Spirit, that Simon wanted? It doesn't say in this particular instance, but in many others, it shows that the sign is that the people speak in tongues, or other languages, as evidence of the baptism in the Holy Spirit.

In Acts 18, a Jew named Apollos came to Ephesus to teach "burning with spiritual zeal." (Acts 18:25, AMP) The Scripture says that he taught about Jesus, "though he was acquainted only with the baptism of John." Priscilla and Aquila, Paul's close friends (with whom he made tents in Corinth), took Apollos aside after one of his messages "and expounded to him the way of God more definitely and accurately."

I believe that at this point, Priscilla and Aquila explained to Apollos about the baptism in the Holy Spirit. The text does not say this specifically. However, it does indicate that he was only acquainted with John's baptism. Elsewhere in Acts, that was the response when believers who had not received the baptism in the Holy Spirit were asked what baptism they were familiar with. I believe that Apollos was baptized in the Holy Spirit after that discussion with Priscilla and Aquila, because then the scripture records, "For *with great power* he refuted the Jews in public discussions, showing and proving by the Scriptures that Jesus is the Christ." (Acts 18:28, AMP, emphasis mine) Earlier, when the risen Christ had told the apostles to wait for the Holy Spirit, in Acts 1:8, Jesus said, "you will receive *power* when the Holy Spirit comes on you; and you will be My witnesses."

4. Why tongues?

God wants to put the perfect prayer into the believer's spirit to speak out loud. However, if He did so in a known language, we would be at risk of altering it. I may pray that God gives me the top position in my company, but God may have a very different plan. If I pray in tongues, I am praying His will, not my own. When I pray in my language, my prayer may be flawed because I am flawed.

I Corinthians 14:2 states, "For anyone who speaks in a tongue does not speak to people but to God."

Acts 2:4: "All of them were filled with the Holy Spirit and began to speak in other tongues, as the Spirit enabled them."

The Bible teaches that when we are baptized in the Holy Spirit we will speak in tongues as evidence. In Acts 10:45, the Jews with Peter were amazed to see that the gift of the Spirit had been given to the Gentiles (Cornelius and his family). But how did they know? Acts 10:46, because... "they heard them speaking in tongues and praising God." Tongues is the evidence.

God instructed us: Ephesians 6:18, "Pray in the Spirit on all occasions." Jude 1:20, "building yourselves up in your most holy faith and praying in the Holy Spirit, keep yourselves in God's love."

What is praying in the Holy Spirit? Paul answers this in I Corinthians 14:15 by differentiating between praying in the spirit and praying in his known language. Paul states (in the NIV), "I will pray with my spirit, but I will also pray with my understanding." Thus, praying in the spirit is distinct from praying with one's understanding. The New Living Translation says, "I will pray in the spirit, and I will also pray in words I understand."

Paul said, "I will sing with my spirit, but I will also sing with my understanding." (I Corinthians 14:15)

Mark 16:17, "And these signs shall accompany those who believe... they will speak in new tongues."

One may wonder if their prayer language is a known language on earth. It actually may be an angelic language. I Corinthians 13:1 says, "If I speak in the tongues of men or of angels...."

Importantly, people frequently will describe this as an ecstatic, emotional state. That is not the case typically. Some people may choose to speak in tongues loudly, but there is no reason to do so. The believer who speaks in tongues does so at will, at his own volume, rate, and pitch. There is nothing overcoming the believer's will with regard to this gift. One can speak in tongues at will and stop and speak in his language, freely.

It is absolutely not a matter of salvation, and there should never be any condemnation for a believer based on whether they have a prayer language or not.

5. Diversity of tongues

I Corinthians 12:10 refers to "diverse kinds of tongues." In other words, speaking in tongues has various manifestations and purposes.

A. Tongues as a sign for unbelievers - I Corinthians 14:22: The best example of tongues as a sign for unbelievers is in Acts 2 on the day of Pentecost, when Jews from all over the known world heard the Galileans speaking in their own language (languages the Galileans did not know). In I Corinthians 14, Paul quotes from Isaiah 28:11-12 in which Isaiah prophesied that "with foreign lips and strange tongues God will speak to this people." That is exactly what happened on that first Pentecost following the resurrection. In the letter of I

Corinthians, Paul was addressing the believers in Corinth. His intention was to clarify the diversities of tongues and encourage the believers to use the gift of tongues appropriately in order to edify each other. Speaking in tongues without an interpreter would not be appropriate in the assembly of believers, because no one would understand. However, it was appropriate, for example, at that first Pentecost, as a sign to the unbelievers.

B. Tongues in the assembly of believers: In I Corinthians 12, Paul explains the gifts specifically for use in the church, to edify believers. For this type of tongues, it is appropriate only when an interpreter is present. Otherwise, the congregation will not understand what is spoken. I address this in more detail below, in section 8.

C. Prayer language: This is the manifestation of the baptism in the Holy Spirit and is available to all believers. When Paul and Jude write, "pray in the Spirit," they were referring to the supernatural prayer language that is spoken by the believer as the Spirit gives utterance. This is available at all times to believers who receive the baptism in the Holy Spirit. This encompasses all types of prayer, including intercessory prayer for others, as the Spirit wills.

6. Why would I want to be baptized in the Holy Spirit and speak in tongues?

A. God instructed us to pray in the Spirit in Ephesians 6:18 and Jude 1:20.

B. Ephesians 6:18: "And pray in the Spirit on all occasions with all kinds of prayers and requests." In Ephesians 6, Paul discusses putting on the full armor of God to withstand the enemy. The final two pieces of the armor are the Word of God and praying in the Spirit.

C. Jude 1:20-21: "But you, dear friends, by building yourselves up in your most holy faith and praying in the Holy Spirit, keep yourselves in God's love...."

D. Tongues edifies us. I Corinthians 14:4: "Anyone who speaks in a tongue edifies themselves."

E. It builds us up and stimulates our faith. Jude 20.

F. For praising God. Acts 10:46: "For they heard them speaking in tongues and praising God."

G. The Spirit helps us to pray in this way. Romans 8:26 (NLT): "And the Holy Spirit helps us in our weakness. For example, we don't know what God wants us to pray for. But the Holy Spirit prays for us with groanings that cannot be expressed in words."

H. Paul said he wished everyone spoke in tongues. I Corinthians 14:5: "I would like every one of you to speak in tongues," (however, not out loud in church without an interpreter).

I. Jesus, after His resurrection, said in Acts 1:8, "You will receive power when the Spirit comes upon you, and you will be My witnesses."

J. Acts 1:4-5: Jesus told His disciples not to leave Jerusalem until they had received the baptism with the Holy Spirit.

K. I Corinthians 14:16-17 says that praying in the spirit[295] is a way of offering thanksgiving to God.

L. Paul said to the church at Corinth, "I thank God that I speak in tongues more than all of you." (I Corinthians 14:18.) This was clearly an important aspect of Paul's life.

M. The baptism in the Holy Spirit was not available to anyone under the old covenant or in the Old Testament. Having the indwelling of the Holy Spirit required Jesus's perfect, sinless life and His sacrifice at the cross, in other words, atonement

---

[295] Some translations capitalize Spirit and some do not. www.BibleHub.com. The prayer of the Holy Spirit is accomplished through the spirit of the believer. Thus, with regard to praying in tongues, praying in one's spirit is equivalent to praying in the Holy Spirit.

for sin, before the Father could send the Holy Spirit to dwell in man. Jesus told the apostles not to leave Jerusalem until they were baptized in the Holy Spirit. This is powerful. This is available to us.

N. Praying in the Spirit is a powerful way to fight the enemy, as Paul demonstrated in the sixth chapter of Ephesians.

7. Can I receive the baptism in the Holy Spirit and not speak in tongues?

The recipient of the gift of the baptism in the Holy Spirit, in general, will speak in tongues as the Holy Spirit gives utterance to the believer. God does not speak in tongues through someone. The utterance is made available by God, but the believer must choose to speak.

The baptism in the Holy Spirit is a gift, freely given, to any believer who chooses to receive. This implies an action on the part of the recipient. Importantly, we need not fear receiving something counterfeit or false. Jesus specifically addressed this in Luke 11:13, "How much more will your Father in heaven give the Holy Spirit to those who ask Him!" All we must do is ask in faith.

Some believers are just too afraid (or hindered in some other way) to proceed with vocalizing the utterance initially. Many believers, even those who initially receive a prayer language, may go years and years without praying in the Spirit. It certainly is a believer's choice. Some do not realize that it is an ongoing gift that is available. Just like a muscle, the more one uses his prayer language, the stronger and more comfortable the believer becomes with this powerful and edifying gift.

Perhaps a believer could be baptized in the Holy Spirit without an ongoing (or even initial) evidence of speaking in tongues. However, it may be that the daily ongoing power of the baptism in the Holy Spirit is in the prayer language. All believers receive power with the baptism in the Holy Spirit, and that may not be directly tied to one's prayer language. However, the edification, the Spirit's help in praying for us, the building up of our faith, are all direct consequences of faithfully praying in one's prayer language.

Again, it is not necessary for salvation. But it is a gift that is offered and was so important to the apostles, that they made sure all new believers understood and received this gift. Jesus did not allow His apostles to leave Jerusalem without receiving this powerful gift.

8. Tongues as a message for the assembly of believers

As discussed briefly above, the Bible refers to "diversity of tongues" in I Corinthians 12:10. There is another type of the gift of tongues, distinct from the prayer language and distinct from tongues as a sign for unbelievers, that is given to a select few. In I Corinthians 12, Paul lists the nine gifts of the Spirit that are given to believers for the edification of the local church body. Those nine gifts are healing, words of prophecy, knowledge, and wisdom, working of miracles, the gift of faith, discerning of spirits, and the gifts of tongues and of interpretation. These operate in the assembly, specifically to edify the body of believers.

There is no benefit to believers in an assembly, in general, for someone to speak in their prayer language out loud without the gift of interpretation. In the church in Corinth, believers would speak in tongues out loud in the church, enjoying this great gift, but not using it appropriately. Paul said,

> When you are praising God in the spirit, how can someone else, who is now put in the position of an

inquirer, say 'amen' to your thanksgiving, since they
do not know what you are saying? You are giving
thanks well enough, but no one else is edified. (I
Corinthians 14:16-17)

One who speaks in tongues as a prayer language does not pray loudly
in the church because there is no benefit to the believers. However,
there may be a situation when God gives an utterance in tongues
specifically for the body of believers to be edified. In that case, it
is only given if that person also has the gift of interpretation, or if
there is another in the assembly with the gift to interpret. (And how
they both know is a spiritual mystery. Sometimes someone will pray
loudly in tongues, and then when it is over, you can hear a pin drop;
several seconds pass, but inevitably, someone from somewhere else
in the congregation will call out the interpretation to the message.
Sometimes the person who delivers the message in tongues interprets
it him/herself right away.)

Thus, among the assembly of believers, the gift of tongues and
interpretation is given for the edification of the assembly. This is
distinct from any given believer's prayer language.

Paul spends a considerable amount of time explaining the gifts
because it is clear that the situation in that early church in Corinth
was a bit chaotic. The believers were so proud to be speaking in
tongues that they did so inappropriately. Paul had to clarify the
purpose of one's prayer language versus tongues for the edification
of the assembly. At the end of I Corinthians 12, he explains that
there are various gifts, but they are given selectively. He writes,
"Do all work miracles? Do all have gifts of healing? Do all speak in
tongues? Do all interpret?" He is referencing four of the nine gifts
of the Spirit for the assembly. In this situation, he is not referring to
a prayer language.

9. Anticipated objections

A. Tongues went out with the apostles.
    a. I Corinthians 13:8 says that prophecy, tongues, and knowledge will cease when perfection comes, that is, when Christ returns. None of these has ceased yet.
    b. Paul wrote in Ephesians 6 to put on the full armor of God, and then, "pray in the Spirit on all occasions." Again, Jude 1:20 also commanded us to pray in the Spirit.
B. Paul wrote (I Corinthians 14:14): "If I pray in a tongue, my spirit prays, but my mind is unfruitful." He answers this, "I will pray with my spirit, but I will also pray with my understanding. I will sing with my spirit, but I will also sing with my understanding." Also, though the mind is unfruitful, the believer is edified. (I Corinthians 14:4)
C. "Tongues is a sign for unbelievers." (I Corinthians 14:22) This is one of the various manifestations of tongues, distinct from the prayer language. The best example of this is from Acts 2, the first Pentecost following the resurrection of Christ.
D. "Do all speak with tongues?" (I Corinthians 12:30) As explained above, Paul was referring to the gifts of the Spirit given for the edification of the assembly. In that regard, only a select few have the gift of tongues, or of interpretation, or of prophecy, or of any one of the nine gifts. This is distinct from the prayer language, which is available to all believers.
E. "I am new in the faith, and this is for mature Christians." As soon as people became believers in the book of Acts, the apostles made sure that the new believers received the gift of the baptism in the Holy Spirit because this is the way to grow in the Christian faith. Jesus said, "you will receive power when the Spirit comes on you." (Acts 1:8) It is by the Holy Spirit that we are led into all truth and in the operation of the gifts of the Spirit. It was vital to the new believers in Acts, and it is no less important today.

F.   Some Christians believe that there are no longer manifestations of miracles. To downplay speaking in tongues, they will point out that "speaking in tongues" simply means speaking "in another language." One preacher stated that when Paul wrote, "I thank my God that I speak in tongues more than you all," that he was simply saying that he was thankful that he knew several languages. The problem with this interpretation is I Corinthians 14:15, in which Paul states, "I will pray with my spirit; I will also pray with my understanding." If Paul were simply praying in another language that he knew, it would be a prayer of his understanding. Thus, there is a prayer that Paul himself prayed and did not understand.

10. How to receive the baptism in the Holy Spirit

The most important thing about any request of God is what the Word says about it. Having studied the baptism in the Holy Spirit according to the Scripture, the believer can understand by faith and study that the baptism in the Holy Spirit is a gift, and anyone who professes belief in the atoning work of Christ on the cross qualifies for the gift.

Some have said, "I am open to this gift if God wants to give it to me." I can assure you that God wants you to have it. The Holy Spirit, through the author of Hebrews, said that God is a rewarder of those who diligently seek Him. If one chooses to simply wait instead of diligently seeking this gift, it will delay or prevent receiving. God is honored when His children receive this gift. He wants us to give the Holy Spirit full reign in our lives. This is an important step in that direction.

Ephesians 5:18 (AMP) states, "Do not be drunk with wine..., but ever be filled and stimulated with the Holy Spirit." Some like to translate the Greek tense of this verb as "be ever being filled" with the Holy Spirit. It is an ongoing infilling of the Spirit that is an action taken by the believer. We are to seek the Holy Spirit's infilling repeatedly, so as to be under His influence, as illustrated by the way one would drink wine and be under its influence.

My pastor recently said, "I think sometimes we need to go into a room and say, 'God, I'm not leaving this room until I hear from You.'" Plan time to be in a private place, and come to God as you usually do, with thanksgiving and praise. Let Him know that you earnestly seek Him and request to be baptized in the Holy Spirit with evidence of speaking in tongues. Understand that you have to vocalize the utterance. The Holy Spirit will prompt you. Speak as you feel led, knowing that it is not unusual at all to feel inhibited initially as you speak in tongues. After you begin, just trust in God. Continue to pray in the Spirit. Once you have a prayer language, it is available at any time. Use it every single day. When you go into your room expecting to be baptized in the Spirit and earnestly request this gift of God, if you do not immediately receive your prayer language, then don't get discouraged. Return the following day with the same request. By faith you can remind the Lord Jesus of His promise, "If you then, though you are evil know how to give good gifts to your children, how much more will your Father in heaven give the Holy Spirit to those who ask Him!" (Luke 11:13) If, after some time, you are not able to receive your prayer language, allow one of the leaders of your church to lay hands on you and pray to receive. If you do not belong to a church that believes in the baptism in the Holy Spirit, stay in faith until you receive your prayer language.

11. Interesting study

There was an interesting study published by researchers at the University of Pennsylvania, in which they performed MRI scans on believers while the believers were speaking in tongues. They concluded that the speech center of the brain is not at work, and therefore the language is not being produced by the individual. The article is titled, Speaking in Tongues; Medical Study Proves Holy Spirit Praying. The link to the ABC newscast is available on YouTube at the following link: https://www.youtube.com/watch?v=NZbQBajYnEc.

12. My testimony

When I was 15, my pastor taught on the baptism in the Holy Spirit at Sunday evening church. Many people went forward and received the baptism in the Spirit with the evidence of speaking in tongues. I did not go forward, but I went home and sat on the floor in my bedroom that evening and asked the Lord for this gift. I received the gift and spoke in tongues quietly. Over time, I developed my prayer language. I strayed from the faith in my 20s and did not use my prayer language until I returned to a close relationship with the Lord 19 years later. When I began to pray in the spirit again, I prayed only a few syllables. After some weeks, I asked God if He wanted me to continue to pray like that, as I was repeating the same prayer. God said into my spirit, you keep praying by faith; I am in charge of your prayer language. So I kept praying what was available by faith. In a short amount of time, within weeks, it became a language. At some point, it becomes very easy for those who use this gift regularly. For some people it can be difficult, especially initially, and should, in my opinion, be diligently practiced by faith, daily. When this gift is available, it is so powerful to be able to pray the perfect prayer, even the perfect intercession for others. It is a constant reminder that the Holy Spirit dwells in us, and that we are not living a life from one crisis to the next, but rather, being guided by Him daily, from faith to faith.

APPENDIX C

SECRET APPENDIX

This is a little essay from my heart, unencumbered by apparent societal rules that should be observed within a publishable book. It is basically an unpolished overview of the whole book from a different angle, that is, the newly affirming traditionalists, in the future.

I do not know God's plan or His timing. I believe that we will soon see mainstream churches become affirming. I honestly imagine staunch traditionalists changing their minds on this, beginning with an "agree to disagree" arrangement. This ongoing rejection of LGBTQ people just cannot continue. Once we have agreed to disagree, we'll recognize that the rejection was wrong from the beginning. I think we'll just agree not long thereafter. (Of course, that's certainly because I think I'm right. I don't mean to diminish the monumentally controversial nature of this topic.)

There are things that really could not be said in this book. Thus, I have created this secret appendix that only a few will ever find.

When we look back on this years from now, as we look back on slavery today, we will question how this happened. It started with the medico-scientific establishment, which determined the gays to be broken, sick, and perverted. The media agreed and shared this sentiment. This widespread understanding led to the mistranslation of I Corinthians 6:9, which led to the mistranslation of I Timothy 1:10. Once we convinced ourselves that "homosexuals will never enter the kingdom of God," we realized, obviously, that Sodom and Gomorrah and the Levitical prohibitions reflected God's view of the gays. Romans chapter one was obviously about the gays. Being gay was so detestable that gay people also hated God. (See what we did there.) Well, since the gays were so condemned in Scripture, every marriage is clearly only between one man and one woman. I mean, look around! We're all, in our little church, paired up as male and female. Anything outside of that is clearly an abomination. Just look at how the sun rises and the sun sets. My goodness, flowers bloom, and bees pollinate the flowers. Male kitty cats are interested in female kitty cats. I mean, just look at nature. All you really need is nature to know that being gay is a sin.

From the time the RSV came on the scene, multiple translators translated. Once the notion was set in place, no one was touching that with a ten foot pole. We won't know until Kathy and Ed's book is out later this year, but I have an idea that translation committees steered very clear of altering Dr. Luther Weigle's initial plan of adding "homosexuals." And why, oh why, didn't Dr. Weigle write an editorial to his local newspaper to right that wrong? I understand his great grandson is affirming. That's really beautiful, and I am thankful to have learned it (from Ed Oxford).

Traditionalists want so badly to hold on to the idea that there really are not people that are different than straight people. They want to believe that that group of people is just confused, that we are really all the same, that we all have the capacity to be straight, but some just have a greater affinity for sinfulness than others. Christ has conquered sin. Thus, there's no real need to refer to a group as gay, or for a given Christian to refer to himself as gay. However, the idea is simply indefensible. We can no longer deny that there are gay people both outside of and within the church. It's just unsupportable to pretend that these are not actual people, regardless of whether you refer to them as same-sex attracted, gay, reprobate, confused, or abominable. It doesn't matter. There are people like this who were actually (as Jesus put it) born that way. Gay people are real.

Later, on the other side of this, being gay will just be a normal variant, as Freud determined in his latter years. It will be as if one is left-handed or right-handed. LGBTQ people will just be people, beautiful people, that are allowed to live, work, and enjoy all the same rights that straight people do. They'll be celebrated and loved. They'll find intimate love and companionship in their communities. They'll marry. Many of them, including those who know Christ and walk in His way, will observe chastity in singleness and monogamy in marriage. Churches will welcome them with wide open arms and love the diversity and creativity they bring to the table.

I visited the Legacy Museum in Montgomery, Alabama in January 2019. While at the museum, I attempted to look at slavery from the perspective of the descendants of the slaves. But I was afraid of how angry that perspective would make me. Worse, I just couldn't do it. I was never able to move beyond the powerful emotions and feelings that I had as a descendant. I mean, I was raised in Alabama. I am... I have difficulty even writing this... I am surely a descendant of slave holders. Obviously, we look back now and have strong sentiments of shame and anger towards our own people who, in their pride and their greed, esteemed our beautiful African American brothers and sisters to be less than us. What a horrifying thought. Talk about "wickedness, evil, greed, and depravity"...

One day soon, rejection of LGBTQ people will be a distant memory. Our grandkids will write senior term papers on this topic. Just as we now look back on slavery, they'll look back on all of this. They'll see Scripture and related things a little differently than we do today.

The following 21 points are from the future, after LGBTQ people are accepted in society and in churches as just as beautiful, loved, respected, and sinless/sinful as straight people. "We" refers to the newly affirming people, looking back at their non-affirming beliefs and their family members, recognizing honestly that their parents, grandparents, and older siblings meant well, but ... what were we thinking!

- Romans 1 described straight people engaging in all manner of promiscuity and wild sexual activity. "They" never referred to gay people; "they" always meant idol worshipers. We're grieved that we ever compared the activity of pagan idol worshipers to our Christian gay friends. How degrading.
- Sodom and Gomorrah was about gang rape. What were we thinking, equating that story to gay couples? Seriously. We should be ashamed.
- The practice of converting any use of "Sodom and Gomorrah" in Scripture to condemn gay people—God, forgive us. That was wrong. That was blatant, egregious, and inexcusable.
- Leviticus was about pederasty, patriarchy, and procreation. The new covenant made that old covenant obsolete. Leviticus was *never* an issue for Christians.
- I Corinthians 6:9-11 and I Timothy 1:9-10 always referred to sexual abuse by means of a power differential. That one mistake back in 1946 threw us off for decades. And somehow we then backtracked and declared that the verses had referred to being gay for the previous 2,000 years.
- How did we miss it when Galatians 3:28 was right there in black and white: "There is neither Jew nor Gentile, neither slave nor free, nor is there male and female, for you are all one in Christ Jesus." There was no distinction before God between Jew and Gentile. Thus a Christian Jew could marry a Christian Gentile, even though the Mosaic law forbade it.

In Christ there is no distinction between male and female. Wait, why did that not solve this issue years ago?! We just assumed it couldn't possibly be true. We greatly preferred quoting "male and female He made them" to "nor is there male and female." 1,000:1.

- Ex-gay ministries failed because gay people's brains are just wired differently. Gay orientation is just a natural, normal variant.

- When God told Peter not to call any man impure or unclean, that was meant for Christians to take to heart as well. What were we thinking kicking gay people out of our churches? We forgot about this story from Acts. We thought the gays were impure and unclean. We thought they brought sin and shame into our clean, Bible-believing church. Yikes.

- We always said that Jesus defined marriage in Matthew 19. Case closed. But that's only because we stopped reading at the end of verse 6. Thereafter, Jesus Himself pointed out that some people would not fit into the creation story model of one man, one woman. Why were we so afraid to consider that openly back when the LGBTQ crowd was being rejected from our churches?

- When kids come out as gay, we used to think it meant that they had chosen some wicked, sinful path. On the other side of all this, when a kid comes out as gay, it just means, they realize they're gay, and they actually need to tell some people. No more clobbering people over the head with nonsense like, "What disgrace you bring to this family!"

- No more shame. What were we thinking shaming people! My goodness, people were committing suicide, and the church couldn't even help them! Pastor Clay Peck quoted a statistic, the reference for which I cannot find: "Teens who are experiencing same sex attraction and come to a religious leader for council are more likely to commit suicide than if they didn't." (Read that quote again. Church, you'll do anything to save the life of the unborn, and appropriately so. But there are also living lives you could be saving. Stop with this "chosen, wicked lifestyle" nonsense! These are *people*.)

- Back in 2018, statistics revealed that "68% of church-going men and over 50% of pastors viewed porn on a regular basis."[296] These Christian men were justified by Christ's atoning blood even if they were habitually practicing sin. But imagine this: a gay Christian couple (picture two Christian women, passionate about serving Jesus) could have been forbidden membership in a church whose pastor was addicted to porn, along with 68% of the men in the congregation. What hypocrisy. How did the church justify it? Why was the church's own porn addiction forgivable, but someone else's homosexuality unforgivable? Because everyone agreed that the porn addict was sinning. Thus, the man who was consciously sinning in his periodic porn habit was justified by Christ's atoning blood, because he agreed he was consciously sinning. But the gay Christian couple was not forgiven because they did not believe they were living in sin. That's almost laughable if it weren't so sad.

- HOW COULD WE HAVE DONE THIS? Paul explained it succinctly: Our consciences had been seared as with a hot iron.

- Remember the next sentence? Those people whose consciences had been seared as with a hot iron forbade people to marry. Ouch. That was us, non-affirming traditionalists, completely convinced that gay marriage was straight from the devil.

- Honestly, we thought we were right. We thought being gay was an affront to God and His design. We forgot that God Himself made these people. We thought the eunuchs in Matthew 19 were metaphors. We thought the two men in

---

[296] TruNews Team. (2018 September 19). "15 Stunning Statistics about Porn in the Church". Retrieved October 5, 2019 from www.TruNews.com.

one bed at night in Luke 17:34 was a cultural thing where there are men somewhere out East who share beds? Wait, what did we think that meant?

- Speaking of, why did translators refuse to translate Luke 17:34 correctly? Shouldn't they have translated the passage correctly and let the chips fall where they may? My goodness, I would be scared to be on the committee that changed something Jesus said. I can understand the need for clarification in translation, but I believe that every word in Scripture is important. Jesus said two men, one bed, nighttime. Translators, we're at your mercy. Please just translate it.

- Had we forgotten, "do unto others as you would have them do unto you"? What about "accept one another then, just as Christ accepted you"? And "love your neighbor as yourself"? We got sidetracked, thinking we had to warn gay people that being gay upset You, God. We were promoting purity in Your kingdom. We were making sure not to fill up the field with weeds. We were doing the weeding for You! Honestly, we thought we were right. We're so sorry we hurt people. We're so sorry if we ever steered anyone away from You. God forbid. God forgive us. God save them.

- The two couples in Luke 17:34-5 really may have just been two gay couples. Jesus certainly was not unaware that gay couples would eventually show up in our churches.

- The natural-born eunuchs Jesus was talking about were just gay people. (Sandy Turnbull knew that years ago. If that doesn't make sense to you, please read her book.)

- Jesus really did tiptoe into the eunuch topic: "Not everyone is going to get this...." And that third category of eunuchs? Those are the hardcore Jesus-serving LGBTQ Christians who have dedicated their lives to the kingdom of God. (Again, Turnbull figured that out first.)

- LGBTQ really is a kind, loving way to refer to queer people. Trans people are beautiful and were just as fearfully and wonderfully made in God's image as the straightest person ever known. God adores all LGBTQ people. Truly, He gushes over them.

- We think back with misery at the idea that we told people, "We love you, but we hate your sin"—your sin of *being gay.*

Thus, the secret appendix. These are things we won't be able to say until years from now, when gay people are just other kinds of normal people, welcome in the church as much as straight people are.

God, from my heart, thank You for allowing me to write this book. Please use it in any way that brings You glory. If I have erred, please God, use it as firewood. I want only to honor You in my life.

I pray for the person who is reading these words right now. Lord, let us, the reader and me, come into agreement with Your heart on this matter. Please reveal Your perfect will to us. We are asking in faith that this matter be settled in our churches so that You get all the honor. We want to come into unity with Your heart and Your plan. We want to bring You pleasure and joy by being full of love for You and for all the beautiful people You have created. Forgive us, God, all of us who have made mistakes on this issue. Forgive those who have rejected LGBTQ people, those who have looked sideways at them and judged them, those who have flat out condemned them for just being different. God, forgive those of us who have judged the traditionalists, who have called them haters for holding to their convictions. God, we're all wrong on this in various ways. Please Lord, right these wrongs for us in Jesus's name. Let us come into unity and agreement just as our Lord Jesus prayed we would. Earnestly we seek You, God. All of our faith and hope are in You.

I trust that my reader won't tell anyone about the secret appendix. Please email me if you made it this far. Did you really read this whole book? I owe you a coffee. IamIncludedinChrist@gmail.com

REFERENCE LIST

Airhart, M. (2009 August 6). "Ex-Gay Researcher Mark Yarhouse Reacts to Repudiation by Psychologists". Retrieved December 2019 from www.TruthWinsOut.org.

Allen, J. (1999 February 11). "Sex doctor David Reuben is back with some new advice". Retrieved September 2018 from www.cnn.com.

Anderson, C. (2019 November 9). "Why the #metoo movement matters for LGBTQ inclusion in the Church". Talk presented at Reconcile and Reform Conference, The Reformation Project, Seattle, Washington. https://www.facebook.com/ReformationProject/videos/464487600847246/, beginning at 1:02:47 into the video.

Ashton, K. (undated). "Survivor Narrative". Retrieved September 2018 from https://BeyondExGay.com.

Associated Press. (2019 May 29). "Maine governor OKs ban on gay conversion therapy for minors". Retrieved May 31, 2019 from www.apnews.com.

Baldock, K. (2019 March 26). "How the Bible Became Anti-Gay: Forging a Sacred Weapon". Retrieved May 2019 from CanyonWalkerConnections.com.

Baldock, K. (2019 June 13). "The word 'homosexual' in the 1946 RSV Bible – a moral wrong based on a factual error". Retrieved June 2019 from CanyonWalkerConnections.com.

Baldock, Kathy. (2014). *Walking the Bridgeless Canyon: Repairing the breach between the Church and the LGBT Community*. Reno, NV: Canyonwalker Press.

Baldock, K. (2019 August 7). "Where Does Christian Anti-LGBTQ Ideology Come From?" Retrieved December 2019 from www. CanyonWalkerConnections.com.

Baldock, K. & Schneider, Y. (2015). "The History of Cultural and Religious Discrimination against the LGBT Community in America". Webinar series. Retrieved October 2019 from www. SistersofThunder.org.

Barker, K. (1985). "Galatians 3:1". *The NIV Study Bible.* Grand Rapids, MI: Zondervan, page 1783.

Barker, K. (1985). "Introduction to I Corinthians: Its immorality" *The NIV Study Bible*, Grand Rapids, MI: Zondervan, page 1732.

Barker, K. (1985). "James 5:11". *The NIV Study Bible.* Grand Rapids, MI: Zondervan, page 1885.

Barnhart, M. (2019 July 27). "Joshua Harris falling away from faith: 'I am not a Christian.'" Retrieved August 1, 2019 from www. TheChristianPost.com.

Besen, Wayne. (2011 October 12). "Former 'Ex-Gay' Activist Admits Gay People Don't Change". *FCNP*. Retrieved September 2018 from http://www.fcnp.com/commentary/national/10288-former-ex-gay-activist-admits-gay-people-dont-change.html.

Besen, Wayne. (2019 June 10). "Ex-Ex-lesbian Yvette Cantu Schneider gives inside scoop on conversion therapy industry -- PART 1" *YouTube*. TruthWinsOut. Retrieved December 26, 2019 from https://www.youtube.com/watch?v=qpTlayQJooc.

Bieber, I., & Bieber, T. B. "Male Homosexuality". *The Canadian Journal of Psychiatry*. 24(5), (1979) pages 409-421. https://doi.org/10.1177/070674377902400507.

Bogle, Bussee, Marks, et al. (2007 June 27). "Apology from Former Ex-Gay Leaders". Retrieved September 2018 from http://www.beyondexgay.com/article/apology.

Bogle, D. (2018 December 7). "Reflection on Conversion Therapy - Former Leaders". Retrieved November 5, 2019 from www.GraceRivers.com/exgayleaders/.

Bradshaw, K., Dehlin, J.P., Crowell, K.A., Galliher, R.V., Bradshaw, W.S. "Sexual orientation change efforts through psychotherapy for LGBQ individuals affiliated with the Church of Jesus Christ of Latter-day Saints". *The Journal of Sex and Marital Therapy*, 41(4), (2015) pages 391-412.

Bratcher, R. (1982). *A Translator's Guide to the Gospel of Luke*. Swindon, England: United Bible Societies.

Brown, M. L. (2018 December 10). "A Short Primer on the Bible and Homosexual Practice". Retrieved December 22, 2018 from www.CharismaNews.com.

Brown, M. (2015 February 15). "Can You Be Gay and Christian? Dr. Michael Brown". *YouTube*. Retrieved September 18, 2019 from www.YouTube.com.

Brown, M. L. (2015 July 10). "Dr. Michael Brown Has 40 Answers and 2 Questions for 'Gay' Christian Matthew Vines". Retrieved December 22, 2018 from https://AskDrBrown.org.

Brown, M. (2018 September 24). "DEBATE: Is Homosexuality Consistent with New Testament Obedience?" *YouTube*. ASKDrBrown. Retrieved September 22, 2019 from https://www.youtube.com/watch?v=EO1-VtCyRvA&feature=youtu.be.

Brown, M. (2018 July 30). "The Revoice Conference and the Danger of a Big Theological Tent". Retrieved August 1, 2019 from www.TheChristianPost.com.

Brownson, James. (2013). *Bible Gender Sexuality: Reframing the Church's Debate on Same-Sex Relationships.* Grand Rapids, MI: William B. Eerdmans Publishing Company.

Brownson, J. What Do We Mean by an Affirming Church? Plenary Session of The Reformation Project annual conference. Seattle, WA, November 9, 2019.

Brydum, Sunnivie. (2013 April 24). "John Paulk Formally Renounces, Apologizes for Harmful 'Ex-Gay' Movement". *The Advocate*. Retrieved September 2018 from www.advocate.com.

Campolo, T. (1996 February 29). "Is the Homosexual My Neighbor?" Transcript of a talk given at North Park College Chapel. Retrieved December 2019 from http://WelcomingResources.org/Campolo.

Campolo, T. (2015 June 8). "Tony Campolo: For the Record. Tony releases a new statement urging the Church to be more welcoming". Retrieved April 26, 2019 from www.TonyCampolo.org.

Carroll, J. (2007 August 16). "Most Americans Approve of Interracial Marriages". Retrieved December 2018 from https://news.gallup.com/poll/28417/most-americans-approve-interracial-marriages.aspx.

CBN News. (2019 April 29). "Jeffrey McCall: From Transgender to Transformed by God". Retrieved May 31, 2019 from https://www1.cbn.com/cbnnews/us/2019/january/jeffrey-mccall-from-transgender-to-transformed.

The Central Carolina Presbytery. (2019 May 28). *Central Carolina Presbytery: Study Committee Report on 2018 Revoice Conference.* [PDF file]. Retrieved May 31, 2019 from https://media.thegospelcoalition.org/wp-content/uploads/2019/05/28130246/Revoice-Report-2019-Final-Draft-Received-by-the-Presbytery.pdf.

Chapman, P. (2007 November 2019). "A Critique of Jones And Yarhouse's 'Ex-gays?' – Part 2". Retrieved December 2019 from www.ExGayWatch.com.

Christsforgiveness. "Ex-LGBTQ Pride March (Washington D.C)". *YouTube.* Live streamed May 25, 2019. Retrieved May 2019 from https://www.youtube.com/watch?v=lf8DsVNcYoA&feature=youtu.be. (This is a recording of the Freedom March.)

Condon, B., Mustian, J. (2019 December 7). "Surge of New Sexual Abuse Claims Threatens Church Like Never Before". Retrieved December 10, 2019 from www.CharismaMag.com.

Congressional Record, *62nd. Congress, 3rd. Session,* December 11, 1912, pages 502–503.

Creasy, Bill. Various lectures covering books of the Bible, www.LogosBibleStudy.com.

Dehlin, John P., Galliher, Bradshaw, Hyde, Crowell, "Sexual orientation change efforts among current or former LDS church members". *Journal of Counseling Psychology*, 62(2), (2014) page 95.

Dimock, M. (2019 October 17). "In U.S., Decline of Christianity Continues at Rapid Pace: An update on America's changing religious landscape". Retrieved October 18, 2019 from www.PewForum.org.

Drescher, Frank, "A History of Homosexuality and Organized Psychoanalysis". *The Journal of the American Academy of Psychoanalysis and Dynamic Psychiatry,* 36 (2008): p. 447.

Drescher, F. (2019 June 21). "Stonewall's 50th Anniversary and an Overdue Apology". Retrieved June 22, 2019 from www. psychologytoday.com.

Foster, David Kyle. (2014). *Love Hunger: A Harrowing Journey from Sexual Addiction to True Fulfillment.* Ada, MI: Chosen Books.

Foster, David K. (2018 April). "Homosexual-Turned-Pastor: What Gay Activists Refuse to Understand About My Ministry". Retrieved August 2018 from www.CharismaNews.com.

Freud, Sigmund, "Letter to an American mother". *American Journal of Psychiatry,* 107 (1951) page 787.

Fritz, R. (2018 July 5). "The LGBTQ Movement and Christianity (Its Threat and Our Response): Part 1". Retrieved December 16, 2018 from https://www.crosswalk.com/faith/spiritual-life/the-lgbtq-movement-and-christianity-its-threat-and-our-response-part-1.html.

Game, M. (2019 August 25). "20 years in ex-gay ministry; I WAS WRONG! Please forgive me!" Retrieved September 22, 2019 from https://www.facebook.com/mckrae/posts/10157639329596563.

Gerig, B. L. (2004). "The Clobber Passages: Re-examined". *www.epistle.us*. Retrieved July 23, 2019 from http://epistle.us/hbarticles/clobber1.html.

Goetz, R. (2011 July 3). "Anti-homosexual Translator Bias". Retrieved August 6, 2019 from https://biblethumpingliberal.com/2011/07/03/anti-homosexual-translator-bias/.

Goetz, Ronald. (2019). *The Galilee Episode: Two Men in One Bed, Two Women Grinding*. El Cajon, CA: Blossom Valley Trumpet.

"Governor Cuomo Signs The Child Victims Act". (February 14, 2019). Retrieved November 15, 2019 from www.Govenor.NY.gov.

Grenz, S. (1998). *Welcoming but Not Affirming: An Evangelical Response to Homosexuality*. Louisville, KY: Westminster John Knox Press.

Groth, A. N., & Birnbaum, H. J. Adult sexual orientation and attraction to underage persons. *Archives of Sexual Behavior, 7*(3), (1978) pages 175-181.

Gryboski, Michael. (2019 May 30). "PCA Presbytery rejects Revoice Conference, says it's not a 'safe guide' on gender, sex issues". Retrieved May 31, 2019 from www.ChristianPost.com.

Gryboski, M. (2018 July 31). "Revoice: LGBT Christian Conference Speaker Rejects Idea That Jesus Supports Gay Marriage". Retrieved May 31, 2019 from www.ChristianPost.com.

Gushee, D. (2019 December 3). "Christian higher ed can't win the LGBTQ debate unless it transforms". Retrieved December 8, 2019 from www.ReligionNews.com.

Helminiak, D. A. (1995). *What the Bible Really Says about Homosexuality*. San Francisco, CA: Alamo Square Press.

Herek, G. (undated). "Facts About Homosexuality and Child Molestation". Retrieved December 22, 2018 from https://psychology. ucdavis.edu/rainbow/html/facts_molestation.html.

Hershey, J. (2019 March 21). "Has 'Homosexual' always been in the Bible?" Retrieved June 22, 2019 from www.ForgeOnline.org.

Hooper, J. (2014 July 28). "Change is possible: Former 'ex-gay' activist Yvette Schneider 'celebrates the worthiness and equality of all people'". Retrieved November 5, 2019 from www.GLAAD.org.

Hooker, E. "The Adjustment of the Male Overt Homosexual". *Journal of Projective Techniques*, XXI (1957) pages 18–31.

Houdmann, S. M. (2019 February 14). "How does the translation process impact the inspiration, inerrancy, and infallibility of the Bible?" Retrieved April 20, 2019 from www.GotQuestions.org.

The Human Rights Campaign. (2020). "The Lies and Dangers of Efforts to Change Sexual Orientation or Gender Identity". Retrieved March 3, 2020 from www.HRC.org.

Iati, M. (2019 September 5). "Conversion therapy center founder who sought to turn LGBTQ Christians straight says he's gay, rejects 'cycle of self shame'". Retrieved September 22, 2019 from www. WashingtonPost.com.

Intersex Society of North America. (2008). "How Common is Intersex?" Retrieved April 2019 from www.ISNA.org.

Jackson, Wayne. (2019). "Don't Judge Me!" ChristianCourier.com. Retrieved July 16, 2019 from https://www.ChristianCourier.com/ articles/637-dont-judge-me.

(Last names unknown), Jake and Matt (co-hosts). (2019 March 31). *Holy Sexuality with Christopher Yuan* [Audiovisual podcast]. *Coffee and Cream*. Retrieved January 10, 2020 from www. CoffeeandCreamPodcast.com.

Jenny, C., Roesler, T. A., & Poyer, K. L. Are children at risk for sexual abuse by homosexuals? *Pediatrics, 94*(1), (1994) pages 41-44.

Jones and Yarhouse. (2007). *Ex-Gays?: A Longitudinal Study of Religiously Mediated Change in Sexual Orientation*. Downers Grove, Illinois: IVP Academic.

Keen, Karen R. (2018). *Scripture, Ethics & the Possibility of Same-Sex Relationships*. Grand Rapids, MI: Wm. B. Eerdmans Publishing Company.

Keen, K. (2018 December). "Dialogue with Preston Sprinkle on Same-Sex Relationships". Retrieved January 5, 2019 from www. KarenKeen.com.

Keen, K. (2019 April 30). "In Defense of Revoice: A Response to Robert Gagnon". Retrieved May 4, 2019 from www.KarenKeen. com.

Klassen, A. D., Williams, C. J., & Levitt, E. E. (1989). *Sex and morality in the U.S.: An empirical enquiry under the auspices of the Kinsey Institute*. Middletown, CT: Wesleyan University Press.

Kuykendall, Aliya. (2019 May 29). "Ex-LGBT People Declare Freedom in Jesus at DC 'Freedom March'". Retrieved May 31, 2019 from https:// stream.org/ex-lgbt-people-declare-freedom-jesus-dc-freedom-march/.

LaHaye, Tim F. (1978). *The Unhappy Gays: What Everyone Should Know about Homosexuality*. Wheaton, IL: Tyndale House.

Law, T. (2019 October 8). "9 Landmark Supreme Court Cases That Shaped LGBTQ Rights in America". Retrieved December 2019 from www.Time.com.

Lee, J. (2012). *Torn: Rescuing the Gospel from the Gays vs. Christians Debate*. New York, NY: Jericho Books.

Lewes, Kenneth. (1995). *Psychoanalysis and Male Homosexuality*. Northvale, NJ: J. Aronson.

Lowe, Bruce. (2001). "A Letter to Louise: A Biblical Affirmation of Homosexuality". Retrieved September 2019 from http://godmademegay.blogspot.com/p/letter-to-louise.html.

Mainwaring, D. (2019 May 27). "200 ex-LGBT men, women rally to show freedom they've found in following Jesus". Retrieved May 31, 2019 from https://www.lifesitenews.com/news/200-ex-lgbt-men-women-rally-to-show-freedom-theyve-found-in-following-jesus.

Mallory, C., Brown, T., Conron, K. (2018 January) "Conversion Therapy and LGBT Youth". The Williams Institute UCLA School of Law. Retrieved December 2019 from https://williamsinstitute.law.ucla.edu/wp-content/uploads/Conversion-Therapy-LGBT-Youth-Jan-2018.pdf.

Marin, Andrew. (2016). *Us versus Us: The Untold Story of Religion and the LGBT Community*. Carol Stream, IL: NavPress.

Martin, Dale. (2006). *Sex and the Single Savior: Gender and Sexuality in Biblical Interpretation*. Louisville, KY: Westminster John Knox Press.

Martin, James. (2017). *Building a Bridge: How the Catholic Church and the LGBT Community Can Enter into a Relationship of Respect, Compassion, and Sensitivity*. San Francisco, CA: HarperOne.

Matlock, Dan. (2020 February 9). *Clarity: Getting Clear*. [YouTube video file]. Retrieved February 27, 2020 from https://www.youtube.com/watch?v=X-k2G_culgM.

McCall, J. (2019 August 22). "Prophetic Word: Eunuchs Trapped in LGBT Community Will Overthrow Jezebel". Retrieved August 26, 2019 from www.CharismaNews.com.

McConaghy, N. Paedophilia: A review of the evidence, Australian and New Zealand Journal of Psychiatry, 32:2, (1998) pages 252-265, DOI: 10.3109/00048679809062736.

Minor, J. and Connoley, J. T. (2011). *The Children are Free: Reexamining the Biblical Evidence on Same-sex Relationships*. Indianapolis, IN: Jesus Metropolitan Community Church.

Mohler, A. (2014 April 22). "God, the Gospel, and the Gay Challenge—A Response to Matthew Vines". Retrieved January 13, 2020 from www.AlbertMohler.com.

Mohler, A. (2018 August 2). "Torn Between Two Cultures? Revoice, LGBT Identity, and Biblical Christianity". Retrieved July 27, 2019 www.AlbertMohler.com.

"The Nashville Statement". (2017). Retrieved August 10, 2019 from https://cbmw.org/nashville-statement/.

"National Security Act of 1947". July 1947. Retrieved from https://www.cia.gov/library/readingroom/docs/1947-07-26.pdf.

Peck, Clay. (2018 May 2). *No Perfect People Allowed - Separation of Church and Hate*. [Video file]. Retrieved April 4, 2019 from https://vimeo.com/266337311.

Piper, J. (2018 August 20). "Is It Wrong for Men to Have Long Hair?" Retrieved July 4, 2019 from www.DesiringGod.org.

Preato, D. J. (undated). "Did Paul Really Say, 'Let the Women Keep Silent in the Churches'?" Retrieved December 5, 2019 from www.GodsWordtoWomen.org.

Ralph, T. (2012 May 18). "Dr. Robert Spitzer, founder of the 'gay cure,' apologizes for his reparative therapy study". Retrieved December 2019 from https://www.pri.org/stories/2012-05-18/dr-robert-spitzer-founder-gay-cure-apologizes-his-reparative-therapy-study.

Renoe, E. (2019 January 16). *Homosexuality and the Bible with Christopher Yuan*. [Audio podcast.] *Abscond* with Ethan Renoe. Retrieved January 10, 2020 from www.AbscondPodcast.com.

Reuben, D. R. (1969). *Everything You Always Wanted to Know about Sex but Were Afraid to Ask*. Philadelphia, PA: David McKay Publications.

Revoice mission statement. Retrieved May 31, 2019 from https://revoice.us/about/our-mission-and-vision/.

Revoice. "Statement on Sexual Ethics and Christian Obedience". Retrieved May 31, 2019 from www.Revoice.us.

Ryan, C, Huebner, D., et.al. (2009). "Family rejection as a predictor of negative health outcomes in white and Latino lesbian, gay, and bisexual young adults". Pediatrics. 123(1), 346-52.

Saia, M. R. (1988). *Counseling the Homosexual*. Minneapolis, MN: Bethany House.

Schlanger, Z. and Wolfson, E. (2014 May 1). "Ex-Ex-Gay Pride". Retrieved October 2018 from www.Newsweek.com.

Schneider, Y. (2018 June 13). "Finding My True Self". Retrieved December 2019 from www.Thrive.lgbt.

The Septuagint, per Biblehub.com: https://biblehub.com/sepd/genesis/1.htm.

Showalter, B. (2019 May 27). "Pulse nightclub shooting survivors: Move of Holy Spirit 'being birthed' among former LGBT persons". Retrieved May 31, 2019 from www.ChristianPost.com.

Siemaszko, C. (2019 August 14) "Hundreds filed lawsuits under Child Victims Act in New York". Retrieved November 16, 2019 from www.NBCnews.com.

Siker, Jeffrey S. (1994). "How to Decide?: Homosexual Christians, the Bible, and Gentile Inclusion". *Theology Today*, 51(2), 219-234.

Slife, J. (2015 April 28). "Professor, author discusses the question: Can you be gay and Christian?". Retrieved August 1, 2019 from www.world.wng.

Smith, W. C. (2017 May 3). "Anne Paulk hasn't given up on ex-gay ministry". *World*. Retrieved September 2018 from https://world.wng.org/2017/05/anne_paulk_hasn_t_given_up_on_ex_gay_ministry.

Sopelsa, B and Ruggiero, R. (2020 January 29) "Wells Fargo pulls Florida voucher donations over anti-gay school policies". Retrieved January 31, 2020 from www.NBCNews.com.

Spiers, J. (2007 October 21). "What Does the Bible Say about Wearing Jewelry?" Retrieved November 12, 2018 from www.WhyILeft.org.

Stone, Michael (2019 June 12). "Baptists Hold 'Make America Straight Again' Conference, Call For Execution Of Gays". www. Patheos.com. Retrieved July 22, 2019 from https://www.patheos. com/blogs/progressivesecularhumanist/2019/06/baptists-hold-make-america-straight-again-conference-call-for-execution-of-gays/.

Stonestreet, J. and Morris, S. (2019 April 14). "Christopher Yuan on holy sexuality: Your desires don't define you". Retrieved January 14, 2020 from www.ChristianPost.com.

Taylor, D.B. (2020 February 7). "Franklin Graham, Dropped by U.K. Venues, Says He Will Proceed With Tour". *The New York Times*. Retrieved February 13, 2020 from www.NYTimes.com.

Tene, W. (2019 June 21). "News: APsaA Issues Overdue Apology to LGBTQ Community". Retrieved June 22, 2019 from www.apsa.org.

The Southern Baptist Seminary Theological Seminary. (2018 December 12). *Report on Slavery and Racism in the History of the Southern Baptist Theological Seminary* [PDF file]. Retrieved December 15, 2018 from http://www.sbts.edu/wp-content/uploads/2018/12/Racism-and-the-Legacy-of-Slavery-Report-v3.pdf.

Throckmorton, Warren. (2012 January 9). "Alan Chambers: 99.9% have not experienced a change in their orientation". Retrieved August 2018 from www.WThrockmorton.com.

Throckmorton, W. (2011 October 27). "The Jones and Yarhouse Study: What Does It Mean?" Retrieved December 2019 from www. WThrockmorton.com.

Trotta, D. (2019 June 21). "U.S. psychoanalysts apologize for labeling homosexuality an illness". Retrieved June 22, 2019 from www.Reuters.com.

TruNews Team. (2018 September 19). "15 Stunning Statistics about Porn in the Church". Retrieved October 5, 2019 from www. TruNews.com.

Tucker, Neely. (2006 June 13). "Loving Day Recalls a Time When the Union of a Man And a Woman Was Banned". Retrieved August 2018 from www.*WashingtonPost.com*.

Turnbull, Sandra. (2012). *God's Gay Agenda*. Bellflower, CA: Glory Publishing.

United States Constitution, Article II, Section 1.

Vallotton, K. (2019 December 8). "Sovereign Providence". Sermon delivered at Bethel Church, Redding, CA. Retrieved December 27, 2019 from https://www.bethel.tv/en/podcasts/sermons/episodes/478. This quote begins at 26.19 in the audio.

Villarreal, D. (2019 May 26). "Ex-ex-lesbian leader slams conversion therapy on eve of 'ex-gay' D.C. Freedom March". Retrieved May 2019 from www.lgbtqnation.com.

Vines, Matthew. (2014). *God and the Gay Christian: the Biblical Case in Support of Same-Sex Relationships*. New York, NY: Convergent.

Wikipedia contributors. (2018 July 27). Charles W. Socarides. In *Wikipedia, The Free Encyclopedia*. Retrieved October 6, 2018, from https://en.wikipedia.org/w/index.php?title=Charles_W._Socarides &oldid=852278358.

Wikipedia contributors. (2018 November 24). Ex-ex-gay. In *Wikipedia, The Free Encyclopedia*. Retrieved October 6, 2018, from https:// en.wikipedia.org/w/index.php?title=Ex-ex-gay&oldid=870349434.

Wikipedia contributors. (2019 November 25). John F. MacArthur. In Wikipedia, The Free Encyclopedia. Retrieved November 26, 2019, from https://en.wikipedia.org/w/index.php?title=John_F._MacArthur&oldid=927970369.

Wikipedia contributors. (2020, March 3). List of U.S. jurisdictions banning conversion therapy. In Wikipedia, The Free Encyclopedia. Retrieved 19:45, March 3, 2020, from https://en.wikipedia.org/w/index.php?title=List_of_U.S._jurisdictions_banning_conversion_therapy&oldid=943734606.

Wikipedia contributors. (2019 February 24). Lost Cause of the Confederacy. In *Wikipedia, The Free Encyclopedia*. Retrieved February 24, 2019, from https://en.wikipedia.org/w/index.php?title=Lost_Cause_of_the_Confederacy&oldid=884921560.

Wikipedia contributors. (2019 November 14). Patriarchy. In Wikipedia, The Free Encyclopedia. Retrieved November 24, 2019, from https://en.wikipedia.org/w/index.php?title=Patriarchy&oldid=926088384.

Wikipedia contributors. (2019 January 16). The Homosexuals (CBS Reports). In *Wikipedia, The Free Encyclopedia*. Retrieved January 2019, from https://en.wikipedia.org/w/index.php?title=The_Homosexuals_(CBS_Reports)&oldid=878640939.

Wong, C. M. (2019 January 23). "Former Conversion Therapist Says He's 'Choosing To Pursue Life As A Gay Man'". Retrieved June 2019 from www.HuffPost.com.

Yuan, Christopher (2018). *Holy Sexuality and the Gospel: Sex, Desire, and Relationships Shaped by God's Grand Story*. Portland, OR: Multnomah.

ACKNOWLEDGMENTS

This book has been a labor of love and great joy for me. I am so thankful to Pastor Garry and my wonderful church, House on the Rock Church, in Rockaway Beach, New York. The church has shown my partner and me nothing but acceptance, friendship, hugs, love, and kindness, despite their long-held, traditional, "one man, one woman" position. I want our dear friends to know that Suzie and I would never dishonor God in our lives. I felt called by God to express from the Scripture why we believe that God brought us together and blesses our relationship in particular and gay Christians in general.

To all the beautiful, loving, kind people in our lives who hold the traditional view of marriage, thank you for your acceptance and kindness toward us. Suzie and I stand firm in our faith in God, but other gay people are constantly wavering, unsure as to whether God accepts them or not. I understand that you must tell me once that you disapprove of my relationship, and I appreciate your honesty. Please understand that if you hold that homosexuality is a sin, then every gay person who believes they are not qualified to come to Christ has potentially been held back from a relationship with God by this ongoing, widespread belief.

Those of you who know me know that I do not like to draw attention to myself. I always sit in the back section at church. I would never take a microphone even on testimony day. I do not hold myself up as a "model Christian" in any way. But consider this—if you honestly believe that I am a sister in Christ, then homosexuality is not a sin, period. Or, let me back up. If you recognize that there are holes in the view that "Scripture is crystal clear on this," do you think it is appropriate to continue to reject gay Christians? Do you think "wickedness, evil, greed, and depravity" describe Suzie and me? If so, do they describe us any more than those words describe you? If not, then would you agree that Romans 1 does not describe homosexuality? If you think that Suzie and I are living in sin, then please return this book with your rebuttals in red ink or just email me. I welcome discussion. If you believe that Christ's atoning work on Calvary extends even to Suzie and me, even today, then please do the work with me to make this right. I believe that if HotRock extended welcome to all people, then we would see exceptional growth in our church.

Glynn, thank you for always listening to me and constantly affirming your love for Suzie and me. We recognize your traditional view of marriage and are humbled by your heartfelt kindness to us, especially in view of your understanding that Scripture does not support our partnership. Specifically, thank you for agreeing to read this manuscript.

Pastor Garry, thank you for agreeing to read this book. I know God is at work in our church. I'm so thankful for the opportunity to worship the Lord and grow in Him with Jesus-loving, Bible-believing, Holy Spirit filled Christians. House on the Rock Church has an enormous influence on my life and in my walk with Jesus. Pastor, I am not asking you or the leadership to change your core theology or definition of marriage. I want to present the scriptural basis for my belief that I, and many gay Christians, serve God wholeheartedly even from within an unapologetically gay relationship. I can't thank you enough for your kindness toward Suzie and me. I appreciate that, as you point out, we can disagree without being disagreeable.

To my closest friends, affirming and non-affirming alike, thank you so much for letting me talk about this for 17 months. Some of you read chapters (or entire manuscripts) and made incredibly helpful edits and provided invaluable insights.

Julie, from the bottom of my heart, I thank you for the professional editing you did, the time you spent editing my first through fourth manuscripts. Hours upon hours you worked and wouldn't let me pay you a dime for your very valuable time. Thank you for your genius emotiwords, which you will soon recognize. You are brilliant, clever, funny, generous, kind, and more. I am honored to call you my friend.

Mom, no one knows better than you and I how important your non-affirming arguments have been for this book. I think I have tackled within the book every single idea you ever mentioned on this topic. I can't thank you and Daddy enough for loving Suzie and me so dearly, despite our "lifestyle," which is in direct contrast to your traditional beliefs.

Natalie, thank you for being a straight ally and for the work you do to include the LGBT+ community in your Catholic church. I am touched beyond words that God brought you into our lives like He did. You became my neighbor when I needed one. A straight Christian ally neighbor. What an amazing orchestrator of every little thing He is.

To my dear, dear peep and crommie, Louisey, you keep me strong and energetic and my head clear with four - five time weekly 5:30am workout sessions and non-stop encouragement, laughter, and friendship. You are an amazing treasure and a dearest, forever

BFF. I can't thank you enough for your love and support. You and I are like the sister version of blood brothers. OMW, orange hearts, 17.5, beautiful rain, the hem of His garment. The final manuscript of the dissy is a *little bigger* than I had planned.

To my hardest-core Bible study friend, Debbie, thank you for studying, discussing, and brainstorming Scripture with me. The day I met you, you were reading your Bible through, as was I. We have motivated and encouraged each other in our Scripture study beautifully. That notebook. God answered a very specific prayer when He brought you into my life. I cannot overstate the impact your trip to that book sale in Brooklyn has had on my life, and perhaps others. Thank you kindly for teaching me that I can end a sentence with a preposition. There's no other option for chapter 16's title, that I know of. (I'm so sorry to my Dad.) Thank you and your people for the "Homonay Heteroyay Happy Conversion Camp." The detailed summary I reference somewhere in this book may make you laugh. Thank you for my New American Bible. My heart loves you and yours dearly and forever. Numbers 26:59.

To Kathy Baldock, Matthew Vines, Ed Oxford, Nancy Bartell, Bishop Randy, Pastor Johnny, Pastors Brenda and Jim Johnson, the fivefold ministry within the Covenant Network, Pastors Aimée and Myriam Simpierre and to so many other gay Christian and our straight ally leaders and authors, thank you for all that you've done to create a way for LGBTQ Christians to belong in the local church. I am honored to refer to your work in this book, and I am so thankful for the foundation you have given me personally, and for the incredible work that you do, day in and day out.

Kathy, thank you so very much for your time and consideration. I am in awe that God gave us, the LGBTQ community, you, as one of the most powerful and tireless straight allies we could have hoped for or imagined. Thank you for answering God's call at that bonfire. We are so very indebted to you for your work.

Thank you, Reverend David. Thank you for being so bold as a young student to address the head of the RSV translation committee and to provide him with meaningful resources to address the translation issue. Thank you so much for allowing us to get to know you and your beautiful story. We love you.

To God's greatest gifts in my life, the Lord Jesus, and His Holy Spirit Who leads and guides me daily, from faith to faith, and puts in me to will and to do for His good pleasure. God almighty, I love and honor You. All of my faith and hope and trust are in You. Use me, God, to Your glory. I am overwhelmed by Your kindness, expressed to me in the most outrageous, exceedingly abundantly above all that I could ever think or imagine, ways. I trust in You. I surrender my life to You. Please Lord, make me a good steward of all of Your countless blessings in my life. Lead me and guide me, that every thought, attitude, word, and action on my part would bring You glory and honor in absolutely every aspect of my life. Correct me, please, when I miss the mark. My God, You are everything to me.

To God's second greatest gift in my life, the love of my earthly life, my precious Suzie. My soulmate, my domestic chores partner, my laughmate, my kitchen dance partner, my dinner partner, my constant companion. What joy you bring to my life every day. Thank you for laboring with me in this endeavor. I'M SO GLAD YOU'RE HERE. God is good. Holds heart, holy hands high, tippy toes, sparkly angels sprinkling rainbow glitter over the ocean in front of us, moonwalk in Times Square, giant orange and red flag, glory to God in the highest, His kingdom come, His will be done, here as it is in heaven! Amen. God loves flags.

ABOUT THE AUTHOR

Cristy and Suzie reside in beautiful Rockaway Beach in New York City. Raised in Alabama, Cristy moved to New York City in her early 20s. She completed a medical degree in her 30s and practices anesthesiology. Cristy enjoys the beach, rollerblading on Rockaway's gorgeous concrete promenade, chess, music, Auburn football, and studying Scripture. She can be reached at IamIncludedinChrist@gmail.com.

jeremiah 33:3